FROM PLASTIC PARROTS TO FLYING KANGAROOS:

Big Boeings and Hovering Helos

GEOFF COWELL

Copyright © 2025 by Geoff Cowell

All rights reserved. This book or any portion thereof may not be reproduced or used in any manner whatsoever without the express written permission of the publisher except in the case of brief quotations embodied in a book review.

ISBN 978-1-7638457-0-1

For my dear father, Athol, my brother, Rodger, and my cherished sons, Alex and Nicholas.

CONTENTS

Introduction 7

PART 1

Prologue 13
1 | First Impressions 17
2 | Getting to Grips with the Giant RAAF Plane 21
3 | Adventures in ~~Paradise~~ Butterworth 33
4 | Bars in Bangkok, Shenanigans in Singapore 43
5 | Fun with Your Friendly Flight Stewards 51
6 | War...What Is It Good For? 61
7 | Arrrrrrrrr...It's Cap'n Ron! 65
8 | I Ordered Escargot and Only Got Snails! 73
9 | Combat Survival Course—The Horror Begins! 81
10 | Deep-Sea Debacle 89
11 | Passing the Beach Bean Soup 99
12 | How Good Are Transpiration Bags? 103
13 | Code of Conduct 109
14 | It's a Trap! 113
15 | The Seventh Circle of Hell 119
16 | Return of the Living Dead 127
17 | Practice Bleeding—A COMSURV Epilogue 131
18 | What You Don't See Can't Hurt You! 135
19 | Bloody Legends! 141
20 | Egyptian and European Extravaganza 145
21 | Ohhhh...Those Russians! 161
22 | Hello Bob and Bye Bye Boeings 181

PART 2

1 | What Have I Got Myself Into? 185
2 | 5 Squadron 191
3 | Gwound School 195
4 | Wokking My Way to Wagga 201
5 | Just Like Riding a Bike 205
6 | The Trials of Training 215
7 | from a Sports Car to a Battle Wagon 227
8 | Sword of Honour 233
9 | How Do Ya Feel? 241
10 | Perils in Paradise 255
11 | Tactical Operations 269
12 | Keeping the Kids Occupied 277
13 | Say Again??? 283
14 | Colourful Characters 287
15 | Going for a Spin 289
16 | Here Comes Santa Claus 295
17 | The Only Constant in Life Is Change 301
18 | Tragedy at Tenterfield 303
19 | Minimum Effort—Maximum Result 307
20 | Army Invasion 309
21 | End of an Era 311
22 | So Long, Farewell, Auf Wiedersehen, Adieu 319
Epilogue 321

INTRODUCTION

My dear mother, rest her soul, always believed that time went by more quickly the older you got, and having (unbelievably) already attained 65 years of age as I write this, I know exactly what she meant. The events recounted here happened around forty years ago, yet they remain so very vivid and fresh in my memory. I guess such is the curse of old age, where youthful memories seem to have been carved in stone while remembering what you ate for lunch can be a challenge. This book began as a way for me to record my flying experiences for my father's enjoyment and undoubtedly, at times, horror. One day not too far away, a kindly nurse may consider reading them to me when I'm lying in the nursing home so that I can be temporarily transported back to the days of my youth.

An old adage goes that facts should never be allowed to stand in the way of a good story, and yet I've deliberately aimed to avoid gilding the lily and, instead, have faithfully recorded my tales as truthfully as I remember them. As I travelled back in time and committed my favourite military stories to the page, there were times when even I had trouble believing that they *actually* happened. Fortunately, like all professional pilots, the aging pages of my logbook provided me with an invaluable portal to the past—providing accurate aircraft serial numbers, places and dates and also, at times, unlocking past events that I'd almost entirely forgotten about. Nevertheless, there may be some minor factual errors in the following pages and, if so, I apologise. A memoir is an account of people and situations *as you remember them* and that is exactly what I've set out to do here.

Of course, like nearly every other job or profession, flying (and military flying, in particular) is full of jargon and slang. While colourful language can, at times, enhance a story (or even comprise an essential element of it) the excessive use of such verbiage can be an annoying distraction. I've tried to avoid doing so here, to make the stories relatable to both pilots and non-pilots alike. Nevertheless, using some jargon and slang has been unavoidable and, to differentiate between official aviation or military terminology and slang, I've emphasised these words and phrases with quotation marks—single quotes for official phraseology and double quotes for slang or phrases in common usage.

I must admit though, that some of this terminology may no longer seem appropriate in the twenty-first century, and so it might be necessary to consider its usage within the relevant historical context. In 1982 (when this account begins), Ronald Reagan was in the early days of his first term as US president and, in the UK, Prime Minister Margaret Thatcher was basking in the reflected glory of a victory in the Falkland Islands War. It was quite a conservative period, where television shows such as *Benny Hill* and *Are You Being Served* pilloried gay culture, and homosexuality was still an offence under military law. The operational Air Force was strictly a male domain, with the first female RAAF pilot not graduating from 2FTS until 1988. In the Australian Defence Force, "political correctness" meant voting for the Liberal/National Coalition, and "woke" was something you did just before you got out of bed. I've tried to avoid stories that haven't aged well, but if any of them cause offence, it was certainly not my intention to do so.

Another aspect of looking back on one's distant past is that, sadly, far too many individuals who played an important part in various stages of your life are no longer alive. When I'm telling a story where this is the case, I've written that person's name in full to pay my respects and help keep their memory alive. And so, in order of appearance, this book is dedicated to the memory of: Charlie Barringhaus, Greg Gibbins, Ron Peters, Harry Wright (DSO, DFC and bar), Ken Vote, Ian Taylor, Mal Cotterell, Glenn Auld, Mark Fallon, Mal Greentree, Gary Criddle and Tim Ellis. Finally, and most importantly, I must express my eternal gratitude to my brilliant and gifted cousin, Adrian Cowell, who provided the original cartoons that complement this account so wonderfully.

PART 1

AIR FORCE AIRLINES

October 1982–May 1985

PROLOGUE

On the evening of Friday, the 29th of October 1982, the sun was rapidly slipping toward the horizon as our Ansett Airlines aircraft approached its descent point into Sydney. Although the flight from Perth had been relatively short, travelling in opposition to the sun meant that our 11am flight would arrive at 6pm local time. Looking out at the changing hues of the darkening evening sky, it seemed surreal somehow, that after nearly sixteen months of continuously moving ever further away from the family home at Kalbar, Queensland, I was finally east-coast bound. I reminded myself though that, for the next few years, home would be at Richmond, north-west of Sydney—the site of my very first operational posting. After more than a year as an itinerant trainee Air Force pilot with a questionable future (at best), now that my flight training was finally behind me, I could begin to experience life as a professional RAAF pilot.

But the demoralizing conclusion to my training had left me with some deep self-doubts. What had the examiner seen on my last flight test that persuaded him to let me graduate and be awarded a set of highly-coveted RAAF Wings? My "Wings Test Mk II" (I couldn't yet bear to think of it as my "Wings Test Repeat") hadn't gone much better than my first attempt and, after landing, I'd fully expected to be greeted with the news that I'd failed and had thus fallen at the very last hurdle. Instead, due to either a stroke of luck or some divine intervention, I'd been handed a Pass for what had been a pretty ordinary flight. Quite frankly, despite all the unrelenting effort, I felt like a bit of a fraud. I now considered myself a tradesman who'd have to work hard to even approach the skills of those craftsmen to whom flying was virtually effortless. But could a tradesman realistically expect to competently handle a big, heavy, four-engined jet like the Boeing 707?

When my posting to 33 FLT had been announced at a function in Pearce, many of the instructors had congratulated me heartily on getting such a "plum posting". No pilot officer had previously been posted straight from 2FTS to 707s, but I was now under no illusions that it came about courtesy of my superior flying skills. My instrument flying was undoubtedly better than my general flying because, on instruments, you dealt in concrete concepts and "flew by the numbers." It was in the vast, three-dimensional arena of general flight—flying "by the seat of your pants" during stalls, spins and aerobatics—that I struggled. While my submission of a preference to fly 707s had been a bit of an idealistic afterthought, the resulting posting to 33 FLT had probably been the ideal outcome.

But as our aircraft dipped its nose and began its long descent into Sydney, I realised how little I knew about 33 FLT. Sure, I knew that it flew all over the world whilst providing transport for royalty, heads of state and politicians, but that was pretty much it. In due course, though, I'd learn that Gough Whitlam (while Prime Minister) had come to an understanding with Qantas that when its 707s were decommissioned in the late 1970s, the RAAF would take delivery of two of them for use as VIP transports. The Boeing 707 offered range, speed and comfort far superior to other aircraft in the RAAF inventory, and its size allowed the incumbent PM to take his staff and a media contingent along with him whenever he ventured overseas. They were about as far removed as you could get from the little single-engine CT-4 "Plastic Parrots" on which I'd started my Air Force flying training at Point Cook in 1981.

Unfortunately for Gough, he was dismissed from office long before the 707s arrived. His successor, Malcolm Fraser, however, (a strenuous critic of the ego-driven purchase while in Opposition) decided to honour the commitment, and the first 707s entered RAAF service in 1979. To limit the exposure of the newly-acquired extravagance to the cynical Canberra press gallery, Fraser's apparent instruction to the military was to "keep them away from Canberra." The RAAF Chief subsequently reasoned that, since the 707 was essentially just another transport aircraft, it should be co-located with the other transport units at RAAF Base Richmond, even though its 7,000-foot runway (sandwiched between the townships of Richmond and Windsor) would severely restrict the new aircraft's payload and range. With only two such aircraft being purchased from Qantas, the 707s initially operated as a Flight within 37 Squadron—a unit that operated a fleet of C-130E Hercules transports. In February 1981, however, to provide the fledgling fleet with a greater degree of autonomy, 33 FLT was formed and, soon afterwards, moved into its own headquarters.

As we commenced our final approach into Sydney, I wondered what the 33 FLT pilots would be like. For such a responsible duty, surely these men would have to be amongst the most capable and professional aviators in the world. How could a newly-minted "boggie" pilot officer (who'd failed his first Wings Test) hope to establish himself and achieve some level of credibility within such an elite and experienced outfit? Although I still ultimately aspired to captain a Qantas 747 someday, I knew virtually nothing about operating multi-engined aircraft and was much more familiar with the world of G-suits, helmets, ejection seats and oxygen masks. Despite my burgeoning feelings of self-doubt, I decided that I would just have to tackle this upcoming conversion course one day at a time.

After landing and collecting our luggage, I received my first taste of life as an officer when my wife and I were met by a cheerful Comcar driver, who'd been assigned to transport us to our temporary accommodation. Almost immediately, we were exposed to one of the bugbears of living in Sydney—the daily peak-hour traffic—and in the typical bumper-to-bumper, stop-start vehicular gridlock, it took well over two hours to cover the fifty kilometres to the Hawkesbury district. Nearing

16 | BIG BOEINGS AND HOVERING HELOS

our ultimate destination, we drove past the Richmond RAAF Base, where I couldn't help noticing one of the big, majestic Boeings sitting, floodlit, out on the flight line. Just what would my future hold onboard these aircraft?

1
FIRST IMPRESSIONS

On Monday morning, I was collected by a RAAF car and driven to my new workplace at 33 FLT. Now, I didn't know what to expect, but I must admit to being a little underwhelmed by the squat, low-set metal-clad building that served as the headquarters of my new unit. It reminded me of the stuffy, demountable buildings that had served as classrooms at Boonah High School, and seemed quite inappropriate for a unit that had routinely transported members of the Royal Family around the world. The building's interior was similarly devoid of charm and character, and there were so few people about that initially I thought it must have been a public holiday. Fortunately, the Orderly Room Sergeant was there, and he explained that the deserted state of the headquarters was due to most of the squadron flight crews being down in Victoria for circuit training at Avalon Airport. After a few days of keeping myself amused, the bulk of the pilots returned, and the CO invited me into his office to formally welcome me into the fold.

The Commanding Officer of 33 FLT, was a shortish, lightly-built fellow with thinning brown hair and a luxuriant, manicured moustache. I instantly pictured him winding his way through the English countryside in a tiny red convertible, cravat flying in the breeze and pipe between his teeth as he rushed to the airfield to climb into his Spitfire and engage the vicious Hun. His clipped and polished tones were just what I expected of the man who was charged with such a weighty responsibility. I stood to attention and saluted smartly. He told me to take off my hat, relax and take a seat.

"Geoff," he said perplexedly, "I don't really know what we're going to do with you, because pilots straight out of 2FTS are rarely posted onto jet aircraft of this size. We're going to have to make this up as we go along, but you shouldn't expect to get a command here, and I'm not even sure yet whether you'll get to sit in a front seat for takeoffs and landings."

Great, I thought to myself gloomily, *I'm here to be a glorified radio operator!*

After the meeting concluded, I was sitting in the crew room, dejectedly contemplating my future, when one of the female flight stewards wandered in and asked me if I cared to head down to the tearoom for a cup of coffee. I told her that I wasn't much of a coffee drinker but, after sensing a little disappointment from her as she was leaving, a few minutes later, I figured I might as well join her and stop being so anti-social. As I walked into the tearoom, it seemed that everybody in the squadron that day was there and on the back wall hung a large cardboard sign that said, "Welcome, Boggie Cowell"—I was late for my own official welcome morning tea.

* * *

A few days later, I was called in to meet Squadron Leader "Woofy"—the Training Flight Commander, and also one of the two squadron QFIs. Just like the CO, Woofy was moustachioed and of a similar height but, unlike the CO, who was a bit standoffish and old-school, Woofy had a constant twinkle in his eye and possessed a great dry wit. Whenever he spoke, he had a perpetual half-smile, as if he was just about to tell a joke or was thinking back on one he'd just heard. He was also gruff and no-nonsense and always got straight to the point.

"What did the CO tell you about your conversion course?" he asked me straight away.

When I told him that the CO had doubted that I'd even be able to occupy one of the front seats after my conversion, Woofy said, "Bull-s**t! As far as I'm concerned, mate, you'll get as far as you want to go. Provided you put in the effort, I intend to give you the same conversion program as the 'retread' on your course. If you can handle the syllabus, I don't see any reason why you shouldn't do the same job as all the other squadron pilots."

A 'retread,' I soon discovered, was the generic RAAF-wide nickname for a pilot who had already been on a couple of operational postings. In effect, Woofy was telling me that I'd get the same opportunities as any other new arrival to the squadron and that what I achieved on this posting was really up to me.

The conversion course was due to start in February, and I was free to use the time remaining before the Christmas stand-down to find somewhere to live, a much more difficult task than I'd anticipated. Between times, I spent the remainder of the year getting to know my squadron colleagues (who, fortunately, proved to be nothing like the aloof elitists I'd feared they might be). During this period, I was also introduced to the 'secondary duty' that would absorb many, many hours of my otherwise free time. Because of its VIP role, 33 FLT could be tasked to fly almost anywhere on short notice, and so a full set of Jeppesen publications (which contained air traffic control procedures, approach charts and airfield information for nearly every country in the world) had been procured. Naturally, these manuals required regular amendment and, naturally, as the most junior pilot in the squadron, it became my duty to plough through the stacks of revisions that arrived regularly in the mail. Although this job was both time-consuming and tiresome, it didn't tax the old grey matter too much and came as a welcome relief from the previous sixteen months of perpetual "brain strain."

2
GETTING TO GRIPS WITH THE GIANT RAAF PLANE

By mid-February, we'd moved into a fully furnished rental house in Castle Hill, and the conversion course was about to kick off. Ground school in a classroom would consume the first month of the conversion course, and we'd then head up to Hong Kong for two weeks of flight simulator training at the Cathay Pacific simulator complex. Some conversion flying and an Instrument Rating Test back in Australia would see the entire process completed by the end of May. It seemed a long time to be in training, but the prospect of a fortnight in Hong Kong was particularly enticing, especially given that my only overseas trip to date had been on a family holiday to New Zealand. My course-mates consisted of just two retreads from a Hercules squadron—Dave (a flight lieutenant pilot) and Charlie Barringhaus (a flight engineer). From the outset, the method of passing on the required 707 systems knowledge was right up my alley.

At Point Cook and Pearce, aircraft systems had been taught by "chalk-and-talk" and passing various components around the classroom. Sitting in the back of the room, by the time some mechanical gadget reached me, I didn't know whether it was a flight instrument, something from the landing gear assembly, or a filter from the crew room coffee machine. It was all "this flange drives this rocker assembly that then opens this valve electro-mechanically" and they may as well have been speaking Greek. But on the 707 conversion course, the aircraft systems were explained by flight engineers using colour slides and schematic diagrams that had been provided by Qantas. Since there were so many complex systems on the 707, the level of detail provided on each system was pretty basic—just the way I liked it. In the classroom, a 707 system would be described to us something like this:

"Using rate gyros, the yaw damper computer senses the aircraft oscillations in yaw that occur at high altitude in what's called 'Dutch Roll.' The computer then sends signals to the rudder servo to move the rudders slightly and cancel out the Dutch Roll. Any questions?"

One of us might then pipe up with, "Yeah, but how does the computer do that?"

To which the instructor would reply, "Using rate gyros, the yaw damper computer senses the Dutch Roll and then sends signals to the rudder to cancel it out. Got it now?"

"Yeah," we would mumble, unconvinced, "but what if the computer fails?"

"Well, then you have to put in the spare computer," the instructor would say. "So, no more questions? All right...let's move on then."

It wasn't that the instructor didn't know the answer—our instructors had lots of experience on the aircraft and knew it intimately—it was just that on this aircraft, and in this squadron, there was a culture that as far as aircraft systems knowledge went, you were only taught what you needed to know to be able to operate the aircraft safely. In the training slide packages, regularly spaced multi-choice questions were used to consolidate the subject matter. It was perfect for me, and I could only feel for the guys undergoing Hercules conversions, where they had to learn the names of every circuit breaker on the (sixty-four position) cockpit circuit breaker panel—by rote and in order.

* * *

After a few weeks of systems lectures, we were instructed on "Aircraft Performance;" a process that involved scrutinising a multitude of graphs and charts to determine the power settings and speeds for take-off, landing, cruise, holding and nearly every other imaginable type of aviation scenario. Of course, this was all new to me, but as long as you didn't query why there was a kink on a graph at a particular point, or why a line was straight in some places, but curved in others, performance wasn't too bad. Eventually, the ground school concluded by having us sit in an aircraft to run through the extensive preflight check that was conducted by the right-hand seat copilot before every flight. There was then a gap of a few weeks before the simulator training started, and I used this opportunity to make notes on the various flying sequences that we'd soon be practicing.

Then, with great excitement, it was time to throw my luggage into the boot of the RAAF car that arrived to take me to the airport to catch my flight up to Hong Kong. Dave and some others had left already, so on this particular Qantas flight, there were six of us—three pilots (Mal, the Operations Flight Commander, Woofy and me) and three flight engineers (Ted, Bill and my flight engineer course-mate, Charlie). Bill was a laconic character who'd earned the nickname "Jaffa" because, whilst touring the ancient city of Petra in Jordan during a VIP trip, he'd dryly described it as, "Just Another F***in' Rock!" Ted had kept us royally entertained during the ground school lectures with his vast collection of hilarious stories and jokes. The movie *Bill and Ted's Excellent Adventure* was still years away, but these two could well have been the movie-makers' inspiration. Right from the outset, it was bleedingly obvious that this trip was going to be an adventure of epic proportions.

We travelled to Hong Kong in business class aboard a Qantas 747 'combi' aircraft that could carry both passengers and freight. When the flight attendant asked Bill and Ted (who were sitting together behind me), whether they'd like a drink before takeoff, they looked at each other briefly before Ted casually said, "Listen, darling, you can spend the next seven hours going backward and forwards to the galley refilling our drinks, or you can make life a lot easier for yourself, by just giving my friend here and I a bottle of scotch each right now!" A few minutes later, Bill and Ted were each handed a bottle of scotch, which they then proceeded to drain before our arrival. It was about 6pm local time when we reached Hong Kong which, being in the northern hemisphere, was still surprisingly cool. We landed at Kai Tak Airport via the infamous IGS approach—a forty-five-degree angle approach over the urban sprawl of Kowloon before turning right quite sharply at about 600 feet to align with the south-easterly runway for landing. Looking out the window, you got the distinct impression that the aircraft was flying *between* the buildings.

Being an inexperienced traveller, once we'd disembarked the aircraft,

I figured I'd better stick close to Woofy and Mal as we headed for immigration and customs. The baggage collection area that awaited us resembled an enormous shed that teemed with seemingly thousands of mostly black-haired Asian folks. It was virtually impossible to make any headway through this churning throng without literally elbowing and shoving people out of the way. When we finally reached the street outside to hail down a couple of taxis from amongst the hundreds of identically-coloured red and cream Toyotas, we noticed that Bill was no longer with us. Without missing a beat, Ted said, "Don't worry, I'll find him" while I thought, *Yeah, good luck with that!*

Ted then proceeded to walk calmly back into the arrivals hall, cup his hands around his mouth and yell out at the top of his voice, "ARE YA' THERE MAAAAAATE?" This bizarre behaviour upset the milling throng not one bit and, almost immediately, a faint voice in the distance responded with, "YEEAAAHH, MATE!" This process was repeated until Bill eventually caught up with us and we all then climbed into our taxis to head for the Hong Kong Hotel in Kowloon—about twenty minutes away. As we drove along, I regarded the ambling masses that clogged the streets whilst browsing in the windows of the shops that seemed to be crammed into every available inch of space. Bright lights and people abounded, with horns blaring constantly as the multitude of cars impatiently manoeuvred along the heavily congested roads. I quickly gained the lasting impression that Hong Kong is just one gigantic human ant's nest. Every few minutes, another passenger jet would roar overhead on its approach to Kai Tak Airport and, as I struggled to take it all in, Woofy played tour guide. He said that strict building codes in Kowloon prevented new buildings from encroaching on the flight paths into Kai Tak and that the only flashing lights permitted in the precinct were those that the pilots used to guide themselves around the abrupt final right-hand turn.

The Hong Kong Hotel was situated adjacent to the Star Ferry terminal which for many years (before the construction of a cross-harbour tunnel) had served as the sole method of travel between mainland Kowloon and Hong Kong Island. As I wearily climbed out of the cab and stood on the kerb, I looked across the harbour towards the island which, along its coastline, was spectacularly jam-packed with a multitude of brightly-lit skyscrapers. It was a breathtakingly unforgettable vista, but by this point, I was feeling decidedly stale and badly in need of some sleep in the room that Charlie and I would share for the next two weeks.

During that period, our training regime would follow a set routine. The other squadron pilots were also cycling through Hong Kong for their six-monthly emergency checks, so the conversion course was given the four-hour morning sessions, while the other crews had the four-hour afternoon sessions. Each morning, we'd meet up with our instructors in the foyer at around 7:30am and then travel together to the Cathay simulator building (near the airport) by taxi. After a thorough briefing, the session ran from 9am to 1pm, before we all caught a taxi back to our hotel. We usually spent the afternoons preparing for the next session but, fortunately, a couple of spare days had been built into the schedule to give us a break from what was a fairly steep learning curve...especially for me.

So, during this period, we saw the inside of a lot of Hong Kong taxis. Now, given that Hong Kong was (and still is) such a tourist Mecca, you might reasonably assume that the local cabbies would possess at least some basic English skills...but you'd be wrong. Business cards on our hotel dressers were accompanied by a nearby notice that read, "When returning to the hotel, please show this card to your taxi driver." Of course, it was in Chinese, and I always suspected that it probably said, "Take this drunken foreigner to the Hong Kong Hotel via the longest way possible, and charge him whatever you like—he won't know any better." Needless to say, every morning it was a challenge to get the taxi driver to understand that we wanted to go to the airport, and it usually required somebody to make jet engine noises and mimic an aircraft before he cottoned on.

As if the language barrier wasn't bad enough, most of the cabbies also habitually carried enough tools, spare parts and oil drums in their boots to allow them to disassemble and rebuild their engines on the roadside, if they were so minded. Consequently, we sat jammed together in the cab nursing our bulky, bulging briefcases. The novelty soon wore off, and on one particular afternoon, after showing the cabbie the obligatory card, the instructor (certain that he wouldn't be understood) proceeded to berate Hong Kong taxi drivers about the junk they had in their boots, the fact they couldn't speak English, how hopeless they all were... etcetera, etcetera. Otherwise, the trip to the hotel proceeded in silence and, after we'd paid the cabbie his fare, in perfect, British-accented English, he said, "Thank you, gentlemen. I hope you enjoy your stay in Hong Kong." We quickly retreated inside.

While Dave, Charlie and I studied every afternoon and evening in our rooms, the instructors hit the town. Because they were such frequent visitors, they knew every bar and nightclub in both Kowloon and Hong Kong Island, as well as their opening and closing times and (for really big nights) which ones served breakfast. These nightspots included such establishments as The Bobbies Arms, Blackies, Ned Kelly's Last Stand, The Stoned Crow and Rick's Café. We'd join them occasionally for dinner, but I was always mindful of why I was there and was usually in bed by midnight. Next morning, we'd see some of the worst night owls wandering back through the hotel foyer just as we were heading out.

When a sim session ended, lunch was the first order of business. For our instructors, there seemed to be only two possibilities—a hamburger (barely-cooked mince patty in a bun with some tomato sauce) at a place they called the *Junior O's* (military slang for junior officers) or a Keema curry at the more upmarket *Senior O's*. In reality, both establishments were far from salubrious, with the curries being consumed whilst seated at fold-out tables and chairs out on the street. At this stage I wasn't particularly adventurous (gastronomically speaking) but, one afternoon, Bill finally convinced me to join them for a hot and spicy Keema curry. I woke up at about 3am the next morning with my stomach churning and just managed to reach the toilet before my digestive tract purged itself spectacularly for about the next half-hour. Feeling weak and wobbly and convinced that I'd contracted food poisoning, I went back to bed and eventually managed to get back to sleep.

Later that morning, I told Bill about what had happened to me during the night.

"Did you look down and see a little brown furry thing fizzing around in the toilet bowl?" he asked.

"Yeah, just about," I said.

"Did you think you'd have to put your bum under the cold water tap to stop it burning?" he continued.

"Pretty much," I agreed.

"My boy," he said wrapping a kindly, almost paternal arm around my shoulder, "You have just experienced the wonders of the Keema Steamer."

But Hong Kong wasn't all beer and skittles (or beer and keema curries) for we trainees—there was also a lot of work to be done. Our workplace (the simulator) was essentially just a big white box atop three spindly, hydraulic jacks that moved and tilted in accordance with the pilot's inputs to replicate the motion of the "aircraft." The only thing that couldn't be reproduced were the 'g' forces that accompany any pushing or pulling of the flight controls. The interior of the box consisted of cockpit controls and instruments at the front, and an extensive panel of red and green buttons at the back that the instructors pushed to induce system malfunctions and create mayhem. Two large black and white monitors clamped to the pilots' windshields displayed runway (and peripheral) lighting so that when you were "in flight," you really felt that you were operating into (or out of) various airfields at night. A massive computer in an adjacent room controlled the hydraulic jacks, the flight instruments and the 'visuals' on the television monitors. When "everything was happening," you almost believed that you were in a 707 aircraft at night.

During the first nine sessions—the tenth would be our check ride—Dave and I alternated as Pilot Flying to learn the various procedures that had to be mastered. Broadly, the sessions consisted of engine start malfunctions and rejected takeoff procedures (preceding a fifteen-minute break) with inflight engine or system malfunctions afterwards. While some emergency procedures required us to carry out numerous checklist actions and operate various system controls from memory, others required us to troubleshoot and analyse the problem as a crew first, before then systematically working through a detailed emergency checklist. The first few sessions were largely introductory, but engine failure sequences soon followed—which, of course, was all new territory for me.

To initiate such a sequence, the instructor pushed one of his many buttons to make an engine either catch fire (accompanied by a very loud fire warning bell) or fail (with an accompanying loss of thrust). So, while some malfunctions were spectacular, others (such as an engine flame-out) could be much more subtle, with the only indication being the need to bank the aircraft into the 'live' engines to maintain a constant heading. Should this occur, the flying pilot then has to quickly introduce rudder in the same direction as the yoke displacement while simultaneously centring the yoke to restore the full range of available aileron travel. It's a skill that requires some practice and, since the rudder displacement is a function of engine thrust, every time the thrust is changed, the aileron/rudder relationship also changes. More thrust, more rudder—less thrust, less rudder. With practice though, this requirement could be anticipated, and the controls could be readjusted almost intuitively. However, despite the rudder being a hydraulically-boosted control surface, the strain of holding in the required inputs for protracted periods usually made my leg start to tremble and shake. After one particularly lengthy engine-out sequence, my leg almost collapsed underneath me as I climbed down the ladder to head for the coffee room.

Engine failures on the takeoff roll came next where, depending on the speed at which the failure occurred, either a rejected takeoff procedure or an engine failure after takeoff (EFATO) procedure was required. Since the simulator belonged to Cathay Pacific, most of our sessions were conducted at Hong Kong, where the surrounding mountainous terrain made EFATOs even more challenging. The simulator was also apparently much more sensitive in pitch than the actual aircraft, and so I was told that if I could fly the simulator well, I'd have no trouble flying the aircraft. Eventually, the day of our check ride rolled around, and I'll admit to suffering some "checkitis" (nerves). But Woofy, our instructor, was very laidback, and the session merely consisted of carrying out sequences and procedures that we'd been practicing every day for nearly a fortnight.

When the check ended (and after we'd both been told that we'd passed), Woofy set up and froze the simulator at 1500 feet on late final approach onto Runway 31. He then jumped into the left-hand seat, released the simulator and said, "Well, my wife has left me, and I've decided to end it all!" He then pushed the thrust levers all the way up and drove the aircraft straight into the runway at about 250 knots. Well, we didn't know what to expect but, looking out the front, we watched the "aircraft" bounce up to about 3,000 feet, roll over onto its back and then fall smack-bang into the middle of Kowloon. The 'visuals' then went blank, and every needle started wildly "spinning off the clock."

"Come on, let's get out of here," Woofy said, unstrapping quickly, "I think we've killed it!"

Hong Kong had certainly been a fascinating cultural experience on so many different levels. From flicking around the local television channels, I'd even learnt from the commercials that Chinese cows don't go "Moooo;" they go "Seeee." I also managed a little local sightseeing and travelled over to the Island and back on the Star Ferry (which cost the princely sum of ten Australian cents each way). Unfortunately, the conditions weren't favourable for taking the cable car to the top of Mount Victoria, because it was obscured by low, thick clouds for our entire stay. We flew home aboard one of our 707s that had ferried the last few squadron pilots up to Hong Kong for their emergency refresher checks. Woofy was the captain, Dave sat in the right-hand seat, and I sat in the observer's seat behind Woofy. It was amazing to be in the actual aircraft and see the real systems in action. Plus, the external "visuals" were fantastic. Now, I just couldn't wait for my turn to fly the aircraft!

That opportunity came a week or so later, during a series of conversion flights that incorporated circuits and instrument approaches at nearly every Australian RAAF base. On the way to Pearce from Alice Springs, much to the delight of the Tower controller there, we flew a circuit and low overshoot at Meekatharra. Whenever we left Richmond, I couldn't help noticing the number of drivers on the busy, adjacent Richmond-Windsor Road, who would pull over to watch us takeoff. The real aircraft, as advertised, was indeed much more stable in pitch than the simulator, however, with the rudder being the only hydraulically-powered control surface, it took some manful control inputs to drive the big girl around the skies. The 707 also had quite a reputation as being a difficult beast to land—something I'd discover for myself on numerous occasions—but my first landing attempt must have been reasonable because, looking back on it now, I have no clear recollection of it whatsoever.

What I do still remember clearly, however, are the circuits at Avalon Airport in Victoria, because it seemed that whenever we went there, the wind was blowing from the west: straight across the long, north-south runway. The maximum permissible landing crosswind for a Boeing 707 was 23 knots of steady wind (with allowable gusts of up to 28 knots) and this limitation must have been known by the Tower controllers. Whenever we asked them for a wind check (usually with the thirty-knot windsock being parallel to the ground and perpendicular to the runway), the controller would instantly respond with a cheery, "crosswind of 23 knots, gusting 28 knots". On final approach in such conditions, it wasn't unusual to experience as much as fifteen degrees of drift and, at times, it felt like you were approaching the runway sideways. To unconsciously compensate, I sometimes found myself twisted around in my seat to make the visual orientation of the runway environment appear more normal.

The technique for landing a 707 in strong crosswinds involved keeping the drift on right up until the flare (about twenty feet above the ground). Then, as the thrust levers were retarded to idle, left or right rudder (depending on the direction of the crosswind) was promptly introduced to align the aircraft with the runway centreline, while opposite aileron was applied to keep the wings level. The engine pods that were slung under the 707's wing were surprisingly close to the ground, and if a landing was mishandled in such conditions and the aircraft wasn't held level on touchdown, it could easily result in the engine pods on the lower wing being scraped along the runway. An hour of crosswind circuits was a real workout, and so I was glad that we got to fly the 707 in our RAAF blue uniforms, rather than in the hot and stuffy Nomex flying suits that featured in nearly every other unit.

Eventually, after nearly a month of flying all over the countryside, my conversion training concluded with the successful completion of an Instrument Rating Test, mostly conducted at Canberra. Again, there was none of the stress and angst that I'd experienced during flight tests at Point Cook and Pearce, and I felt that I might have finally found my spiritual home on the big, four-engined jet. Now I just couldn't wait to get away on some of those exciting overseas trips that I saw appearing regularly on the big tasking board in the Operations Room.

3
ADVENTURES IN ~~PARADISE~~ BUTTERWORTH

In 1983, RAAF Base Butterworth, in Malaysia, was the home away from home for two permanently deployed RAAF Mirage fighter squadrons, which patrolled the Malay Peninsula and the Straits of Malacca as part of the Five Powers Defence Arrangements (between Australia, the UK, New Zealand, Malaysia and Singapore). The 2,000 personnel stationed there to support these two squadrons (along with the occasional deployment of Orion maritime patrol aircraft) resulted in Butterworth being Australia's second-largest RAAF base—only Amberley was bigger. One of 33 FLT's regular "milk runs" was a fortnightly service to Butterworth that ferried deploying personnel and their families to the base, and then returned those who had completed their postings back to Australia. The base at Butterworth also had an Australian School attended by the servicemen's children and therefore many young civilian teachers, usually fresh out of college, also travelled with us regularly.

The flights operated out of (and back into) Sydney International Terminal so that customs and immigration formalities could be efficiently carried out for the large numbers of passengers that we carried. On the return journey, the 8,000-foot runway at Butterworth wasn't long enough (in the high ambient temperatures) to allow us to uplift enough fuel to reach Sydney direct, and so a refuelling stopover was always conducted at Darwin. The Butterworth Charter, as it was known, was a three-day trip that left Richmond for Sydney at 3pm on Monday, flew to Butterworth direct on Tuesday, and then returned to Richmond via Darwin and Sydney on Wednesday, arriving back home just before the unofficial Richmond curfew commenced at 11pm. While Monday evening involved a nice dinner and a night's accommodation in a King's Cross hotel, these luxuries were more than offset by the long and tiring return legs back to Richmond on Wednesday.

Being the most junior squadron pilot (in terms of both rank and experience), I flew a lot of these trips—so many that I decided I wouldn't tally them up until I left 33 FLT on my next posting. Carl was the captain on my very first Butterworth Charter (BC) in late May 1983, but over the ensuing two years, I would fly to Butterworth with nearly every other pilot in the outfit. The very short leg from Richmond to Sydney (little more than ten minutes in the air) would usually see us check into our hotel at about 5:30pm. Most of us then ate dinner together at a restaurant in the Cross, where I soon fell in love with their delicious Oysters Kilpatrick and Filet Mignon. But we were free to eat wherever we liked, and a funny story circulated within the unit about Tim (one of our more colourful characters), and his dining experience one particular evening.

Tim was a pocket dynamo who marched to the beat of his own drum. A keen mountaineer, he'd earned himself the nickname of "Sherpa" due to his ambition to one day tackle Everest. It wasn't unusual for Tim to take his camping gear on a trip and, rather than sleeping in his hotel bed, set up a tent in his room and then sleep on the floor. Tim also enjoyed vegetarian meals so, while most of us were scoffing steaks in the Cross, Tim would head off, alone, to his favourite organic restaurant in Darlinghurst. One night, a contingent of Rajneeshis (the followers of a controversial Rolls-Royce driving, multi-millionaire Indian cult leader referred to at the time as "The Bhagwan") walked into the restaurant attired in their flowing, bright orange robes. Tim must have been feeling a bit lonely that evening because he tried to engage them in a little casual conversation.

"Who are you guys?" Tim asked innocently.

"We're the Orange People," the nearest one replied.

"Oh, okay," Tim replied chattily. "I'm from Bathurst, myself."

On the Tuesday morning that followed, we were always up bright and early, with the transport arriving at about 7:30am to pick us up and take us to Mascot for our 9:30am departure. During these flights, I soon discovered what a "Boy's Own" adventure flying the 707 was, with the hijinks usually starting just as soon as passenger boarding was underway.

To my knowledge, every large airliner has its cargo doors on the right-hand side, with the passengers boarding from the left. While I can't say why this is the case, as a consequence, the captains on early passenger aircraft began occupying the left-hand control seat so that they could check out the passengers (particularly the pretty girls) as they climbed the stairs to board the aircraft. Of course, enclosed aerobridges eventually came along and ruined everything. The 33 FLT 707s had five seats in the cockpit—two pilot seats, a flight engineer's seat, a first observer's seat (behind the captain) and a second observer's seat (behind the first observer's seat—the long-unused navigator's station). Because a BC crew normally consisted of three pilots and one flight engineer, there was always a spare seat in the cockpit for every takeoff and landing. Sometimes, the newly graduated teachers travelling with us to Butterworth included some very young and very attractive ladies. But it was also a convention for any spare cockpit seat to be offered to the highest-ranking military passenger. This situation could have presented a conundrum elsewhere; but not in Air Force Airlines.

When boarding commenced, the aircraft loadmaster (who travelled with us on trips in the passenger compartment) was charged with the important task of identifying the prettiest girl onboard the aircraft and noting her seat number. When he subsequently presented the captain with the completed weight and balance loadsheet just before departure, he would say something like, "A gorgeous girl is sitting in 10C". Shortly afterwards, as we were taxiing out for departure, it was customary for the third pilot to make a PA to the passengers detailing the direction of turn after takeoff and the planned flight time, and then concluding with the instruction for the cabin crew to be seated for takeoff. On a BC though, the pre-takeoff PA would be more like this:

"Well good morning, ladies and gentlemen, boys and girls. Shortly we'll be taking off from the northerly runway and turning left to set course for Butterworth with a flight time of about seven and a half hours. Now today, we happen to have a spare seat on the flight deck, and to be fair to everybody, we've decided to put all the seat numbers into a hat and whoever's seat number is drawn out can come up and join us for the takeoff, as well as for the descent and landing into Butterworth. Okay, so...I've drawn a number...and the winning seat number is...10C!"

The whole thing was a sham, of course, and just as soon as the announcement had been made, the pretty young thing down the back would let out a squeal of excitement before being met and escorted to the flight deck by the courteous and attentive loadmaster. So, instead of having to play host to some stuffy old group captain or air commodore, we instead got to enjoy the company of a delightful young lady...and nobody ever seemed any the wiser. On departure, the 707 was a noisy old girl thanks to her inefficient Pratt & Whitney JT3D-3B engines that not only made an ear-splitting racket but also left a stream of black sooty exhaust in the aircraft's wake.

The departure track out of Sydney usually passed very close to Bankstown Airport—an airfield used predominantly by light aircraft for charter work and pilot training. It was protocol on departure to set the right-hand VHF radio to the emergency 'guard' frequency so that a distress call could quickly be transmitted if something went badly wrong on the climb-out. But one day, as we overflew Bankstown Airport, we heard a very excited voice call up on the guard frequency:

"Heavy jet aircraft overflying Bankstown...you have black smoke coming out of all four of your engines," he reported breathlessly.

"Thanks," replied Woofy indifferently. "We certainly hope so!"

Once we were in the cruise and our passengers had eaten their meals, there would usually be a steady stream of visitors to the flight deck (if the captain was feeling in a sociable mood). Without fail, they would comment on the plethora of switches, knobs, buttons and dials in the

ADVENTURES IN ~~PARADISE~~ BUTTERWORTH

flight deck, and we would try to reassure them by saying that, fortunately, we only ever had to operate them one at a time. Unlike the 'glass' cockpits of modern aircraft, there were no television screens in the 707 flight deck and, instead, every conceivable system component—leading edge flaps, trailing edge flaps, utility hydraulic pumps, auxiliary hydraulic pumps etcetera, etcetera—had its own controls and indicators. The most dated piece of equipment on the flight deck was a 24-hour clock which had to be checked, manually wound, and set for every departure.

Oftentimes, "baby knucks" ("baby knuckleheads")—newly qualified fighter pilots—would travel with us on their very first operational postings. Woofy loved to kid these impressionable young rookies that the 707s were built in France. "No...they were built in Seattle!" the young knuck would reply unhesitatingly. "Oh yeah? Well, how do you explain this then?" said Woofy. "Le flaps," he said pointing to the leading edge flap indicator (labelled LE FLAPS), "and aux pumps," he added, pointing to the auxiliary hydraulic pumps switch (labelled AUX PUMPS).

With his "mark" now momentarily confused, he'd move in for the kill by saying, "And you probably think that the 707 is an old piece of junk, but this aircraft is so advanced, that the clock even takes the wind

ADVENTURES IN ~~PARADISE~~ BUTTERWORTH | 39

into account." Leaning forward, he'd point to the winder on the 24-hour clock that had an arrow above it labelled WIND.

The penny would usually drop at this point but, for all I know, there might still be some middle-aged pilots around who believe that the 707 was built in France, and that time can be adjusted for the wind.

Butterworth Airmovements (the military equivalent of a passenger terminal) was nearly always a hive of activity, both for our arrival on a Tuesday evening and for our departure at 8am the following morning. With only fourteen hours on the ground, we usually stayed overnight in the Butterworth Travelodge on my early BCs, and there was only ever enough time to check in before quickly heading over the road to an outdoor eating area to sample the local fare. On my first Butterworth trip, I was convinced to try the chilli crab, but just the heat from the sauce was enough to make my lips burn. Being in no hurry to ever experience another "Keema Steamer," I offered mine to the grateful flight engineer. I did, however, immediately fall in love with the local delicacy of Malaysia—the satay stick.

Beef and chicken satays are sold by the dozen, and there was great honour accorded to anyone who could consume a hundred satays in a single sitting, thus becoming entitled to automatic membership of the illustrious "Hundred Satay Club." The authentic Malaysian peanut and chilli sauce is delicious, and I must say that I haven't had satay sauce anywhere else in the world that comes close to replicating that unique flavour.

Back on that first trip, one thing I couldn't help noticing as I ploughed through my satays was that nearly every stray cat that was wandering around foraging for food scraps had had its tail docked. One of the crew offered the explanation that, in local folklore, cats are considered perfect creatures, and so their tails are docked to prevent them from occupying space in the afterlife that might otherwise go to less-than-perfect human spirits.

It all sounded a bit suss to me, but I couldn't help wondering aloud to my dining companions, "I wonder what happens to all those tails?"

"Where do you think the satays come from?" one of them mischievously replied.

Early morning departures allowed us to maximize our takeoff weight in the cooler temperatures that prevailed before the onset of the typical steamy Butterworth afternoons. There were always crowds of people at the terminal (either saying goodbye to others or being farewelled themselves), and for particularly esteemed colleagues, there could be some elaborate ceremonies. Sometimes, we carried more cargo than passengers, and on one particularly sorrowful occasion, we transported a serviceman back to Australia in a flag-draped coffin. He'd fallen victim to the notoriously lethal traffic on the Kuala Lumpur-Bangkok highway that passed by just outside the base. His parents and a RAAF chaplain accompanied him, and the cockpit that day, unsurprisingly, was devoid of its usual hijinks. Eerily, every landing on that flight was as smooth as any I ever felt on the 707.

On happier days, the return legs usually saw us transporting joyful service families home who could have been in Malaysia for as long as three years. Often, the servicemen's children would visit the flight deck and they'd always be excited by the prospect of seeing their grandma and granddad again very soon. Greg "Gibbo" Gibbins devised an ingenious way to have a bit of fun with these kids that involved the Passenger Address handset, which looked exactly like a big black telephone, and the Max Airspeed Warning System that, when tested, sounded just like a ringing telephone. The purpose of this latter system was to warn of an impending exceedance of the maximum permissible airspeed—known colloquially as "ringing the bells"—and it was tested before every flight by pressing a switch on the overhead panel just above the right-hand pilot's head.

When Gibbo was in the mood for some fun and a youngster was visiting the cockpit, he would look over to the pilot in the right-hand seat and wink. The copilot would then pretend to yawn and stretch his arms up over his head—pressing the Max Airspeed Warning System test switch in the process. The bell would ring, Gibbo would pick up the PA handset to answer the imaginary call, and then tell the incredulous child that it was their grandparent on the line calling from Sydney. Gibbo would then pretend to pass information back and forth between the non-existent grandparent and their grandchild, in what could sometimes be quite a lengthy conversation. One day, however, things didn't quite go according to script. Gibbo gave me the signal, I yawned and pressed the test switch and Gibbo answered the "telephone"—just as I'd seen him do many times before.

"Your name's Johnny, isn't it?" Gibbo asked the young fellow standing beside him.

"Yeah," said Johnny dubiously.

"Well, I've got your grandma on the phone here, Johnny—your Mum's mum. She said she can't wait to see you in Sydney, and she wants to know how you're going," said Gibbo.

"That's not grandma on the phone!" replied Johnny with a surprising degree of certainty.

Looking sidelong at me with an expression on his face that said, "This kid's pretty smart—I think he's onto us," Gibbo then asked sweetly, "Why's that, mate?"

"Because grandma's dead," said Johnny succinctly.

Night had always fallen by the time we finally descended into Sydney, and if we were lucky enough to have clear skies and a southerly breeze blowing, the passengers would be treated to one of the world's great spectacles—the city, the Opera House and the Harbour Bridge all spectacularly illuminated and sliding slowly down the aircraft's left-hand side. The only entertainment system on the 707 was a largely unused and ancient eight-track sound system that could pipe music through the PA. Rags, one of our loadmasters, managed to track down an eight-track recording of Peter Allen's *I Still Call Australia Home* (long before Qantas unofficially "acquired" it) and to welcome home the passengers after their long absence, he would dim the cabin lights and play the song for them. There was rarely a dry eye in the back of the aircraft (for both passengers and crew alike).

4

BARS IN BANGKOK, SHENANIGANS IN SINGAPORE

My first non-Butterworth overseas trip was to Bangkok in early June 1983. Bangkok is sometimes referred to as the "Venice of Asia;" not so much because of any particularly elegant architecture, but because this city of eight million sits only a few feet above sea level, and any tropical downpour can render large portions of it navigable only by boat. Before leaving Richmond, I was warned that, although the Thai people are gentle, courteous, and friendly, you never make a joke about their king—ever! Thailand in 1983 was still a developing country and its capital was (and still is) most usually associated with the infamous "girlie bars" that proliferate in the Patpong district of the city. My crewmates decided that, because I was a young man without a great deal of worldly experience, I should broaden my horizons by visiting Patpong and witnessing the gaudiness and decadence for myself. Naturally, they would be happy to accompany me during my educational and cultural enlightenment.

Even in May, the nighttime air in Bangkok was hot and humid, and the atmosphere in Patpong was a suffocating assault on the senses. The girlie bars practically pulsated from the volume of the pop music that blared out of each bar's sound system. Through the doorways, you could see lithe, bikini-clad young women illuminated from above and below by multi-coloured lights or by pulsating white strobe lights as they gyrated around floor-to-ceiling brass poles behind the bar. Pause for a second, or make eye contact with one of them for an instant and they'd try to lure you inside with a broad knowing smile, a beckoning finger or a particularly suggestive gyration. On the second floor of many of these bars were the notorious "Tiger Shows" that featured the girls in cabaret acts that you'd never see in your local RSL on a Saturday night.

We ended up visiting the second floor of the Kangaroo Bar—an establishment that had gotten its name because of its popularity with Australian servicemen on R&R during the Vietnam War. One of the older unit pilots had told me all about the place and said that, as a young RAAF Caribou pilot, he'd been a frequent customer while overnighting between the flights that shuttled the troops back and forth between Bangkok and the war zone.

"It was a wild, old place during the war," he told me. "One afternoon when we were finished flying for the day, my copilot and I went to the downstairs bar for a coldie, and suddenly a grenade appeared, rolling along on the floor...without its pin."

"Geez," I said. "What did you do?"

"We dived over the top of the big, wooden bar just before the grenade went off. We weren't hurt thank goodness—unlike some of the other people in the bar—but there was dust and debris everywhere!"

"I bet you got out of there fast," I said.

"Naaah," he said, "it was hot, we were really thirsty, and we reckoned that the chances of it happening again were pretty slim. So, we just ordered another couple of beers."

The intriguing thing about the Tiger Shows was that, even though they were common knowledge worldwide (with shady hawkers constantly roaming Patpong drumming up business), as far as the local authorities were concerned, they simply didn't exist. The reason why became apparent when, in the middle of the floorshow, a bell suddenly rang loudly. In an instant, the stage lights went out, the music stopped, and the performer snatched up her discarded costume and fled backstage.

"What's happening?" I asked the barman.

"Police raid," he said, boredly.

Sure enough, about ten seconds later, a uniformed policeman appeared at the top of the stairs, took a cursory glance at the unoccupied and unlit stage, turned on his heels and promptly disappeared back downstairs. A few seconds later, the bell rang again, the stage lights came back on, the music resumed, and the performer returned to the stage. It was quite a bizarre example of "out of sight, out of mind."

When a girl had had her turn on stage, she roamed amongst the patrons, soliciting drinks and tips…or just soliciting. Most of us avoided them by claiming to be married to Ruth, one of the more matriarchal flight stewards who had come along out of a sense of morbid curiosity. I have to say that, in retrospect, the guilelessness of it all made it not in the least bit titillating and, to be honest, it was all rather sad. Many poor rural families sold their daughters into prostitution, and these poor souls invariably ended up working in the girlie bars along Patpong Road. Many of them would tragically succumb to the AIDS epidemic that would sweep the world within just a few years.

* * *

Throughout these early trips, I never stopped learning, and on my first trip to Singapore, I was taught a very valuable lesson…although it had nothing to do with flying. In civilian accommodation, RAAF crews normally shared rooms and, sometimes, this universally-despised aspect of transport operations had some unforeseen consequences. The usual complement for a 707 overseas crew was three pilots, one flight engineer and a loadmaster and so, typically, the captain had his own room, the other two pilots shared a room, and so did the flight engineer and loadmaster. On this particular trip however, for some reason, I was sharing a room with Nev, the loadmaster, a man who was a rarity in the squadron because he didn't drink, and hardly ever went out. Nev's favoured activity in a slip port allegedly consisted of little more than staying in his room and watching television. I'd been warned of Nev's preference for a quiet life, but I wasn't about to be deterred from partaking in the cold beers that were traditionally consumed by the crew together in one unfortunate person's room.

Therefore, just as soon as we'd checked in that evening, I threw my bags into the room that Nev and I were sharing and headed off to the "room party" for some frosty refreshments and the lively chat that usually accompanied them. The session turned into a long one, however, and after several hours I decided to skip dinner altogether and go straight to bed. I fumbled my key into the lock, stumbled into the darkened room, peeled off my clothes, collapsed onto the bed and immediately fell into a deep, inebriated sleep. Naturally, a few hours later, I awoke with a bladder that was on the verge of exploding if I didn't immediately open the floodgates. The problem was, Nev had drawn the blackout curtains, and the room was pitch-dark. Not wishing to disturb him by turning on a lamp, I sat on the end of my bed with no clue as to whether to turn left, turn right or go straight ahead. In desperation, I stood up, held my arms out in front of me and, like Frankenstein's monster, blundered around in the darkness in the hope of finding the doorway to the bathroom by sheer chance.

Now you may recall an old Looney Tunes cartoon where a cute little puppy creeps up behind a cat and barks very, very loudly right in the cat's ear. The cat gets such a fright that it rockets up to the ceiling. When I stumbled over the edge of Nev's bed in our darkened hotel room and almost landed right on top of him, Nev's "blast off" would have done that cat proud. But I had no time for explanations and no choice but to continue my quest. Crawling about on my hands and knees, I eventually located the bathroom and finally achieved some blessed relief. Throughout the entire episode, not one word passed between us—either that night or the next morning. I mean...what could you say? I'm not confident that my roommate got much more sleep that night, but I'd certainly learned a valuable lesson. Unless you're sharing a room with someone who doesn't mind you falling into bed next to them in the middle of the night, always know where the bathroom is!

* * *

Another eventful trip to Singapore occurred a year later when the OPSFLTCDR (Mal) and I flew there overnight via Amberley. A passenger with us that night was Air Commodore "Tex" (Officer Commanding RAAF Base Richmond) who was taking advantage of his position to go along on an overseas junket as an "observer." Tex was an intimidating character—a big bear of a man who, in his younger days, had been a fighter pilot. But now, approaching the end of his career, he'd inexplicably been put in command of a transport base. It was a bad fit, since "trash haulers" and "knuckleheads" had little in common and rarely saw eye-to-eye about anything. Tex's lack of any operational transport experience also irked some of the Richmond squadron commanders but, to the rest of us, he was far more notorious for his strict insistence on monthly formation parades.

Younger pilots often wondered what happened to the minds of senior officers as they aged, and I well-remembered the cryptic utterings of the air commodore who attended the daily morning brief at 1FTS. But surely the prize for bizarre behaviour belonged to an air commodore at RAAF Base Edinburgh (outside Adelaide) who, just before his retirement, arranged to be towed slowly around and then out of the base whilst standing in the cockpit of a Mirage fighter. All base personnel were ordered to stand to attention on the side of the road and salute him as he rode past in his "chariot." While Tex never seemed this delusional, he did take the opportunity at his monthly parades to display his superior knowledge of most things—a not uncommon trait in the knucklehead fraternity. A typical Richmond parade would see over a thousand service personnel formed up in their dress blues, and the sheer wastage of man-hours must have been extraordinary. Nobody enjoyed parades and the level of absenteeism was such that the service police would search the base for absconders—often even checking under the toilet cubicle doors. The best we could hope for was to be legitimately absent on the day of the parade by being away on a trip somewhere.

And so it came to pass that I avoided the parade where Tex famously told the Band Commander of the (full-time and professional) Operational Command Band that the tempo of the music had been too slow during the march-past—when the formation exits the parade ground and salutes the OC on their way past. But I was on parade the next month when, after the order to begin the march-past had been given, the band played so fast that a flat-out sprint ensued, and the parade ground seemed to empty in just minutes. As the troops flashed past the OC on his dais, I could visualize the Band Commander pumping his baton thinking, *Is this fast enough for you, Tex? Is this fast enough?* By the time we'd cleared the parade ground I was exhausted, and I hoped that the Band Commander had gotten his point across—otherwise, I'd be needing some serious training before the next parade.

Tex was still a few years from retirement when he accompanied us on our moonlit jaunt to Singapore. At the time, the customs laws were such that you could take as many bottles of spirits as you liked *out* of the country, but you could only bring one 1125ml bottle back in. Tex had taken along two 1125ml bottles ("forty-pounders" in RAAF slang) of gin with him, which meant that one had to be consumed during our two days away—a challenging task for just one person. We landed in Singapore around 8am, and after checking into our hotel, Tex invited Mal and me to his room to assault one of his forty-pounders. Even though I'd only ever seen Tex on the parade ground, I was well aware of his prickly reputation. Surprisingly, though, away from the office, he seemed quite affable and relaxed, and the gin flowed copiously. Initially, we started with gin, tonic and ice...then the tonic ran out...then the ice ran out. But the gin just kept on flowing, and between us, the bottle was drained in around ninety minutes flat. Given that I was already extremely fatigued (and probably at about .05 before we even started drinking), the strong white spirit soon went straight to my head.

Staring at Tex (and barely comprehending what he was saying), his face suddenly doubled, and I knew that I was in serious trouble. A strange look must have come over my face, because the two Texes asked in unison, "Are you alright, Geoff?" I made my apologies, said that I was pretty weary, and headed for my room, breaking into a trot just as soon as I was outside. By the time I reached my door just down the hall,

I had my hand over my mouth, and barely made it into the bathroom before spectacularly purging myself of Tex's gin by "laughing into the big white telephone." Fortunately, Mal (a squadron leader), was entitled to his own room, and so I was able to endure the ensuing twelve hours of abject misery on my own. Undoubtedly, my peers at Richmond would have thoroughly approved of how I'd dispatched Tex's gin (both on the way in and the way out), but that evil, white Devil's brew was now strictly off my list (and has remained so ever since). As for Tex, he retired from the Air Force when his Richmond posting ended, and bought a small hobby farm near Amberley to keep him busy. He died of a heart attack just a short time later, and I can only hope that he didn't try to tell the Choir of Angels that they were singing too slowly.

5
FUN WITH YOUR FRIENDLY FLIGHT STEWARDS

While base parades at Richmond were commonplace, unit parades were a rarity. Nevertheless, the solitary unit parade that I attended during this posting was truly unforgettable. By way of setting the scene, I should explain that there were once two brothers—Don Donnelly, and his younger brother Dave—who were born only a year apart. Each brother had joined the RAAF at fifteen, and, in 1984, both were, by coincidence, based at Richmond. By now, both men had also attained the rank of sergeant, with Don being a member of 33 FLT and one of the unit's more senior flight stewards.

At this time, military medals were scarce and hard to come by, with one Chief of Air Force Staff having only three ribbons on the left breast of his service jacket to show for more than thirty years of service. It must have been extremely embarrassing to encounter his American equivalent, who'd probably received that number just for completing basic training. Therefore, in the 1980s, getting a medal...any medal... was a pretty big deal. Even the National Medal (for fifteen years' service) fit into this category, its blue and gold stripes (reminiscent of the colours of Parramatta's rugby league jersey) seeing it dubbed the "Parramatta Medal." When a National Medal arrived at 33 FLT inscribed to SGT D. DONNELLY, the CO decided that a unit parade would be an appropriate setting at which to acknowledge Don's service and present him with his "gong."

On the appointed morning, we all duly assembled on the tarmac between two hangars, just across the road from the squadron headquarters. After the obligatory inspection, the CO addressed the parade.

"Ladies and gentlemen," he said, "it gives me great pleasure this morning to present the National Medal to Sergeant Don Donnelly."

Don snapped to attention and, with his voice ringing out clearly and concisely across the ad hoc parade ground, channelled Monty Python from a decade earlier when he replied, "THANK YOU SIR...BUT I'VE ALREADY GOT ONE!"

The medal for Don's younger brother had been sent to the wrong unit and so, after a few muffled exchanges between the CO and his ADMINO, the order was given to march past. By the time we'd done so and then "fallen out," we could barely breathe for laughing so hard.

* * *

The flight stewards haven't received much attention here so far, but they truly were an integral part of the operation. By attending to the needs of our passengers—be they civilians, service personnel, Prime Ministers or members of the Royal Family—they were very much the "public face" of 33 FLT. But despite their full-time role aboard military aircraft, most had had little operational experience before re-mustering from their previous duties as Mess Stewards serving meals in the dining room and cleaning rooms in the "blocks." Since the majority of the lower-ranking flight stewards were also young women, some of these "public faces" were more attractive than others.

One of the prettiest faces of all belonged to Leanne (not her real name), a petite young lass with dark, bobbed hair and big, beautiful eyes who was so gorgeous that she'd once appeared as a contestant on a television dating show called *Perfect Match*. In this formulaic program, a male contestant would sit behind a screen and ask questions of three concealed, aspiring dates. Then, based purely on their responses, the contestant would select one of the young ladies to accompany him on an exotic, romantic getaway. Unfortunately for Leanne, while she was physically striking, her speaking voice was a little nasal, and so she always sounded just a little whiney. So, despite being easily the most attractive of the three hopefuls, it wasn't really surprising that she wasn't picked. But when she emerged from behind the screen to give the contestant the customary peck on the cheek, he looked at her and his expression was obvious: "Uh oh! I've screwed up, haven't I?" And indeed, he surely had.

Leanne was a beautiful young woman but sadly, and in all honesty, she wasn't the "sharpest tool in the shed." This shortcoming became obvious on a Sunday afternoon flight to Woomera in South Australia. The airfield there had been constructed to support the joint Anglo-Australian scientific project team that had tested experimental long-range weapons systems in the area during the 1950s. By the 1980s, the program had long since been wound down and the base bore little resemblance to the hive of activity that it had been during its halcyon days. After the aircraft had landed at Woomera, it taxied onto one of the large parking areas and was shut down to await the arrival of its passengers. During this lull, the crew took the customary opportunity to stretch their legs and walk around outside the aircraft. One of the pilots immediately noticed Leanne standing apart from her colleagues with a very confused expression on her face.

"What's the matter, Leanne?" the pilot asked.

"It's really windy," she said, looking around.

"Yep," said the pilot absently.

"But there aren't any trees!" said Leanne (with a little more concern in her voice as she surveyed the barren, desolate terrain around her).

"Yep," said the pilot, with a little more interest.

"But you can't have wind without the trees, can you?" Leanne asked perplexedly.

It took a moment for the pilot to realise that Leanne thought that the wind was generated by the movement of trees. So how could you possibly have wind if there weren't any trees? Unwilling to contradict Leanne's entire understanding of the universe, he just quietly moved away.

* * *

There was also a yawning cultural divide between the technically-oriented, all-male flight crew (at the time), and the welfare-oriented (often female-dominated) cabin crew, with this distinction becoming very apparent on my inaugural trip to Honolulu in June 1983. Already being quite familiar with the uniformly overcrowded and smelly cities of Asia, I was thrilled to be heading for the iconic holiday destination that would soon become one of my very favourite locations. Most pleasing was the fact that I could easily understand the American controllers over the radio.

Now, I should explain at this point that various types of radios are used in aviation, depending on the distance that the transmissions must travel. Military aircraft at RAAF bases used short-range Ultra High Frequency (UHF) radios, whilst at civilian airfields and in civilian airspace, we utilised the slightly longer range Very High Frequency (VHF) radios. But, in the pre-satellite era on flights that traversed unpopulated landmasses or vast expanses of open ocean, there was a far greater reliance on the very long-range High Frequency (HF) networks that had been developed after Amelia Earhart's disappearance over the Pacific Ocean in 1939.

Often, a "nest" of frequencies serviced several geographically proximate ATC agencies and, if the frequency was busy, making a HF call was like shouting a message to somebody across a crowded bar. On my early flights to Butterworth, we'd normally switch over to HF off the northwest coast of Western Australia. Through the squeal and static, I'd give my position report and, in reply, I'd hear just a garbled bunch of gibberish that I knew was meant for us only because I recognised our callsign. The other pilot would then jump in quickly and say, "Roger, Jakarta, maintain Flight Level 350 and report again at KEVOK." I'd then turn to my colleague and say, in utter amazement, "How the hell

FUN WITH YOUR FRIENDLY FLIGHT STEWARDS | 55

did you work that out?" He'd then assure me that, in time, I'd be able to understand them too...and ultimately, of course, he was right. But on my first trip to Hawaii, my initial call to Honolulu HF was greeted by a young female voice with a very cheery "Honnnnolulu," which was instantly understandable and confirmed for me that I was on my way to Paradise. Before its decommissioning, contacting Honolulu on HF always invoked the feeling of "Party Town...here we come!!"

But I digress.

This first flight to Hawaii was an all-nighter, and I'll never forget watching the sun come up over the Pacific and the woolly, tropical clouds being illuminated in pink and orange hues above the sparkling, tranquil waters. Hawaii already seemed a much better proposition than the steamy, dirty cities of Asia. When we reached our downtown hotel (just before noon), we were more than ready for a few cold nightcaps, and were soon convened in the captain's room doing exactly that. Among the assemblage were several flight stewards, including one very brave female (Corrie) and "Berongadilla Dave"—a sergeant who, if the "f-word" had been banned, would have had very little to say. As the drinks flowed, so too did the stories, jokes and anecdotes, and Dave quickly turned the air blue with his colourful language. Corrie stoically tried to ignore it for a while, but eventually, it got the better of her and she stood up and let forth with an absolute tirade:

"To have a few drinks with you blokes, do I have to sit here and be subjected to your filthy, disgusting language? Can't you show ME some consideration and remember that there's a female in the room? YOU ALL MAKE ME SICK!!!" she screamed.

Having said her piece, she stood up, stormed out the door and slammed it so hard behind her that it practically came off its hinges.

In all likelihood, Berongadilla Dave at this point would probably have said "F***!"

Corrie's dramatic exit brought a temporary lull to proceedings, but the captain just sat quietly in the corner, next to Corrie's now-vacated chair, with a wry, knowing smile on his face. After just a few minutes, there was a quiet knock on the door, someone opened it, and Corrie's sheepish face appeared. "Hey Corrie," the captain said with a sly grin, "you forgot your f***ing keys," and he tossed them to her across the room.

Then it was time for some sleep before setting off to explore the place that I would soon consider the most climatically blessed place on Earth. Except for the occasional typhoon and the three or four weeks a year when the Kona winds blow, Hawaii averages around thirty degrees every day and twenty degrees every night—"short-sleeved shirt weather" all day, every day. Visiting the island for the first time, you just can't help but be blown away by the beauty of Waikiki Beach, with its stunning turquoise waters and the towering presence of Diamond Head (an extinct volcano) as a backdrop. While Honolulu exudes a perpetual holiday spirit, what I didn't enjoy on this visit was my first serious encounter with jetlag. Despite having just a few hours' sleep on arrival, I wasn't really tired enough to go to bed until the early hours of the following morning.

In the interim, I found myself in a downtown Honolulu bar with Berongadilla Dave, chatting to some of the locals who'd noticed our Aussie accents. Australia II's nation-stopping victory in the America's Cup Finals was still a few months away, but Men at Work's anthem, *Down Under* had already achieved commercial success in the United States, and they wanted to know what Vegemite was. Despite my enthusiastic endorsement of it as a sublime accompaniment to hot buttery toast, my description of Vegemite's black colour, axle-grease texture and bitter taste (like the dregs from a beer vat—which, indeed, it is) they remained sceptical. I promised to send one of them a jar in the mail but never did—for which, I'm guessing, they were probably very grateful.

Mind you, this was in a country that combined peanut paste with grape jam ("peanut butter and jelly") and whose inhabitants often consumed a breakfast of bacon, pancakes and maple syrup all together on the same plate. Not only is there a vast chasm between the culinary palates of Australians and Americans, but I soon discovered that there were different rules of etiquette involved when ordering a meal too. After perusing the menu in a café one day, I decided on a simple turkey sandwich. But when my order was taken by the very attentive waitstaff, the conversation went something like this:

Waitress: "Have you decided on your order, sir?"

Me: "Yes, I'd like a turkey sandwich please."

Waitress: "Will that be on white, wholemeal, rye, pumpernickel or sourdough?"

Me: "Aaaaahhhhh...white bread, please."

Waitress: "Would you like mustard or mayonnaise on your sandwich, sir?"

Me: "Ummm...mustard and mayonnaise, please."

Waitress: "And would you like a side salad with your sandwich, sir?"

Me: "Yeah, okay. Why not? That'd be nice. Thank you."

Waitress: "Would you like a Greek salad, Caesar salad, Waldorf salad or garden salad?"

Me: "Just a garden salad I think."

Waitress: "Would you like some dressing on your salad, sir?"

Me: "Sure...why not!"

Waitress: "Would you like French dressing, Italian dressing, Thousand Island dressing, Ranch dressing or balsamic vinegar?"

By this time, you're thinking, JUST GET ME THE DAMN SANDWICH WILLYA! but in the Land of Good Service, such prolonged exchanges (which transform mild peckishness into looming starvation) are considered "Superior Service" and deserving of a tip of at least ten percent of the cost of the meal. Tipping in the US is essentially a parallel economy, whereby tour operators and the owners of hotels and restaurants minimize their labour costs by passing them directly on to the public in the form of a "service charge." Bag to your room? Tip the bellboy. Room service meal? Tip to the staff member delivering it. Guided tour? Tip to the tour guide. Everything effectively costs ten percent more than you expected and, over time, a healthy tip has simply become an expectation by those who work in the service industry on, admittedly, very low wages. And woe betide anyone who doesn't tip—even if the service has been perfunctory at best. Whether by a withering gaze or a snide, "And you have a lovely evening too, sir," you'll know if you haven't lived up to your end of the bargain. Considering that Australians didn't customarily tip for anything in the 1980s, it was all a bit intimidating and, after a while, you just felt like handing out dollar bills to strangers at random on the assumption that if you hadn't yet tipped them for something, then you soon surely must!

But there were many other differences too, and some appeared in the unlikeliest of places. We Australian simpletons only have HOT and COLD taps in our showers but, in the US, there's usually one lever to divert the water from the bath to the showerhead, another to adjust the flow from a trickle to a torrent and, yet another that (through painstaking trial-and-error) adjusts the temperature to anywhere between freezingly cold and blisteringly hot. After visiting the 'restrooms' in Waikiki's enormous Ala Moana shopping centre, I discovered that the toilets were different as well. Having "done my business" I stood up…at which point the toilet flushed itself, almost causing me to involuntarily repeat the bodily function that I'd gone there to do voluntarily in the first place.

Notwithstanding the interminable food orders, the plumbing that requires a degree in mechanical engineering and the self-flushing toilets, Hawaii offers some fascinating sight-seeing opportunities. Naturally, Pearl Harbour was at the top of my list of must-sees, and during our two-day stay, I joined my colleagues for a visit to this iconic Navy base, about a thirty-minute drive away from downtown Honolulu. As I stood looking at the US Navy combat ships sitting quietly at their moorings, it was difficult for me to reconcile the tranquil scene that I was witnessing with the devastation that had occurred at that exact spot almost forty-two years earlier. It was a feeling that would become quite familiar over the years—where it is difficult to equate a place's placid present with its colourful (and sometimes horrific) historical past—and I eventually dubbed it "Is This Really It Syndrome".

The exhibit that had the biggest impact on me at Pearl Harbour was the USS Bowfin—a World War II-vintage submarine maintained in pristine condition by an army of volunteers. After paying your admission, you could pay a little extra for a self-guided audio tour that explained the function of each of the sub's compartments as you moved through the boat from the bow to the stern. In the cramped and claustrophobic forward torpedo room, I was informed that not only did this area provide storage space for most of the boat's torpedoes, but it also provided the living quarters for about twenty enlisted men. At the very height of the war, the Bowfin had penetrated the defences of Tokyo Harbour, and I could only imagine how nerve-wracking it must have been for the crew of this windowless craft to realise that they were in the very heart of enemy territory and that they were completely alone. Somehow, though, they and their boat survived—unlike fifty-two other US submarines that were lost during the war, mostly with all hands and often without trace.

Hawaii offered such an appealing blend of history and holiday that I simply couldn't wait to return. But I'd have to wait a year and, in the interim, I'd have to endure my own "wartime" experience.

6
WAR...WHAT IS IT GOOD FOR?

Every few years throughout the 1980s, a major military exercise (usually involving all three Australian services, as well as contingents from other countries) would be conducted somewhere in Australia's north. These joint manoeuvres were designated 'Kangaroo' exercises, and "Kangaroo 83"—the largest such exercise yet held in Australia—was scheduled for six weeks during September and October. Such exercises allowed senior military commanders to trial aspects of joint service doctrine and inter-service cooperation that were otherwise never utilised in peacetime, and so little expense was spared (with the participants often numbering in the thousands).

One capability that the country lacked at the time was that of air-to-air refuelling and, to remedy this shortcoming, two more ex-Qantas 707s were to be purchased with the future goal of converting all four aircraft into aerial refuellers. In June 1983, a month before the two new aircraft were due to arrive, "No 33 Flight" was re-designated "No 33 Squadron", an occasion which I figured would at least justify a parade of some sort. However, despite 33 Squadron's previous proud military history as a transport unit during World War II, the event was marked by nothing more than some money being put over the Richmond Officers Mess bar one Friday afternoon.

As Kangaroo 83 drew closer, Matt, one of our pilots, was notified that he'd be a participant and to say that he was unimpressed would be an understatement. As luck would have it though, on a night when Matt had been Orderly Officer, an airman had been charged with an offence and the charge was slated to be heard while Kangaroo 83 was underway. As a potential witness, Matt had to be present at the base to give evidence if required. A replacement therefore had to be found, and who do you think was the lucky sod who got the job? The Attachment Authority that I duly received said that I could expect to be deployed tactically in the field as a member of the "MAOT" for up to six weeks. Now, I didn't even know what a MAOT was (and nor did anybody else in the squadron), but the prospect of living tactically in the heat of Northern Australia didn't exactly fill me with joy.

The Area of Operations (the AO, in military slang) was a huge tract of northwest Western Australia that encompassed Port Hedland, Karratha and Broome and extended for hundreds of kilometres inland. I was booked to travel on civilian flights and, at Sydney Airport, I met up with the squadron leader who would be my boss in our two-person MAOT—a Mobile Air Operations Team that moves tactically with the Army to arrange whatever air support is necessary for the re-provisioning of food, ammunition and supplies, and whose duties may include the preparation of ad-hoc landing strips. It didn't sound like my idea of "fun in the sun," and so I thought I'd better enjoy every creature comfort that came my way during the Ansett flight to Perth and the subsequent Airlines of Western Australia flight up to Karratha. It was just closing in on dusk when we finally arrived at our temporary, demountable accommodation at Dampier, and were soon informed that a Caribou would transport us out to "Camp Anderson" about 250 kilometres inland early the next day. Being all too familiar with the grandiose designations that the Army afforded their primitive "camps," as I drifted off to sleep, I wondered what god-forsaken hell-hole I would find myself in on the morrow.

The next morning, after two hours aboard a dreadfully slow Caribou, we were finally delivered to our destination out in the wilds of the Pilbara. Although the associated red-dirt airstrip had been pretty rustic, the Camp itself, set against a spectacular backdrop of ragged, scarlet ranges under cloudless blue skies, came as quite a pleasant surprise. Camp Anderson, a Railways of WA maintenance camp, had been commandeered for the exercise and consisted of about a dozen sturdy, demountable buildings (each room with air-conditioning), interconnected by covered concrete walkways. A large central building contained a full-sized kitchen and dining area, and within a green oasis of mowed grass amidst the abundance of red dirt, there was even an outdoor swimming pool. The camp would serve as a Field Headquarters for senior military staff, and an R&R facility for infantry troops on a rotational basis. I couldn't believe my luck, but figured that this place was probably just a brief stopover. The colonel who was our superior wouldn't be returning until the following day, so we were invited to enjoy the facilities which included delicious hot, roast dinners and frosty, cold beers. *If only we could stay here*, I thought to myself that night as I contentedly drifted off to sleep.

The next morning, resplendent in our olive drab tactical uniforms, we reported to the Colonel to find out what was in store for us over the next six weeks.

"Who are you guys?" he asked, as we stood to attention before him.

"We're the MAOT, sir—the Mobile Air Operations Team," said my boss.

"And what are you supposed to be doing while you're here?" the Colonel continued.

"Well, we're here to coordinate whatever air support you might need for re-supply, sir," said the Boss (quoting the information he'd read in the Joint Forces Manual).

"Well, I don't need any re-supply," said the Colonel to our utter astonishment. "All of our supplies were pre-positioned here weeks ago by road. We've got enough stuff stashed away to last us for the whole exercise. I don't see any need for re-supply at all...especially by air."

There was a long pause before my boss said, "So...what do you want us to do then, sir?"

The Colonel pondered this question for a while before saying, "Well, you may as well stay here for a few days while we work out whether there's anything for you to do. But if we can't come up with anything... you may as well go home."

I was simply stunned. I'd expected to be out in the "boondocks" somewhere, eating hard rations and carving out landing strips while talking to aircraft on hand-held radios. Instead, our routine quickly became one of sleeping in until about ten o'clock, reading whatever we could find until noon, having a hot roast meal for lunch, playing a game of cricket or having a swim in the afternoon, before having a hot roast dinner, cold beers and then watching a few movies before bedtime. After four days, we were bored rigid and rapidly growing out of our uniforms. "How about we ask the colonel if we can go home?" I suggested one afternoon. The colonel readily agreed, and so we consulted our Joint Forces Manual and finally drafted and dispatched our first operational Air Support Request message...the one that requested our extraction from the field. War was hell!

7
ARRRRRRRRR...IT'S CAP'N RON!

Having survived the warzone free of any post-traumatic stress or psychological flashbacks, I resumed my flying duties with...what else, but several more trips to Butterworth. If truth be told, I was probably serving my unofficial apprenticeship with some more regional experience before being let loose on the rest of the world. In February 1984 though, someone must have decided that I was finally ready for the "big time", and I was programmed to accompany Ron Peters (the captain) and Dave on a trip to Seattle in the American north-west.

At the time, the Royal Australian Navy was taking delivery of some frigates that were being constructed under contract at a shipyard in Tacoma, the twin city of Seattle in Washington State. As each new ship was being built, its complement of officers and men (along with their families) were flown over to Tacoma and then accommodated while the crew received their training. When the ship was subsequently commissioned and the crew's training was complete, the family members were flown home while the ship was sailed over to Australia. 33 Squadron's task was to periodically take the next crew in the rotation (along with their families) over to Seattle and then about ten days later transport the families of the previous group of trainee crewmen back to Australia.

This process must have been a very costly one at a time when the military budget was under heavy scrutiny. Historically, Qantas Executive Air had booked all our accommodation, but in the face of increasing budgetary pressure, we duly received word from "on high" that, henceforth, military accommodation (including foreign military accommodation) should be used whenever possible. Accordingly, when this trip to Seattle via Honolulu was in the planning stages, messages were sent to the United States Air Force (USAF) bases at Hickam in Hawaii and McChord (near Tacoma) through military channels requesting that accommodation be provided for our crewmembers while we were in port. In the era before the widespread use of fax machines, however, communications via the AFTN (Armed Forces Telecommunication Network) were notoriously unreliable, and no confirmation had been received from the USAF before we departed from Richmond.

The flight to Honolulu was an overnighter (after loading our passengers in Sydney), and we didn't arrive in Hawaii until about 10am local time. Understandably, we were feeling pretty tired by the time we eventually arrived outside the BOQ (the Bachelor Officers Quarters) at Hickam USAF Base. We were none too pleased when they had no idea who we were and were even less impressed when they told us that all their rooms were in use accommodating transit personnel for a major defence exercise that was underway in Guam. "So, there's nothing available for us at all?" we asked tiredly, to which we were told, "No sir. Sorry." There was no alternative but to ring the local Qantas agent, who was eventually able to organize some accommodation for us at the Ilikai Hotel in Honolulu (which had provided the rooftop from which Jack Lord fixed his steely gaze on the camera during the opening credits of *Hawaii 5-O*). By the time we checked in, we'd been on the ground for four hours and were well beyond exhaustion. USAF accommodation had been an abject failure so far, and Ron was determined that the situation not be repeated on the next leg.

Twenty-four hours later, we were back in the air, and during the much shorter flight to Seattle, I was amazed at the sheer volume of air traffic that plied the airways between the US West Coast and Hawaii. To transmit my obligatory position reports, I sometimes had to wait more than ten minutes for a gap in the constant HF radio chatter, at which point it was almost time for the next one. We crossed the coast near Portland, Oregon, and on descent passed close by Mount St Helens, which had spectacularly erupted three years earlier, killing over fifty people. Once all our passengers had disembarked, we were supposed to fly across to the nearby McChord USAF base and remain there, but Ron had already decided that, before we went anywhere, he was going to investigate whether our accommodation arrangements were in place. A quick phone call confirmed, again, that there was no record of our request and that, again, there were no vacant rooms available. McChord was in the middle of an Operational Readiness Inspection and was effectively in lockdown. As aircraft captain, Ron decided to leave the aircraft at Seattle airport and rang the closest Qantas office to request some accommodation in town. Another three hours passed before we could check into our lodgings and, between us, we were convinced that the experiment of using USAF accommodation had been a frustrating and dismal failure.

In early February, the US ski season was still underway and Seattle, not far from the foothills of the Rocky Mountains, had some major ski fields nearby. Ron and Dave were both keen skiers—I'd never seen snow in my life, but with ten days to kill before we headed back, they decided to arrange some ski gear and I decided to tag along. But before we headed up into the mountains, we took a few days off to adjust and spent a day at the mightily impressive Boeing aircraft factory at Renton, on the outskirts of Seattle. At the time, the Boeing factory had the largest cantilevered roof in the world, covering 65 acres of floor space. Within that colossal space, we watched gigantic 747s being put together and moved around the factory like children's toys. As I recall, in 1984, Boeing was close to peak production, and a complete 747 was being rolled out of the factory roughly every five days. In the paint hangar, we noticed some 767s being painted up in Qantas colours before their delivery into service the following year. My other clear memory of this visit was when our engineer tour guide told us that they had examined the feasibility of extending the upper deck of the 747 all the way back to the fin (which actually made the aircraft more aerodynamically efficient). At the time, however, there were simply no engines in existence that could lift such an enormous aircraft, and so the concept would remain just that until the maiden flight of the double-decker A380 in April 2005.

The next day, it was time to head for the ski fields. Along the way, we stopped in to hire some gear. Soon after, we reached the snow line—the elevation where the ambient temperature never rises above freezing—and I was gobsmacked by the natural beauty of the snow-covered pine trees and the majestic mountains that now flanked us on both sides. Our day was spent at Snoqualmie Pass, where the instructor who conducted my half-hour introductory lesson simply couldn't believe that I'd never seen snow before. I soon learnt the basics of walking sideways up a slope and "snow ploughing"—where you point your toes inward to slow your acceleration—and by the end of the day, I could navigate the "bunny slope" reasonably efficiently. But I also took my fair share of tumbles and when we finally got back to the hotel that night, I had muscles aching that I never even knew existed. We adjourned to the hotel hot tub for a while, and as I looked up through the glass roof at the twin towers of the hotel that rose steeply on either side of us, I couldn't help but think, "I wonder what the poor people are doing?" Life was pretty sweet, we agreed and later, on television, we watched spellbound, as two young English skaters—Jayne Torvill and Christopher Dean—won the ice dancing gold medal at the Sarajevo Winter Olympics.

What we didn't know yet was that the Richmond headquarters staff were apoplectic at Ron's decision to leave the aircraft parked in Seattle and move the crew into a hotel. It'd taken them several days just to find us and, for a time, they had anecdotally considered charging Ron with Air Piracy. When they finally got in contact with him in what, I'm sure, would have been a very animated phone call, they informed him that the RAAF staff in Washington were now in the process of finding us some military accommodation and that, when that accommodation had been confirmed, we would fly our 707 there and stay in that accommodation until it was time to return to Australia. This development didn't go down at all well with the rest of the crew who had, by now, adopted the Long Horn Bar & Grill—a Tex-Mex joint complete with continuous country music, hay bales and a pretty mean chilli—as their watering hole of choice. I'd joined them there for dinner on "Amateur Talent Night" where, without much encouragement, our flight engineer Ted had gotten up on stage to tell a joke. He started by telling the audience that he'd use an American accent because, sure as hell, nobody would be able to understand his Aussie one. The bar's owner latched onto this comment and, with his profits skyrocketing thanks to his newfound clientele, he decided to hold an "Australian Accent Competition," with the RAAF crew acting as judges. He even advertised the event on local radio...but since we'd now been ordered elsewhere, his gala event was in jeopardy. He even offered to pay our hotel bill, but the powers that be refused his generous offer and insisted, on principle, that we relocate.

While we awaited word from Washington, Ron and Dave decided to go skiing again but, with my body still aching, I offered to stay behind and take the call that would seal our fate. When it finally came, the RAAF officer on the other end of the line said that they had rung nearly every USAF base on the US West Coast before finding us some accommodation at Fairchild, just outside Spokane (about 350 kilometres to the east of Seattle). An extraordinary amount of effort had gone into saving accommodation costs of about four thousand dollars all up—especially when the extra turnaround at Seattle would cost the RAAF about half as much again. But in military logic, since operating costs came out of a different "bucket of money" than the politically-sensitive accommodation costs, it was entirely appropriate to spend six thousand dollars to save four thousand dollars—a classic case of the "penny wise, pound foolish" attitude that proliferates in the aviation world.

The following afternoon, we flew east to Fairchild USAF Base where, just as soon as we'd landed, our flight engineers and loadies jumped into a rental car and drove west, straight back to Seattle, for the "Australian Accent Competition." Fortunately, the accommodation at Fairchild—the cause of so much angst so far—was a pleasant surprise, because it really was of a hotel standard and far superior to anything on offer at the RAAF Officers messes back home. After a quiet first night on base, I awoke the next morning and pulled back my curtains to behold the incredible sight of a heavy snowfall underway outside. The tiny white flakes swirled and whirled past my window, changing direction with each minuscule wind shift in such a mesmerizing display that I simply couldn't resist watching it until the grass and trees were all covered in a fresh, white blanket of snow.

A few days later, Ron and Dave continued their skiing marathon at Mount Spokane, with Ted and I joining them for the day. Unfortunately, the conditions were pretty awful up on the mountain with leaden grey, overcast skies and a light freezing rain falling. I was unable to rent any overalls and so, not wishing to get soaking wet in such frigid conditions, I decided to just sit it out and have a few quiet drinks in the chalet instead. Again, the language barrier reared its ugly head when I went to the bar and ordered a local beer that was named after the nearby Mount Rainier (as featured on a large poster that was on prominent display behind the bar). The conversation went something like this:

"Can I help you, sir?"

"Yes. I'd like a Rainier beer, please," I said (pronouncing the name as in the sentence "it was much rainier today than it was yesterday").

"Pardon me?" he replied.

"A Rainier beer," I repeated, gesturing in the direction of the poster behind the bar.

"Oh, okay! One Ra-neeeerr coming up," he said.

After about thirty minutes, Dave, Ron and Ted returned to the chalet complaining that it was virtually impossible to ski in the freezing rain without wearing goggles. A couple of nearby, middle-aged ladies overheard this conversation and considerately offered to loan them a few pairs. After my colleagues had headed back outside, I thought I'd better reward the ladies' kind gesture by offering to buy them a drink. They each asked for a "red beer" and when I admitted that I had no idea what that was, they said that it was beer with tomato juice. Now, this concoction sounded pretty disgusting to me, but as I headed for the bar, I thought, *If the barman couldn't understand me when I asked for a "Rainier" beer, how's he going to cope with a beer with "to-mar-toe" juice?*

At the bar, I put on my best faux American accent and drawled, "Three beerrrrs thanks buddy, two with to-may-toe juice." They appeared instantly and with no clarification required.

This little incident was very illuminating with respect to the Australian and American interpretations of the (then) Queen's English. In Australia, we're subjected to so much US television that we can understand every one of their various accents, regardless of whether it's a Texas, Boston, Deep South, California or New York inflection (and believe me, they're all very different). Conversely, Americans rarely ever hear an Australian accent, and so it's very difficult for them to understand us. Aussies who spend a lot of time in the States probably acquire their faux American twang not out of any pretentiousness or disloyalty to Australia, but rather simply out of the need to be understood without having to endlessly repeat themselves.

Finally, after twelve days in Washington State, it was time to return home to Australia via Seattle-Tacoma and Honolulu airports. This time we didn't even bother going to the Hickam BOQ on arrival and, instead, went straight to the Qantas office (where a telephone call to Hickam confirmed that, once again, they had no available accommodation). The Qantas agent then handed us a local newspaper with a front page headline that read "THREE 747 LOADS OF TOURISTS SENT BACK HOME DUE TO NO HOTEL SPACE". She then took out three local phone books, and, between us, we proceeded to call every potential source of accommodation on Oahu. Eventually, the Qantas duty manager got us some rooms by calling in a favour, and thus narrowly avoided the need for us to spend a night in the luxurious Hotel 707. I then flew the penultimate sector from Honolulu direct to Sydney, where we carried every drop of fuel that we could squeeze into the tanks. We took off on Honolulu's "Reef Runway" at the aircraft's maximum permissible takeoff weight and the takeoff roll (with the engines roaring away at full thrust) was timed at an incredible 65 seconds. It had truly been a trip of firsts—the first time I'd seen snow, the first time I'd been on skis, the first time I'd taken off at maximum takeoff weight, and the first time that I'd flown with a pirate!

8
I ORDERED ESCARGOT AND ONLY GOT SNAILS!

The year I arrived at 33 Squadron (1982) marked twenty years since the RAAF had taken delivery of its first Iroquois helicopter. Much of 9 Squadron's early flying during the Vietnam War had been in the 'Bravo' model Iroquois, but in 1968, the heavier and more capable 'Delta' models replaced the underpowered Bravos (which then became the basic trainer for trainee helicopter pilots at 5 Squadron in Canberra). In 1982, the Defence Department decided to replace the aging Bravo trainers with eighteen French-built Aerospatiale Squirrel helicopters. Two years later, the first few of these aircraft were ready for delivery, and 33 Squadron was given the job of transporting five of them from Marseilles to their new home at RAAF Base Fairbairn. For this unusual task, all of the passenger seating (as well as the forward galley) was removed to provide the maximum amount of cargo space. What I didn't initially realise was that the squadron loadmasters had spent weeks calculating the amount of space that could be made available in the cabin, and then confirming that this space would be adequate for the job. Their ingenious solution was to load the Squirrel fuselages obliquely onto cargo pallets and transport them upstairs, while the rotor masts, rotor blades and tail booms would travel in the cargo holds downstairs. When we finally departed Richmond for Marseilles, the loadmasters assured us that there would be "at least half an inch" of clearance available in the cabin.

Owing to a technical problem, however, our departure was delayed, and it would take us fourteen hours to finally reach Butterworth (after brief stopovers in Darwin and Kuala Lumpur). Even so, bright and early the next morning, we departed Butterworth and, instead of tracking south-east for Darwin (as I'd done so many times previously), this time we headed west. What a novelty it was to be heading somewhere different, and how exciting it was to be bound for Europe!

Out over the Bay of Bengal, the weather was poor, and the HF communications were worse. In the 707, we'd inherited a HF SELCAL (Selective Calling) system from Qantas, whereby each SELCAL-equipped aircraft is allocated a discrete four-letter designator. When a crew has established contact with ATC via SELCAL on HF, rather than having to continuously monitor the awful HF hash and static, ATC agencies merely need to transmit this code to trigger an aural cockpit alarm to advise the crew that the aircraft is being called. SELCAL, therefore, was an absolute godsend, and we pilots were forever grateful that Qantas had insisted that the RAAF pay a charge for it to be removed (as the RAAF had originally requested and which, of course, they then baulked at paying). On this particular day, though, the weather was so bad that even the SELCAL proved ineffective and, for several hours, we had no choice but to do things the old-fashioned way. The weather only cleared once we'd rounded the southern tip of India, whereupon normal operations were blissfully restored.

Then it was across the Arabian Sea to the coast of Oman where, instead of being greeted by the anticipated expanse of featureless desert, we were met with a range of dramatic, barren mountains that rose steeply to an elevation of nearly ten thousand feet. As this hostile, jagged landscape slipped quietly by far below us, I could almost feel the heat of the desert on my face and visualize the trader caravans and bandit gangs who'd roamed this region for millennia. Approaching Abu

Dhabi, on the north coast of the Arabian Peninsula, the mountains finally subsided into flat desert sands. Ahead lay the waters of the Persian Gulf, teeming with ships of all sizes, including the super-tankers that waited patiently at anchor for their turn to draw up their precious cargoes of oil. Also visible on the eastern horizon was the dusty coastline of Iran which, at the time, was engaged in both a bitter land war with its neighbour, Iraq, and an equally bitter philosophical war with "The Great Satan" (the United States). Iran still possessed a potent (although aging) Air Force and, as a military aircraft, we were particularly careful to remain on track and avoid Iranian airspace. The Persian Gulf was an extremely volatile region and, four years later, a US warship would mistakenly shoot down Iran Air Flight 655 with the loss of 290 lives.

Fortunately, our passage across the Gulf was uneventful and, finally, we began our descent into Bahrain. Now, some archaeologists claim that Bahrain may have been the site of the Garden of Eden, but the drab, barren island that I saw bore little resemblance to any lush, biblical paradise. The next day was free, and so I headed off for the Gold Souk (market) in search of a small gold chain for my father-in-law who, years earlier, had lost one in the Gold Coast surf. The wealth that I saw on display when I got there was simply mind-boggling! The Souk was a three-story block with about ten or fifteen shops on each level and every shop selling just one thing—gold. There was gold cutlery, gold crockery, gold bathroom fittings, gold lamps, gold ashtrays, gold statuettes and, of course, gold jewellery...acres and acres of gold jewellery. Every shop window was filled from floor to ceiling with gold chains and bracelets, and the merchandise in each store alone must have run into the millions. Islamic law requires the hand of a thief to be cut off as punishment, but this place would surely be enough to make you wonder, "Are hands all that indispensable?"

Entirely overawed by the astonishing wealth on display, I eventually wandered into a shop and made a tentative enquiry about buying a gold chain. At the counter, a middle-aged American lady was trying on a particularly gaudy necklace of gold studded with emeralds. When she asked the shopkeeper the price, he replied matter-of-factly, "Two hundred and fifty thousand American dollars, madam." My imposed budget of about a hundred dollars made me feel like a charlatan...and an impoverished one at that. Nevertheless, when I told the proprietor what I had in mind, he showed me a variety of chains in my price range and asked me to pick one. I selected a particular style, and he then placed examples of differing lengths onto a small scale until he found one that would cost what I wanted to pay. In the gold Souk, you didn't pay for the craftsmanship, you just paid for the gold.

The next morning, we headed off for Marseilles and the realisation that I'd soon be seeing Europe for the first time kicked in in earnest. Along the way, we overflew Cairo and Crete and passed close by Athens and Rome. The flight took just seven hours, but during that time we traversed three of the great ancient civilizations—Egypt, Greece and Rome. I didn't want to leave the cockpit for rest breaks, even though talking to ATC on the radio was, admittedly, a bit of a distraction. As the flight progressed, I thought about the rich and fascinating history of the regions passing by below us—the construction of the pyramids, the epic sea and land battles of ancient Greece and the rise and fall of the Roman Empire. Travelling between these distant capitals would have taken weeks or months in ancient times: we were crossing them all in just a few hours. As I looked down at every piece of land and every body of water, I wondered whether a battle may have occurred there. How many different languages had been spoken? How many different cultures had fought for supremacy? In a little longer than it takes to fly from Sydney to Perth, we had covered the sites of six thousand years of recorded human history. It was, truly, both a fascinating and humbling experience.

Our ultimate destination, Marseilles, France's second-largest city after Paris, has its own interesting history. The city was initially established by the Greeks as a Mediterranean trading port in 600 BC and has retained a strong maritime focus ever since. In books and films, however, the city's proximity to North Africa sees it portrayed as a tough place that plays host to smugglers, mercenaries, drug-runners, gun-runners and other similarly shady characters. In the city centre, the old port is still the focal point, and small fishing boats tie up at the marina to sell freshly caught seafood directly to the strolling members of the public. Overlooking the old port and town is the Notre Dame de la Garde (Our Lady of the Guard), a limestone Catholic Basilica consecrated in 1864, although the original church on the same spot dated back to the 13th century. With a long seafaring tradition, the local people of Marseilles traditionally view the church as the guardian of both the city and its sailors.

As in most other European cities, while the historic city centres are largely preserved, modern urban developments are relegated to the city's peripheries. By the time we'd landed, secured the aircraft at Marseilles-Marignane Airport, travelled to our inner-city hotel and settled into our rooms, it was almost dinner time. A squadron leader involved in the Squirrel project met up with us at our hotel and escorted us down to the old port for a traditional French dinner. At a waterfront restaurant, many of the crew dined on escargot (snails) and bouillabaisse (a traditional Provencal fish stew that originated in Marseilles)... I wasn't one of them. During the meal, we discussed the chaotic local traffic flow, and the project officer let us in on the French definition of a millisecond—it's the time between when a traffic light turns green and when the first local taxi driver blows his horn.

The next day was Anzac Day and, mid-morning, most of us assembled in the hotel foyer to venture into town and explore the Notre Dame de la Garde. While climbing the steep hill on which the church sits, we were surprised to see an American-built Sherman tank sitting on the side of the road. Operation Dragoon (August 1944) was one of the lesser-known campaigns of the war, where US and Free French troops made an amphibious assault across the beaches of the French Riviera to capture the key ports of Toulon and Marseilles. The Notre Dame de la Garde had become a heavily fortified observation post under German occupation, but when Free French troops battled to reclaim the city, they used only tanks and infantry when assaulting the hill so as not to damage the cathedral. One of these tanks (Joan of Arc), was hit by heavy German fire and all three of its occupants were killed. The French assault was ultimately successful, however, and the Joan of Arc was left where it was hit as an enduring monument to the French soldiers who'd died during the battle. The cathedral itself was also surprising because its Byzantine-style interior was more reminiscent of a mosque than a church. On the walls were a multitude of plaques dedicated to various ships and their crews in the hope of ensuring their protection by a higher power. It was an impressive place to visit, but it was now time to wander down the hill and get some lunch.

We dropped into a small waterfront eatery (intriguingly named The New York Brasserie) for a quick snack and a beer…and then stayed on for about six hours. The mild temperatures, sunny skies and perfect late-spring weather along with the picturesque setting made it almost impossible to leave. Vincent, our waiter, cheerfully served us round after round of drinks and eventually joined us for one at the end of his shift. We couldn't speak French, and he couldn't speak English, so when Ted tried to explain the purpose of our visit to Marseilles by imitating a kangaroo, a big aeroplane and then a helicopter, Vincent probably thought that we were all quite mad. When he'd cheerfully bid us farewell and left for home with a hefty tip, Charlie (the other flight engineer) and I headed to the railway station at Gare Saint Charles to enquire about catching a train to Cannes the next day.

A popular television show around this time was *Lifestyles of the Rich and Famous* and so Cannes seemed the perfect place to take a break from my usual "Lifestyle of the Poor and Insignificant." The Cannes Film Festival was due to begin just a fortnight later, and Charlie and I figured that we should visit the French Riviera and go on the lookout for some of the attendant "Beautiful People." At the station, there was, again, a significant language barrier, but we eventually managed to get a copy of the railway timetable that detailed the stops along the two-hour route (including arrival and departure times at each of them…to the minute). "Yeah, right," we thought cynically, "arrive Saint-Raphael 1:02pm: depart 1:04pm". We bought tickets for a mid-morning departure the following day and then returned to The New York Brasserie for "just one more" before dinner.

The next day, the weather was perfect! Charlie and I headed off to the station where, before long, the Cannes-bound train pulled in (exactly at the time shown on the timetable…to the minute). The carriages were comfortable and, apart from their generous legroom, the seats resembled airline economy-class seats (complete with fold-down tray tables). Vendors circulated throughout the train pushing large trolleys full of drinks and snacks for purchase, and at each stop along the way, the train arrived and departed right on time...to the minute. From the carriage's large windows, we got some excellent views of the countryside of Provence, which was not as green and lush as I'd imagined, more akin to the rockier, scrubbier lands of Mediterranean countries like Italy and Greece that I'd seen on television. The train hugged the coastline for the final part of the journey, offering us a spectacular view of the Mediterranean, before depositing us in Cannes exactly on time.

The side streets of the town were crammed with designer stores, and before long we emerged onto the palm-tree-lined Boulevard de la Croisette that parallels the shoreline for about 600 metres. The sand was slightly darker than the bleached white sands of home, but under clear skies and in bright sunshine, the beach was heavily populated. Each of the waterfront hotels—including the iconic, white-washed Carlton Intercontinental—had a section of beach reserved for its patrons, complete with blue-and-white striped chairs and umbrellas. The French tricolour flew everywhere, immaculately coiffed and attired people in sunglasses browsed the windows of the chic designer stores and luxury cars and limousines cruised slowly up and down the Boulevard. Offshore, multi-million-dollar pleasure cruisers and yachts bobbed quietly at anchor, while helicopters on scenic flights buzzed restlessly up and down the shoreline. It was a stunning display of wealth and opulence, and we spent an hour or so just strolling along the footpath, admiring the scenery and people-watching. At one point, I was certain I saw Yannick Noah (the black French tennis star who'd won the French Open the year before) stroll past with a small entourage in tow. At lunchtime, we sat at a beachfront restaurant and dined on avocado seafood washed down with glasses of white wine. It was a difficult place to leave and proved to me, once and for all, that while money may not buy happiness, it must certainly make being miserable a lot more fun.

The next day, we returned to the airport and prepared for departure to Bahrain. The planning by the loadmasters had paid off, and five Squirrel "shells" now sat snugly on their pallets in the main cabin. Once again, there were stopovers in Bahrain and Butterworth before we finally arrived back in Canberra late on the evening of the 30th of April. The little helicopters were unloaded early the next morning, and all those who'd gathered to watch the proceedings couldn't help noticing the large hand-written signs that the loadies had placed inside the Squirrel's windshields. "FIRST HELICOPTER TO FLY AT 37,000 FEET" read one. "FIRST HELICOPTER TO FLY FOR EIGHT HOURS WITHOUT REFUELLING" read another. "FIRST HELICOPTER TO FLY 3600 MILES NON-STOP" read yet another. The 33 squadron loadmasters were justifiably proud of their accomplishment and all those assembled appreciated their wry sense of humour. For me, it was yet another unforgettable trip, with the visit to Cannes being undoubtedly the highlight. But as I watched the little blue and white helicopters being unloaded, I couldn't have imagined that in just a little over twelve months, I'd be flying some of them.

9

COMBAT SURVIVAL COURSE— THE HORROR BEGINS!

After graduating from 2 FTS, I'd been lucky enough to find myself posted to a squadron that was the military equivalent of my sought-after dream job of flying for Qantas. But the RAAF insisted on reminding me that I wasn't yet "flying for fun and profit" and, instead, was actively employed in the defence of my country. One avenue by which this obligation was demonstrated was the necessity for newly qualified military pilots to complete Combat Survival Course: a course intended to provide both commissioned and non-commissioned aircrew of all three services with the skills necessary to live off the land in the event of being downed over hostile territory.

Most of my course-mates from No 117 Pilots Course had been hustled off for such training within a year of our graduation parade but, initially, I'd been spared. Even so, every time that some official correspondence arrived at 33 Squadron seeking nominations for the next COMSURV course, I knew that the clock was ticking and that my time was running out. These courses were held in North Queensland and, having never been a fan of tropical heat (or any kind of heat really, for that matter) I'd pleaded with my superiors to delay my nomination until a course came up during the winter months. I'd become extremely spoilt by the over-eating and under-exercising sedentary lifestyle of a globetrotting 707 pilot, and I assured my flight commander that being packed off to COMSURV in the middle of summer would almost certainly kill me and thus result in a lot of paperwork for him—I suspect that the latter part of the argument was probably the most convincing. My aircrew colleagues in the squadron knew that I was only delaying the inevitable, and rejoiced in telling me (in great detail) of the many hardships that they'd endured during their training.

In the 1970s, Combat Survival Courses had been conducted at Canungra (in the Gold Coast hinterland), but successive hordes of hungry survivalists had depleted the local flora and fauna to such an extent that the course had been shifted to the ranges behind Townsville to provide the trainees with at least some chance of avoiding starvation. But even during the Canungra years, sustenance had been hard to come by. On his static survival phase, Charlie (my conversion course colleague) had been encouraged to consume as little as possible from his spartan combat ration pack, since points would be awarded at the end of the phase for each item that remained uneaten. When the instructor duly opened Charlie's ration pack at the end of his five days of deprivation, he was shocked to discover that the little olive-drab metal box was empty.

"What happened to all the stuff in your ration pack?" he asked incredulously.

"I ate it all," said Charlie (a big bloke who always enjoyed his tucker).

"What about the water purification tablets?"

"Yep. Gone!" said Charlie.

"...and the anti-malarial pills?"

"Yummy!" said Charlie, guiltily.

"If I could swallow it, I ate it," he told me. "And I probably would've eaten the tin as well if I'd been out there a few more days."

Other enterprising individuals found more imaginative ways to avoid malnutrition. A 9 Squadron helicopter crewman based at Amberley (just outside Ipswich) was very familiar with the nearby exercise area.

Just a few days before he was due to commence survival training, he and his girlfriend had driven separate vehicles there and left one of them hidden in the scrubby brush with the keys buried nearby. When he subsequently commenced the static survival phase (during which, at the time, the trainees were pretty much left to their own devices), he proceeded to dig up his keys, drive to the Gold Coast and spend four carefree days with his girlfriend in a luxury hotel. He was careful, however, to return to the exercise area well before the instructors arrived for their final inspection, and even rolled around in a puddle of mud to dirty up his otherwise pristine flying suit. Nevertheless, his instructors were somewhat suspicious when the weigh-in of the trainees at the end of the course revealed that he'd *gained* two kilograms while "roughing it" in the bush.

By the early 1980s, changes to the course protocols had rendered such legendary shenanigans an impossibility, and when a Routine Order was received from Operational Command asking for nominations for a COMSURV course that was being conducted in June 1984, I knew that I'd finally run out of excuses. The Attachment Authority that arrived in the squadron a few weeks later did little to assuage my apprehension about what awaited me in Townsville. The training, I was informed, would include a Deep-sea/Sea Coast Survival phase, a Semi-arid Survival phase, an Escape and Evasion phase and, finally, the dreaded Static Survival phase. Participants were advised that achieving an elevated level of physical fitness before the course commenced would be highly desirable and that for the Deep-sea/Sea Coast Survival phase, the ability to tread water for twenty minutes would be assumed by a candidate reporting for training.

At twenty-four, I was still relatively trim and joked that "I love sport—I spend all day on the couch watching it." I also managed to convince myself that I still had some innate level of physical fitness, despite my ongoing love affair with tacos and satays whilst on the job at 33 Squadron. So, despite my inexorably expanding girth, I deluded myself into thinking that too much exertion in the gym beforehand was probably an unnecessary inconvenience. The requirement to tread water for twenty minutes, however, was another matter entirely. Having never been a strong swimmer—or, more accurately, always being a very poor swimmer—I hustled off to the base pool to see if I could fulfil this requirement without drowning. After several sessions of holding each breath for as long as possible (for buoyancy) and then minimizing my arm and leg movements, I found that I was able to eventually do so in the becalmed waters of the RAAF Richmond pool. But in the open ocean? On balance, I reasoned that it would probably not be wise to admit to having all the sea-going capabilities of a house-brick...after all, I was in the Air Force, not the Navy.

Thus, with a feeling of impending doom, I reported to Airmovements Section at Richmond a few weeks later for the long flight up to Townsville. In the departure area, I bumped into "Dicko", a Caribou pilot from a few Pilots Courses behind me, who was also heading north for COMSURV training. Dicko was taller and wirier than me, but in our opening exchanges, he confessed to a level of distaste for physical exertion that very nearly rivalled my own. As a firm adherent to the Limited Heartbeat Theory, I resolved to form an alliance with Dicko against those who would otherwise try to unnecessarily reduce my allocation. By early afternoon, we were settling into the on-base accommodation that was reserved for COMSURV inmates...err, trainees.

Mindful of my predecessors' tales of deprivation, I'd resolved to attack every meal on offer with gusto. So, the next morning, after a hearty breakfast of everything on the menu at the Officers Mess, I waddled off to the COMSURV School with the other trainees. Once assembled in the classroom, we were addressed by the school's CO—a Ground Defence Officer (the RAAF equivalent of an infantry officer) who I'd heard described previously in terms usually reserved for the sadistic commandants of World War II POW camps. I also got to know a little bit more about my fellow course-mates, who were indeed drawn from all three services and included within their number (for the first time, apparently) a female—a RAAF Intelligence Officer I'll refer to as "Sharon."

Sharon was short and full-figured with pale skin, freckles and closely-cropped, bright red hair. In the 1980s, 'active service' positions were (as a matter of military policy), denied to female members of the Defence

Force. But it was Sharon's openly stated ambition to become the first female INTELO in the MFO—the Multinational Force & Observers, who were actively engaged in monitoring the fragile ceasefire between the Israeli and Egyptian armies in the Sinai Peninsula. And so, after much lobbying, her superiors had finally relented, on the strict proviso that she complete a COMSURV course that made no allowance, whatsoever, for her gender (in either its curriculum or its physical demands). I begrudgingly admired her for her determination, particularly when it became immediately and glaringly obvious that she would be receiving zero preferential treatment from her instructors.

No sooner had we been welcomed to the school than we were headed back to the blocks to change into our sporting attire for a session of "circuits"—not the flying kind of circuits, but rather a circuitous sequence of calisthenics that was completed at a cadence determined by a supervising PE instructor. On the way from the blocks to the circuits area, Dicko and I hurriedly conversed and convened the inaugural meeting of the *Gentlemen Jogger's Club* with the express intention of achieving maximum effect with minimal effort. The circuit included areas for push-ups, chin-ups, sit-ups and other "-ups," with a sign in each area stating how many repetitions of each exercise should ideally be completed within the allotted time (with ten being the most typical stipulation).

After we'd distributed ourselves around the various exercise areas, our sinisterly cheerful PE Instructor blew his whistle to indicate that the circuit training had begun. The "conshs" (RAAF slang for conscientious types)—consisting of all the Army trainees and Sharon—tore into their tasks ("one, two, three, four") while the Gentlemen Jogger's Club deliberately pursued a much more leisurely pace ("one......two...... three..."). Soon, the whistle blew again to tell us to move on to the next exercise in the rotation, with the conshs racing off and feverishly launching themselves into the new activity and the Gentlemen Joggers shuffling off to eventually labour through another three or four fairly torturous repetitions before the whistle blew again. Despite our conscientiously unconscientious efforts, Dicko and I were still pretty well knackered by the end of that first session, and our spirits weren't lifted

any by the news from our grinning tormentor that circuits would now be a daily ritual whenever our course activities were on-base. And as if that wasn't bad enough, he also cheerily informed us that a pre-breakfast run up Castle Hill would be added to the exercise regime, starting the next morning. *Oh, what joy!* I thought.

After a quick shower and change, it was back to the classroom for our first theory lessons. Now, the theory instructors launched into the coursework by pointedly telling us that they considered their jobs done if we only ever remembered that the survival priorities (in decreasing order of importance) were "protection, location, water, food." Since that's pretty much all of the classroom theory that I can still remember, those instructors did their jobs admirably. After the first couple of lessons, we were given the news that the Deep-sea/Sea Coast survival phase would commence first thing on Friday morning. We would be required to survive aboard a liferaft for several hours, and then be relocated to a semi-tropical island to participate in an overnight training exercise that would run until the following afternoon. In the meantime, we would get to know the circuits area well, and discover that Castle Hill (a poor relation of Ayers Rock that didn't quite reach a thousand feet above sea level) could seem as precipitous as The Eiger when tackled on an empty stomach.

10
DEEP-SEA DEBACLE

Bright and early on Friday morning...well, early at least...our happy little band found itself being transported by truck to the Townsville jetty to board the RAAF "crash boat" that would transport us out to the Deep-sea Exercise Area. While some islands in the area have such alluring and exotic names as Curacoa Island, Havannah Island and Orpheus Island, we'd be spending the night on the enticingly-named Rattlesnake Island, which the RAAF routinely attempted to blast to smithereens during its primary function as an Air Force aerial bombing and gunnery range. Being only too aware of the efficiency of some RAAF units in coordinating their activities, we hoped that hunger and the elements would be the only things that we'd have to survive during our brief stay there.

To supposedly make our training more "realistic," we were each provided with the resources that would typically be available to any downed military airman—a parachute and a metal box of hard combat rations. Now, as a 707 pilot, I told them that, if realism was truly their goal, I wouldn't have a parachute, but I *would* have access to at least a hundred meals (and just as many bottles of booze). My protestations fell on deaf ears. We were then bluntly told that only the barley sugars and the beef stock cubes in our ration packs could be consumed on any given phase and that the anti-malarial pills and water purifying tablets were strictly off the menu. We'd also been advised to dress warmly (to counter the recent chilly nights) and so I'd decked myself out in my complete winter rig—flying suit, jacket, boots and gloves. Dressed in such bulky attire, I suspected that I'd sink like a stone just as soon as I hit the water, and so I was particularly relieved when we were each handed a bright yellow lifejacket to inflate just before we stepped off the crash boat to swim to our liferaft. We were also issued with some sea-sickness pills because, we were assured, bobbing about in a liferaft for hours on end could be quite nauseating...which it certainly was, but just not in the way I initially imagined.

As the crow flies, Rattlesnake Island is about thirty kilometres to the north-north-west of Townsville. As the crash boat sails, it took about ninety minutes for us to traverse the choppy waters between the Townsville Marina and the Deep-sea Exercise Area. During that time, we were split up into groups of eight or nine and in Group Three (which included both me and Sharon), Sharon (as she probably anticipated) was appointed Raft Commander. When the boat began to slow, we were given some advice on how we should step off its deck to minimize our immersion time in the water—one foot slightly in front of the other, with arms folded across our lifejackets. The boat then shuddered to a standstill and a Zodiac inflatable with two instructors aboard was launched to act as a roving safety, communications and shark lookout post. The orange liferaft for Group One was then inflated, inverted and tossed into the sea. With the rest of us watching on, the members of Group One fitted and inflated their lifejackets, stepped off into the pitching waters and struck out for the upturned raft (which had drifted away surprisingly quickly). It took several minutes for their most capable swimmer to reach the raft, right it, and then help his struggling colleagues aboard. Watching closely, Group Three consulted to determine who was our strongest swimmer...fortunately for us, it wasn't me!

After Group Two had been similarly dispatched, it was our turn, and we quickly took our place at the side of the boat so that we could reach our raft before it drifted too far. With some trepidation, I pulled the inflation toggle on my lifejacket, which reassuringly filled itself with air and constricted itself tightly around my upper torso. Believing that I now had at least some hope of eluding a watery grave, I stepped off the deck and plunged into the waters of the Coral Sea. When I surfaced, I could see our group's strongest swimmer striking out for his objective as it bobbed up and down in the passing swells. Circling us, the Zodiac kept up a watchful, but stand-offish vigil. Everything went quite well... for about the first thirty seconds. By adopting a sidearm stroke of sorts, I could make reasonable headway while keeping my face out of the stinging brine. But then Fate stepped in to reveal that it had either a very sadistic sense of humour or a viciously vindictive streak. The poorest swimmer that day (me) had been handed the only defective lifejacket, and as I painstakingly worked my way towards the raft, I noticed that I seemed to be settling ever lower in the water that now, disturbingly, was starting to wash over my upturned face.

Valiantly attempting to remain calm, I began to tread water and discovered, to my horror, that my lifejacket was now a bit floppy...and getting floppier by the second! Thanks to many past pre-flight safety briefings, however, I instinctively remembered that the jacket also had an oral inflation valve. I started feverishly blowing air into the protruding red valve stem, only to watch it bubble out uselessly through a gash in the jacket where the valve had partially torn away. The last of the air remaining in my lifejacket would soon escape, and I'd need lungs like an air compressor to have any chance of staying afloat. Wearing my bulky flying gear, I could feel myself beginning to slip below the surface...but all was not yet lost. The Zodiac (circling not too far away) offered me salvation but, even in my desperate, waterlogged state, I was faced with a moral dilemma. I was an officer and a pilot, and it would *not be cool* to thrash away and scream for help in front of any enlisted personnel. So, despite my impending demise, I rallied my remaining strength, kicked my feet as hard as I could and, struggling to breathe, called out to my would-be rescuers (as calmly as I could):

"Ummmm...could you help me please? My lifejacket's faulty."

My performance must have been pretty convincing because I saw them turn hesitantly towards the crash boat and seek instructions from their superiors.

"Should we pick him up?" I heard them ask tentatively.

Mentally, I was screaming "YES! GET ME OUT OF HERE YOU IDIOTS!! CAN'T YOU SEE I'M DROWNING!!!" but instead, I merely upgraded my pleas to a slightly-less casual "Ummmm...help!" and started to wave an arm above my head...but not too high...and not *too* frantically. If I was about to die, I was determined to retain at least some degree of dignity and decorum throughout my final moments.

Just as I felt certain that they were prepared to watch me sink into the abyss, they must have finally registered my desperation and hefted me out of the water and into the Zodiac. Thankful to be alive, I lay coughing and spluttering, pointing to the mostly-detached oral inflation valve and cursing the manufacturer of the lifejacket for all I was worth...but calmly, and in the dignified manner befitting an officer. Then they sped me back to the crash-boat, where I was tossed a bulky, solid buoyancy vest. As I donned it, I remembered the tale of a Hollywood movie star who'd served in the oppressively hot engine room of a US Navy warship in the Pacific theatre during World War II. Despite the heat, he'd been ordered to wear a cork buoyancy vest around the clock in case his ship was ever torpedoed. When the war finally ended, this unfortunate rushed up onto the deck, tore the wretched thing off, flung it into the ocean...and watched it *sink like a stone*. I hoped that the design of buoyancy vests had improved since then, and I can say now with perfect clarity that *this* was the defining moment that snuffed out any remaining affinity that I may have ever felt for the sea!

While its consequences could well have been eternal, the whole demoralizing incident probably only took a few minutes, and I was soon unceremoniously dumped near our liferaft to join my exhausted colleagues. Still coughing up seawater, we settled ourselves into our rhythmically bobbing short-term refuge as best we could. To establish her authority, Sharon formally introduced herself to our sodden and dishevelled little group.

"I'm your Raft Commander," she began authoritatively before

pausing, saying "Excuse me a moment," and then leaning out of the raft to throw up spectacularly for several minutes.

Not wishing to jeopardize her credibility, Sharon quickly regained her composure and began directing our activities. The priority was to take off our boots and tie them up outside the raft so that we wouldn't put a hole in the floor. Our instructors had warned us that, undoubtedly, there were sharks about, and that some careless groups in the past had been required to precariously balance themselves atop their raft's flotation chambers for hours before their eventual rescue. With our boots now securely stored, we distributed our water supply and dried our home as best we could. Inevitably, the sun rose higher into the tropical skies, transforming our fully-enclosed little orange cocoon into a floating orange sauna bath. Now, a "ten-man raft" is badly named, because our group of eight was pretty squeezy and with an extra two people aboard it would have been unbearable. The only respite from rampant claustrophobia was the brief rotational period spent sitting in the raft's doorways "on watch." In a genuine survival situation, the lookouts are kept alert by rotating them regularly but, in this situation, it merely provided us with the opportunity to breathe some wonderful fresh air and confirm that the outside (non-orange) world still existed.

Understandably, it didn't take long for the novelty to wear off, and we were soon engaged in a battle against a very real and persistent enemy...grinding boredom. Initially, we told jokes and stories of past adventures, and there was even a half-hearted attempt at a sing-along at one point. But, almost inexorably, we all succumbed to the onslaught of the mind-numbing, spirit-sapping tedium. Minutes passed like hours and hours felt like days as we drifted into a state of suspended animation inside our little orange world that bobbed, never-endingly, up and down...up and down...up and down.

Occasionally we drifted close enough to another raft to exchange some verbal pleasantries:

"Hey, you guys! Have you felt a shark bump into your raft yet?" one group called out to us.

"F*** OFF," we wittily replied, before nervously re-appraising our fragile temporary home.

The Zodiac also passed by every few hours to uninterestedly enquire about our welfare.

"How are you going, Group Three?"

"F*** OFF" we again replied...but with less humour and more than a hint of malice.

After several hours (days...weeks...somehow it didn't seem to matter anymore) the boredom was alleviated by a novel experience reserved for the devotees of rafting—the inability to relieve oneself, even when one's bladder feels like it's about to explode. We'd been slowly sipping away on our water bottles to prevent dehydration when nature (inevitably) took its course.

"I gotta pee," announced one of our number suddenly. He shoved his way over to one of the doorways, stood up and then balanced himself precariously in preparation for the relief ahead. But after a minute or so, nothing seemed to be happening.

"I can't do it!" he said frustratedly, before slumping back down into the raft.

"Here...let me have a go then," said somebody else (now that the power of suggestion had firmly taken hold). But again, the result was the same.

After yet more futile attempts by a few others, the odds finally caught up with Sharon.

"Sorry guys," she said. "My turn!"

I just happened to be sitting next to the doorway when Sharon awkwardly barged her way over. To provide her with a modicum of privacy, we males all gallantly looked away as she thrust her lower half out over the side of the raft. But when she grabbed hold of my shoulder for added stability, it became increasingly difficult to ignore the milky-white, freckled caboose that was hovering just on the edge of my peripheral vision. But Sharon had no more success than her predecessors. Eventually, the instigator of the entire situation quietly stripped down to his underwear and leapt out of the raft. We thought he must have "lost the plot," but his immersion in the tepid seawater soon did the trick, and he almost cried with relief as the painful pressure in his bladder was finally eased. Now feeling much happier, he merrily thrashed about until somebody gently reminded him that it was lunchtime and there might be a hungry shark about. Nobody followed his lead, and so another uncomfortable hour or so would pass before the rest of us could finally achieve our goal conventionally.

I guess this strange inability to pee could have been due to several factors—the stress and embarrassment of the situation or the instability of the raft (with the corresponding need to brace one's lower half continually to stay balanced). Whatever the reason, the fact that we all experienced it confirms for me that it was more than just a manifestation of our imaginations. I would recount this experience two decades later (during Qantas Emergency Procedures Training) and our instructor would tell us about a staff member who'd experienced the same thing during a prolonged dinghy drill in the waters off Mascot. Feeling increasingly uncomfortable and frustrated, he'd unwisely tried to force the issue by drinking even more water, which eventually resulted in him being transported by helicopter to a nearby hospital for emergency medical treatment. At least our shared discomfort had provided a brief distraction, and, in retrospect, I have no doubt whatsoever that just a few days in a liferaft would drive me stark, raving mad. I can only marvel at the resilience of some brave souls who've had to wait weeks before their eventual rescue. Our suffering only totalled about six hours, but it's a six-hour period that is indelibly etched in my memory.

By mid-afternoon, we received the joyous news that we would all soon be rescued. A Search and Rescue (SAR) Iroquois helicopter from RAAF Base Townsville was on its way to winch the members of each group aboard, in turn, and transfer them to Rattlesnake Island for the Sea Coast phase. When the helicopter approached our group, we were instructed to climb up onto the raft's roof, put our boots back on and then wait for the 'stole' (the rescue harness) to hit the water before attempting to retrieve it. Not letting the stole 'earth' before touching it could result in a nasty shock from the static electricity that it accumulated during its descent. We were also warned to put the stole on properly, otherwise, we could fall out...not a particularly desirable outcome when the helicopter would most likely be hovering at about fifty or sixty feet. Suddenly, the atmosphere aboard our little craft was transformed from one of grinding boredom to tense expectation. I'd experienced a water hoisting exercise at Geraldton on Pilots Course in 1982 and so, while I knew what to expect, I hoped I'd be spared a "tea-bagging" (getting repeatedly dunked into the water) by the helicopter crewman.

Soon, we heard the unmistakable "Wok...Wok...Wok" of the inbound Iroquois helicopter as it approached the area and then went into a hover over Group One. It took about ten minutes for the survivors to be winched onboard, and we all craned our necks to get a better view of the unfolding spectacle through our raft's doorway. Then it roared off to Rattlesnake Island before, just a little later, returning once more to repeat the exercise with Group Two. We were next, and when we heard the faint "wok...wok...wok" starting to grow ever louder, it triggered a flurry of activity that almost bordered on panic. The next few minutes would prove to us that getting eight people out of a tightly-packed liferaft and onto its roof is a surprisingly difficult exercise. At one point, I became trapped under the suffocating orange canopy, but eventually managed to extricate myself and, puffing and panting with exertion, scramble onto the roof to join the others. All around me, people were struggling to undo the tight knots that secured their boots to the raft, with one unfortunate soul swearing loudly as his boots slipped their moorings and plunged to the bottom of the Coral Sea.

I was still struggling with my boots when the helicopter roared into a hover right over our heads. "WOK...WOK...WOK" screamed the rotor as it whipped up a massive downdraft of stinging spray that made seeing and communicating with each other virtually impossible. Fortunately, we'd worked out a winching order beforehand, and when the stole touched down in the water beside us, the pre-determined "first survivor" retrieved it, donned it, gave a thumbs-up signal and disappeared into the sky in a cascade of whipped-up seawater and flailing flying boots. The raft emptied rapidly as the winching sequence was repeated and, from memory, I was the second-last survivor to abandon our orange torture chamber. The ensuing short flight to Rattlesnake Island offered just the briefest opportunity for us to bid farewell to the little cluster of rafts as they retreated into the distance behind us. Ahead loomed a flat, sparsely vegetated island that had some expanses of sandy beach as well as some stretches of rocky coastline. Sadly, the flight was over all too quickly and we were soon back on terra firma... although I swear that island bobbed up and down just as much as our raft had done.

11

PASSING THE BEACH BEAN SOUP

After delivering its final load of passengers, the helicopter took off, circled around and then roared off low over our heads towards the RAAF base. We were now all alone on Rattlesnake Island...and it was suddenly just so incredibly quiet. Only the sound of the breeze, gently rifling through the leaves of the island's foliage, broke the all-enveloping silence. That, and the collective gurgling of our empty stomachs. The instructors arrived all too soon, though, and summoned us all together to hand out some parachutes for us to use as shelter for the night. Some practical instruction followed on how to erect a "para-tepee," which was like a regular tepee, but laid over on its side. The top of the canopy was weighted down on the ground with rocks, and the base of the parachute was then splayed open by tying the riggers (strings) to some nearby vegetation to provide both a floor and a roof (of sorts). Each para-tepee could accommodate two or three people in relative comfort, and after six hours spent cramped together in a tiny liferaft, it was great to simply be able to stretch out fully again.

Then it was time to build a fire and dry out our clothes and boots (if they hadn't been lost at sea). Some practical instruction followed on the food sources that were available nearby. Naturally, the coastline provided the richest potential bounty—fish, crabs and sea cucumbers (which, we were assured, were like eating old rubber tyres)—but the large woody pods that hung thickly from some of the island's scrubby vegetation also contained large edible seeds (called "beach beans"). When the ad-hoc lesson ended, some intrepid souls headed off for the shoreline to forage for crabs and sea-cucumbers, or to try out their improvised fishing lines. But for our group, boiling up the plentiful beach beans with some beef stock cubes seemed a much easier proposition. The resulting concoction tasted so good that, after having gone without food for so long, we simply gorged ourselves on the stuff before heading back to our para-tepees for a little lie-down. What the instructors didn't tell us, however (either through ignorance or omission), was that beach beans possessed all the laxative properties of mildly diluted Drano, and that our distended stomachs were now ticking time bombs.

Not long after getting horizontal, our stomachs began gurgling and cramping up in the most alarming manner imaginable. An afflicted sufferer of "beach bean belly" had just enough time to register the onset of acute abdominal discomfort before having to sprint off somewhere private to commence the inevitably explosive voiding process. After several such excursions in very quick succession, our poor tortured bowels were only capable of producing tremendous blasts of wind and pathetically miniscule quantities of water. Collectively, we decided that we may as well wade out waist-deep into the ocean and admire the sunset together until the gripping sensations had passed...spaced out from each other at suitable intervals, of course. At times, the conversation was understandably a little strained, but eventually, the urge to purge abated and so we weakly retreated to our makeshift shelter to collapse onto the sand and finally drift off into the blessed, black oblivion of sleep.

The next day, we returned to Townsville to recuperate from what had been, at different stages, a terrifying, nauseating, boring and sh***y experience. And yet there were still nearly two more weeks of torture ahead! I began to wonder whether I could survive Survival Course and resolved that, to get through this, I'd just have to focus on taking it one day at a time. To do otherwise, would be to invite surrender to the increasingly prevalent feelings of impending doom. Besides, after narrowly avoiding drowning, and then bobbing about on the ocean for hours on end in a liferaft, a few days without water during the Semi-arid phase might prove to be a blessing in disguise.

12

HOW GOOD ARE TRANSPIRATION BAGS?

Sunday, my day of rest, was mostly spent in the Officers Mess laundry, soaking, scrubbing and washing my flying gear to remove the accumulated saltwater from it and render it clean and serviceable before we "headed bush" again the following Wednesday. In the interim, Monday and Tuesday were occupied with increasingly perilous scalings of Castle Hill, exhaustingly concluded sessions of the Gentlemen Joggers Club and some forgettably-conducted theory classes that focused on "Protection, Location, Water, Food" in water-deprived environments. While protection from the elements is paramount to ensure your immediate survival, indicating your location to SAR agencies is vital if you ever hope to be rescued. During the two-night Semi-arid phase, we'd be expected to construct more robust forms of protection than the para-tepees used on Rattlesnake Island, and we'd also be required to construct signal markers that indicated our location.

Of the two remaining survival priorities, we were cheerily informed that in a real-life situation, we'd probably only last about four or five days without water. Comfortingly though, if we did find water, we'd probably stay alive for about three or four weeks before we succumbed to starvation. This phase would be all "Burke-and-Wills" where we'd gain some practical experience in procuring water and, if we were feeling particularly adventurous, catching and eating some bush tucker to overcome our innate "food aversion." In COMSURV jargon, food aversion described a person's natural tendency to view slimy, slithery or crunchy critters as just that, and not as a potentially tempting source of sustenance. My food aversion had always been off-the-charts and, as a youngster, I was so fussy that Mum or Dad had often had to read me stories to entice me to eat anything that wasn't meat or potatoes. While my culinary palate had expanded considerably since then, it was still going to take a lot more than two-and-a-half days in the bush to get me to crunch on a cricket, sauté a snake or grill a galah. No sir! Two days of barley sugars and beef stock-cube soup was going to suit me just fine.

By Wednesday afternoon, we were ensconced in the Semi-arid exercise area, somewhere in the foothills of the Great Dividing Range. The rocky landscape suggested that there had once been a watercourse flowing through the area, and the scattered trees and shrubs were typical of those that can be found in the creek beds and gullies along Australia's temperate coastline. This time, we were split up into groups of about five or six, with each group being geographically separated from the others. The leader of each group was handed a map that showed his group's location, the locations of the other groups and the existence of a large river (just outside the western edge of the exercise area) that was marked "OUT OF BOUNDS" in large red letters.

This phase was 'non-tactical' which, in military parlance, meant that we were in friendly territory, with no enemy about. Therefore, we could make as much noise as we liked and build fires for warmth, illumination and cooking. In tactical situations, to reduce the risk of detection by the enemy, both of these activities are strictly prohibited by observing "noise and light discipline." On arrival at our new home, we divided ourselves into two working parties: one to construct our accommodation, and the other to collect firewood. By early afternoon, we'd erected a liveable parachute tent and stockpiled enough firewood for both our main fire and our smaller signal fires (we hoped). In the remaining daylight, we replicated the methods of producing water that had been taught to us in the classroom. Firstly, we placed large, clear plastic "transpiration" bags onto some of the leafier-looking tree branches around the campsite. Secondly, we constructed a solar still by placing a cup in the centre of a dug-out area of damp soil and then laying a large, circular piece of clear plastic over the soil (with a small rock atop the plastic, directly above the cup). The theory behind both apparatuses is the same: when heated by the sun, the plastic causes either the leaves or the damp soil to sweat water, which is then captured in the bottom of the transpiration bag, or the solar still's cup.

It'd been a very busy first day, but by sunset, we had an established campsite, a blazing campfire and some water-collection devices in place. Unfortunately, despite the fairly mild winter temperatures, our exertions had led to us drinking quite a bit of our available water and, if our present consumption rate continued, our supply would be exhausted with nearly a full day remaining. We resolved, therefore, to be thriftier with our water supply. As the sun fell soon afterwards, so too did the temperature. By about nine o'clock we were all shiveringly huddled around the fire, getting just as close to the flames as we dared without running the risk of involuntary self-immolation. And BOY, DID IT GET COLD! By midnight, the temperature must have been in the low single digits, and sleep was only possible in about twenty-minute bursts. Why twenty minutes? Well, that was the amount of time it took for the side of you facing the fire to become unbearably hot and the other side to become unbearably cold. When you were "done" on one side and frozen on the other, you merely woke up, rolled over and reversed the process. Had Sharon been amongst our number, we might have explored the concept of shared body heat, but we were an all-male group, and we weren't prepared to forego our masculinity just for the sake of avoiding death by hypothermia. Dawn saw us barely rested and feeling just as wretched as we'd been on Rattlesnake Island just a few days previously.

The next day was spent collecting more firewood and preparing our signalling devices. To indicate our presence to search aircraft, we could spell out "HELP" (using logs or rocks), construct a large "X" (if materials were scarce) or lay out signal fires (in a triangular shape) that would emit copious amounts of smoke when lit. Essentially, the larger your markers, the better your chances of discovery and, by the end of Day Two, we'd tried to emulate all of these methods. The instructors would be assessing our efforts the following afternoon but, by this point, our remaining energy reserves were nearly spent. More worrying was the fact that the transpiration bags and solar still had produced little more than a few miserable thimbles full of water and that our water supply would be exhausted by morning. Drastic times require drastic measures, and, in our hollowly hungry, sleep-deprived and nearly dehydrated state, we were prepared to take drastic action. "Out-of-Bounds River," we decided, was just too tempting a resource to let go to waste. After all, we reasoned, following animal tracks and birds were valid ways of locating water and if, in doing so, they led us to "Out-of-Bounds River," then so be it! We'd move out at dawn (which would be easy, seeing that we couldn't sleep) and have lookouts ranging ahead and beside the main party (who'd be carrying the empty water bottles).

None of the local wildlife had yet been foolish (or suicidal) enough to offer themselves up for our sustenance, so after yet another cold, hungry, thirsty and largely sleepless night, we assembled our raiding party just as the first faint glow of dawn appeared on the eastern horizon. Moving off quietly, we discovered that there were, indeed, animal tracks headed for the river and that following them was relatively easy. Twenty minutes later (near the edge of the exercise area) we hastily convened another tactical planning conference. The main party (of which I was a member) would stay put while the two scouts fanned out ahead to search the riverbank for any enemy (instructor) encampments. Just as the sun was broaching the horizon, the scouts returned with the news that a RAAF truck was parked on the riverbank up ahead and that, despite a cooking fire smouldering nearby, there were no obvious signs of any activity. The main party then quietly edged forward, just within visual range of the truck so that we could quickly "bug out" if there were suddenly any signs of movement. We didn't know what'd happen if we were caught but, by this point, we couldn't have cared less.

At the riverbank, we used what little natural cover was available for camouflage, and began silently refilling our water bottles. We then retreated to where the scouts awaited us and, as the first signs of activity became evident near the truck, we bolted back towards our campsite just as fast as we dared in the soft, early-morning sunlight. It was crazy. It felt like we'd infiltrated an enemy camp and escaped undetected! We felt re-invigorated! We felt euphoric! We were undoubtedly almost delirious from accumulated hunger and fatigue. But at least now we wouldn't be thirsty! Back at the campsite, we boiled up our contraband to avoid using up our delicious water-purification tablets. Then, when it had all been rendered drinkable, we lay down in the gloriously mild midmorning sunshine and finally got some much-needed "shut-eye." When we finally awoke, we realised two things: firstly, it wouldn't be long before the instructors arrived to assess our efforts and, secondly, we were now faced with a very different problem...we had *too much* water!

"If we have as much water now as we had two days ago, they'll know that we went to the river for sure," said one of the brighter members of the group.

"Yeah...you're right!" said our group leader. "Quick! Everybody, have a good long drink. We should keep about half our water, but what'll we do with the rest?"

"The transpiration bags and the still!" somebody else suggested. "Pour some of the water into each of the bags and some into the cup in the solar still!"

More frantic activity followed as we divvied up the water bottles, gulped down a few long mouthfuls, and then poured the rest into the transpiration bags and the solar still. No sooner had we settled ourselves down again, it seemed, than the instructors arrived with their clipboards in hand.

"Okay. So how did you guys go with your water management?" they asked us.

We all mumbled something guiltily before our group leader (lying through his long un-brushed teeth) said, "Well...we were pretty careful, but we were *really* surprised at how effective those transpiration bags were!" He gestured in the direction of the various bags as he said this, one of which had been placed over a tiny, mangy-looking sapling that was now practically doubled over under the weight of water that it had supposedly produced.

"Mmm. Yessss," said one of the instructors inscrutably, as he wrote down some notes.

On command, we ignited our signal fires—not much of a challenge given that it hadn't rained in weeks—and we were soon joyously on our way back to RAAF Base Townsville. Had the instructors suspected some shenanigans? We knew we'd be in trouble if somebody "talked," but we'd sworn an oath of secrecy and were now well past the halfway mark with the end finally in sight! Our little raiding party to "Out-of-Bounds River" had just been a bit of a giggle, and had provided us with some light relief. We suspected that there wouldn't be too much to laugh about when Escape and Evasion kicked off on the following Monday morning...and we were right!

13
CODE OF CONDUCT

The penultimate Escape and Evasion phase would simulate the aftermath of being brought down in hostile territory, where the survivors must trek on foot to a location from which a rescue can be affected. Enemy patrols would be actively scouring the area, and so the classroom theory was focused on what we could expect if we were ever captured by enemy forces during an actual conflict. And this is where the subject matter became very real and quite confronting. As a child of the 1960s, I was quite familiar with the old black-and-white movies that were set in World War II POW camps, where the sinister German interrogator attempts to extract information from the wily, captured British officer who, stiff upper lip firmly set, states that the Geneva Convention only requires him to disclose his "name, rank and serial number...old boy." Frustrated by the superior moral fibre of this fine up-standing example of English manhood, the German interrogator sulkily orders his prisoner back to "The Cooler" to reconsider his position.

More recent actions, however, have brought the US and its allies into conflict with enemies who have little interest in (or regard for) the principles of the Geneva Conventions. Many Western politicians also have a proclivity to avoid being labelled "war-mongers," by deploying their forces into conflicts that are never actually formally declared as "acts of war." Instead, these sometimes-bloody military engagements are obtusely described as police actions or armed interventions. Arguably, if Western troops are thrust into undeclared military actions, their adversaries are somewhat justified in ignoring the Conventions that, technically, relate purely to the treatment of prisoners of "war." In 1984, the two most recent large-scale military campaigns had been the Falkland Islands War in 1982, and the long-running involvement of US forces in Vietnam (that had finally concluded with their withdrawal in 1973). Neither of these actions had been "declared" wars and in Vietnam, in particular, downed US airmen had suffered terribly at the hands of their North Vietnamese captors. Mind you, so too had the North Vietnamese populace suffered during the sustained US bombing campaigns that had dwarfed the raids conducted against Nazi Germany during World War II.

In the COMSURV classroom, video-taped interviews with some of these former USAF POWs were screened, during which they described (in harrowing detail) what they'd endured in the infamous "Hanoi Hilton." The interrogations immediately after their capture had been particularly brutal since they were still in possession of intelligence that was extremely valuable. One vivid account came from an American pilot who, with his hands tied behind his back, had had a second rope looped around his elbows, which was then pulled so tight that his elbows almost touched. He was then suspended from a girder by a third rope (attached to the one around his elbows) and was left hanging there until he passed out from the searing pain radiating from his dislocated shoulders. But the torture wasn't just limited to physical intimidation. After particularly heavy bombing raids on Hanoi, the prisoners were sometimes roused from their cells and paraded through the streets of the battered city so that the angry townspeople could hurl abuse at them, spit on them or beat them. To break the Americans' spirits, their captors might tell them that their wives (believing them to be dead) had remarried, or that their children had been murdered or killed in accidents. They were often kept awake for days and were only ever given enough food to keep them alive. Time meant nothing and some POWs lived like this for years. In one recorded propaganda interview staged by his captors, a resourceful US airman had famously blinked his eyes to spell out "torture" in Morse code, indicating that his otherwise traitorous performance was only given under extreme duress.

We watched in silence as these haunted men related their distressing tales. For some of them, it was a cathartic experience, but for most, it was still an extremely upsetting and emotional one. For us, though, it was deeply confronting, and there was none of the typically light-hearted banter or bravado in the classroom afterwards. I began to reflect on how I could ever hope to live through what one of these poor captives had endured for nine years before his eventual release (along with all the other US POWs) in 1973. In the 1976 movie, *Marathon Man*, Laurence Olivier tortures Dustin Hoffman by ramming the point of a dental probe repeatedly into a cavity in one of Hoffman's teeth. Because of the many painful hours I'd spent in a dentist's chair myself as a child, just hearing the sound of a dentist's drill during an interrogation would probably be enough to have me "spilling my guts." The instructors finally broke the prevailing introspective silence by initiating a discussion on how military law views those who have disclosed classified information to the enemy. Under US law, those POWs who'd done so, even under torture, were technically guilty of treason. As we'd already witnessed in their interviews, most of these men, themselves, felt that they'd betrayed their country, even though they'd only succumbed after being subjected to ongoing acts of almost intolerable physical and psychological cruelty. Thankfully though, to my knowledge, no charges were ever laid against them.

Australia's official policy, we were soberingly informed, had changed little since the advent of the "name, rank, serial number and date of birth" credo of the late-1920s. But officialdom had also acknowledged that it was practically inconceivable to expect Australian captives to resist the effects of prolonged and persistent torture. And so, the unofficial policy had become one of "hold out for as long as you possibly can, and let your conscience be your guide." Would my conscience excuse me for divulging military secrets at the mere sound of a dentist's drill, or just the *prospect* of suffering excruciating pain? Such questions can provoke a lot of soul-searching, particularly when, on a modern battlefield, most sensitive military information may well be out-of-date within just hours of its inception. The US military was so concerned about protecting its military intelligence that it required many of its front-line personnel to undergo a Code of Conduct course.

Such specialised courses exposed trainees to restricted levels of physical and psychological intimidation and gave them a greater understanding of both what they could expect, as well as where their personal resistance limits lay. Anecdotally, I'd heard that the Commandant…err, Commanding Officer of the Combat Survival Training School was eager to introduce some form of resistance training into the COM-SURV curriculum but, thankfully, that hadn't yet come to fruition in 1984. Undoubtedly in wartime, acquiring detailed knowledge of an enemy's dispositions and intentions is extremely valuable, but where is the honour in using fear, intimidation and beatings to extract information from somebody who can't protect themselves or fight back? Would not a prisoner be capable of "breaking" his interrogator if the tables were turned? When the session ended, we headed off to prepare ourselves for the final phase of the course (with the underlying threat of capture during the Escape and Evasion portion). "If one of those bastards so much as touches me, they'll be up for a court-martial," I said to nobody in particular. And I sincerely meant it!

14
IT'S A TRAP!

After a Sunday spent gorging ourselves on anything edible within reach, we reported to CSTS at 8am on Monday with the grim prospect of a strict diet of barley sugars and beef stock cubes for the next week...plus whatever dim-witted wildlife we could catch or trap. The mood was sombre, particularly after we'd been individually summoned into the building and ordered to strip down to our underwear to ensure that we weren't smuggling illicit foodstuffs either on our person or in our clothing. Thankfully a cavity search was deemed unnecessary...and I could only imagine:

"Hey guys...anybody want a nibble on this Mars bar?"

"Where have you been hiding that?

"Don't ask!"

Still in just our underwear, we were then ordered onto a set of scales for a weigh-in, knowing that this process would be repeated when we returned...if we returned...to see how much weight we'd lost whilst engaged in surely the most unpopular and unwelcome crash diet of all time. Resplendent in our uniforms once more, the course was reassembled for a final briefing that did little to lift the prevailing mood. While the preceding phase had focused on saving water, we were now ordered to drink enough at all times to prevent the deadly onset of dehydration. Just within the previous year, one COMSURV trainee—a lean, fit and conscientious individual—had pushed his water conservation efforts to the extreme and had subsequently succumbed to severe heat stress. Assistance had been promptly sought, but by the time the trainee had been evacuated, his organs had begun to shut down and he died soon afterwards. Consequently, hand-held UHF emergency radios ("yellow bricks" in RAAF jargon) would be issued to each group to call for immediate help, if required.

For the coming ordeal, each five-man group was issued with backpacks, some very basic equipment and just one precious combat ration pack per person. "If your group is captured during the Escape and Evasion phase," we were warned, "you'll have to forfeit one of your ration packs. If you're caught again, you'll lose another one. I'd advise you not to get caught for a third time! Now the trucks are ready...so let's go." With that, we despondently gathered together our meagre possessions and gloomily piled into the backs of the awaiting vehicles. Our first challenge would be to determine where we wound up using just a map and compass and so, to ensure that we couldn't cheat, we were driven to the drop-off point with the tarpaulin covers on the rear of the trucks firmly secured closed. As our noisy transports bumped and jolted along during their slow ascent into the ranges west of Townsville, we felt like prisoners being hauled off somewhere to work on a chain gang. *And so, it starts*, I thought to myself miserably, as we all rocked and rolled in unison on the hard wooden bench seats. Understandably, there was little of the usual banter during this all-too-brief ninety-minute respite before the real fun began.

Eventually, the trucks braked to a halt, the tarpaulin flaps were hauled back, and we were ordered out into the bright morning sunshine. After our eyes had adjusted, we found that we were now in a clearing on the side of a dirt road high up in the Great Dividing Range. Surrounding us was a sawtooth array of mountain peaks covered in dense, green vegetation. The instructors then handed out a map and compass to each group so that we could pinpoint exactly where we were. Having used nothing but these tools for navigation during my years in the Army Reserve, I was confident that this task would be reasonably straightforward. I was wrong. In such situations, you can determine your position by taking magnetic bearings from several prominent natural features and then plotting these bearing lines on a map. By triangulation, your location is the point on the map where these bearing lines intersect. However, to triangulate successfully, you have to be certain that the features that you've taken the bearings from are the same as those you've identified on the map. Our problem that day was that there were peaks and valleys everywhere and that the map was just a swirling tangle of contour lines where all the hilly features looked identical. After a few failed attempts using this method, we tried to find a spot along one of the roads where the topography on the map matched what we could see around us. But again, we had no success and, as we watched the other groups heading off, we realised that we were losing valuable time.

Eventually, the instructors had to provide us with some pretty obvious clues and, once we knew our location, we were given the coordinates for where we'd be "rescued" at midday Wednesday. After plotting that point, we saw that we had about fifteen kilometres to cover on foot over the next few days. From the map, it appeared that the terrain would initially be very steep and heavily wooded, but would open out onto flatter and clearer ground once we'd descended out of the ranges (at around the halfway mark). The map didn't lie, because just as soon as we stepped off the road, we promptly lost our footing and slid, rolled and tumbled about ten metres down the side of the road's very steep embankment. Fortunately, our descent was quickly arrested by some heavy underbrush. But the tangle of vines, creepers, shrubs and saplings that had initially been our saviour soon became our mortal enemy. Without a machete to blaze a trail through the dense undergrowth, we simply had no alternative but to barge our way through. It was incredibly hot and tedious work, and to conserve our energies, we took turns in the lead position. At times, the vegetation was so thick that a frontal assault proved futile, and we had to concede precious ground by backtracking and finding another way through. Progress was painfully slow, and although we knew that there were six other groups somewhere in the dense foliage around us, all we could hear were the sounds of our exertions and those of the native birdlife above our heads. During one brief break, we tried out our yellow brick, but our test calls went unanswered. Essentially, we were completely on our own!

As evening approached, we figured that we'd only covered a few kilometres, and began to wonder how we'd ever make the RV (rendezvous) point in time. When it was simply too dark and dangerous to continue, we stopped. But because we were in a tactical environment, building a fire was out of the question...even if we'd had the strength to do so. We simply slept where we dropped...in my case, face-down amidst a pile of rocks. I was dirty, sweaty and on the verge of both hopeless despair and utter exhaustion. Despite my rumbling stomach and uncomfortable bedding, the blessed oblivion of sleep came quickly. In bleak circumstances like this, dreams can sometimes provide some light relief but, when you then re-awaken to your ongoing reality, the situation can seem doubly depressing. This is precisely how I felt when I awoke the next morning and slowly remembered that I was sprawled in my flying suit amongst the rocks and dirt of some very heavy bushland in far North Queensland. For a few precious moments, I tried to forestall the inevitable but, around me, I could already hear my colleagues beginning to stir. Since we still had a lot of distance to cover, we knew that the sooner we got going, the better. Fortunately, it didn't take long for us to pack up, simply because we hadn't unpacked anything the night before. After swallowing a few swigs of precious water, we re-oriented ourselves on the map, took a compass bearing and set off for a new day of hell.

We feared at least another half-day of solid bush-bashing but, astonishingly, after only fifteen minutes or so, we burst through a thick screen of underbrush to discover that the countryside ahead was suddenly far less heavily wooded. If we'd pushed on just a little longer the previous evening, we could have rested a lot easier, but at least we realised that we could now cover the remaining distance a lot faster, and our collective mood lifted considerably. While it was tempting to cheer like idiots at having finally escaped the jungle, we were now in open countryside where we were far more likely to encounter enemy patrols. Therefore, we decided to spread ourselves out in an extended single file, with a gap of as much as fifty or sixty metres between each one of us. While our field of vision the day before had been down to just a few metres at times in the almost impenetrable underbrush, the challenge now was not to lose sight of the person far ahead of you in the column. We regrouped and took breaks every hour or so, and were making such good time that, by evening, we were within striking distance of the RV...and our full complement of ration packs was still intact.

The next morning, the final part of our trek required us to follow a broad, gently downward-sloping valley that was mostly grassland at its centre and was only lightly wooded from about midway up the ridgelines on either side. We had three ways in which to cover the remaining distance: we could walk through the grassland at the bottom of the valley (where we would be easily spotted), we could walk along the top of a ridgeline (where we would be silhouetted against the morning sky) or we could walk along the mid-point of the escarpment (where we would have at least some natural cover). The first two options provided the easiest going, but the latter option was the technique recommended by COMSURV. Naturally, our adversaries must have anticipated this move, because, after only a few hours of our final assault, we were intercepted by an enemy patrol and captured.

Sulkily, we sat around in a little dishevelled cluster, avoiding eye contact with our captors, as they circled us, demanding to know our unit and our final destination. I just remember sullenly thinking, "DON'T YOU TOUCH ME! DON'T YOU TOUCH ME!" and I'm not sure how I would have reacted if they'd tried some rough stuff. By this point, we were all feeling pretty cranky—we'd done the right thing by taking the tougher route, and yet we'd still been captured. Plus, we'd soon suffer the humiliation of having to hand over one of our precious ration packs. Eventually tiring of their nonsensical interrogation, the enemy said, "Righto! Give us one of your ration packs and you can get going." We reluctantly handed it over—silently wishing each of them a long, lingering death—and got underway again.

Approaching the RV, we could see some of the other groups also quietly making their way towards the spot where we would all soon be rescued. Thankfully, we weren't intercepted again and, when we were all re-assembled at the RV point soon afterwards and comparing notes, we discovered that the only group that hadn't been caught was the one that had taken the easiest route...right down the middle of the valley. And so, it seemed that there were two likely possibilities. Either the instructors had directed the enemy to patrol our most likely route so that we'd be captured and interrogated, or they'd wanted to ensure that we were complying with the advice given in the classroom. In either case, the captured groups felt set up, while the group that had evaded capture felt smug (by having applied some reverse psychology). In a training environment, punishing the recommended method while rewarding the ill-advised one is referred to as 'negative training,' and it caused a lot of resentment amongst those of us who now had even fewer supplies for the days ahead. Soon we were back in the trucks again, heading off to our ultimate place of torture—the Static phase.

15

THE SEVENTH CIRCLE OF HELL

As the truck rumbled along to our next undisclosed location, I silently took stock of my physical and mental well-being. Despite my footwear being called "flying" boots (and not "walking" boots) I'd managed to complete the arduous Evasion phase without developing any potentially troublesome blisters. All things considered, I felt in remarkably reasonable shape...physically. It was the psychological aspect of the upcoming Static phase that had me worried. I tried convincing myself that three of the four phases were now over and that all I had to do was just exist for the next four days and I'd be on my way home. My self, however, remained staunchly unconvinced. The Static phase would initially be focused on the Protection element of the four survival priorities, and we'd need to clear an area to bare earth, suspend a parachute tent from a tripod of sturdy wooden poles and dig a drainage ditch to prevent us from drowning in the event of any substantial rainfall. Thankfully, the weather so far had been nothing but a succession of spotless blue-sky days that the tropical north can produce over the winter months. To keep us elevated above the damp jungle soil, we'd also have to construct a sleeping platform by driving some large wooden stakes into the ground and then intricately weaving parachute string tightly around them to create a "mattress" of sorts. Any spare parachutes could then be used as both base sheets and blankets.

When the trucks finally came to a halt about thirty minutes later, we found ourselves back up in the mountains in an area that could be loosely described as a temperate rainforest. We piled out of the transports and, after collecting our meagre kit, headed off with one of the instructors down a well-beaten dirt track to be shown where we'd be living (existing?) for the next four days. It soon became obvious that the staff were going to use this final phase to exact their retribution on passive resistors like me who'd been putting in little effort.

"Okay, Group One. This is your area," our guide said after a few minutes. The indicated spot was situated under a leafy canopy of high overhanging tree branches, already cleared to bare earth (complete with a large circular drainage ditch) and had some "wild" tent poles conveniently lying nearby. Sharon (who'd met the required standard by this point) and her group peeled off, while the rest of us continued down the trail.

"Group Two. This is you," we heard a little later. Once again, the site had been completely cleared, and although there was no already-excavated drainage channel this time, there were again some tent poles lying in the bush not too far away.

Group Three's location was in another shady spot, but it was sparsely covered in patches of short grass that would need to be removed. Even in my understandably diminished mental state, it didn't take me long to figure out that there was a trend developing here. Each area was getting progressively more "rustic," and I was a member of the very last group... Group Seven! After parting company with Groups Four, Five and Six, the track was also becoming noticeably more poorly defined.

"Group Seven. This is your spot," said the instructor finally, with just the slightest hint of satisfaction in his voice. We all stopped dead in our tracks, gawped at the site of our proposed "campsite" and collectively thought, "YOU'VE GOT TO BE SH***ING ME!"

Our new home was an exposed site amidst a veritable sea of thick, waist-high grass. Immediately, we knew that it would take hours of backbreaking work just to clear it, and no wild tent poles were lying around nearby either. Instead, one tall, slender but sturdy palm tree (swaying gently in the afternoon breeze) would serve as the only potential source of lumber. For this final phase, we'd been allocated a few heavy-duty tools (including a hammer and a machete) but establishing any liveable accommodation by dusk would have required a bobcat and a chainsaw. Undoubtedly feeling quite pleased with himself, our instructor departed with a cheery, "Have fun, you blokes. We'll be back to check on you tomorrow afternoon." Despite being tempted to tell him to "SHOVE IT," we realised that to get home, we had little choice but to get into it. Within our group was a burly NCO from the Royal Malaysian Air Force, and although he didn't speak a lot of English, it didn't take him long to figure out what was needed when we handed him the machete and pointed at the swaying palm tree. Both our tent and our sleeping platform relied on us cutting down that tree, and so this job became the number one priority. Over the next few hours, we all took turns hacking away at that obstinate tree trunk, while our "breaks" were spent collecting firewood and clearing the campsite.

Ultimately, it took us until the following afternoon to get to where Group One would have been after about thirty minutes or so. Just clearing the site took a day's unrelenting effort, and when we finally lay, exhausted, on our newly constructed sleeping platform, Group One was probably well advanced in installing their jacuzzi. The instructors paid us a social call on the second evening and, when they berated us on our slow progress, their comments (most assuredly) weren't particularly well received. After they'd left, we lethargically lay around our campfire, discussing the gruesome ways in which we'd like to see them die—a rather pleasant distraction for a time. But if truth be told, the exertion of the first thirty-six hours had probably been a bit of a blessing in disguise: it had kept us occupied and had prevented us from thinking too much about our predicament. Once the campsite was fully operational, however, there was little to do but endure the passage of time and reflect on just how badly we felt, both physically and psychologically. Some routine jobs remained—we had yet to build our signal fires and constantly needed more firewood—but we were so physically exhausted by this point that the prospect of yet more physical labour was almost too much to bear.

Day Three of the Static phase—Friday...or was it Saturday...we didn't know (or care) anymore—was the toughest of the entire course. We'd now been without any substantial food for about five days and, while my stomach had rumbled constantly on the first day, with time, that sensation had given way to gnawing emptiness and then, finally, to a perpetually hollow feeling (in my gut) and a constant craving for food (in my head). But the most noticeable symptom of looming starvation was the inability to stand up for any longer than just a few minutes at a time. By

Day Three, our earlier exertions would have been beyond us, because just a few minutes on your feet now resulted in sensations of light-headedness and dizziness. In the past, I'd joked that my motto was "Never stand when you can sit, never sit when you can lie down." Well, from Day Three onwards, this slogan became Group Seven's default state. Any spare time—and there was plenty of it—was spent horizontally, either lying in our tent or propped up on one elbow around the fire.

We still had a few of our ubiquitous barley sugars and beef stock cubes left for an emergency "energy hit," but having endured a steady diet of the wretched things for five days straight, most of us simply couldn't stomach them anymore. Adding to our misery was a perpetually rancid taste in our mouths—the consequence of weeklong uncleaned teeth, and the lack of any flavourful variety in our diet. To achieve some degree of psychological relief from our pitiful existence, we'd often lie around the campfire and discuss what we'd eat when we got back to Townsville.

"Me? I'm gonna go to the first pub I can find and order the biggest steak on the menu, with pepper sauce, chips and corn," somebody would say dreamily.

"Oooh, yeaaah," everybody else would groan, blissfully imagining that big, thick, juicy slab of meat just lying there on the plate all hot and steaming and smothered in thick, pepper sauce with golden, crunchy chips and hot buttered corn on the side.

I added my culinary fantasy to the conversation. "Well, I'm gonna go to Pizza Hut and order a Family Size Supreme, a big Coke (with lots of ice) and some garlic bread!"

"Ooooh, yeaaah," everybody would blissfully moan again, as the mental image shifted, and we began feasting on this latest imaginary course.

For the first time in our young male lives, Food had supplanted Women as our Number One Fantasy. If that stunningly good-looking sort wearing the red bikini in the Tab cola ad (Elle Macpherson) had strolled up to us on Day Three bearing hamburgers and chips, it would have been the food that got our attention. During this longest of all long days, our rambling campfire dialogues included such memorable forums as "My Best Meal," "The Fullest I Ever Felt" and, most popular of all, "The Hugest Christmas Buffet Ever." Occasionally, lying on our backs during our fantasy feasts, we'd spot an aircraft weaving a contrail of gossamer thread across the infinite blue vault high above our heads. We speculated about what its passengers might be eating (and complaining about) as they sped over our little clearing tucked away in the rolling green carpet of the Great Dividing Range far below. How we wished that we were up there with them! How we wished that they were down here instead of us!

Early that afternoon, one of the instructors arrived on an impromptu visit.

"You guys haven't built your signal fires yet!" he snarled.

"No," we replied, astonished at his powers of observation. "We can barely stand up."

"Well," he said, "you'd better have them ready for the final assessment tomorrow."

"We will," we groaned in exhausted unison.

"And where's your latrine?" he asked, looking around the campsite.

"ARE YOU KIDDING?" we protested loudly. "We haven't eaten anything in FIVE DAYS! Why the f*** would we need a latrine?!?"

"Well, it's a hygiene requirement. So, you'd better have one dug by tomorrow!" With that decree issued, he turned on his heel and left.

A latrine? Seriously? My bowels hadn't moved since we'd started the Escape and Evasion phase, and I'd probably need a pair of pliers to open them now. But again, there was nothing to be done but to summon up our last meagre energy reserves and attempt these final tasks. If somebody felt unsteady, he recovered by lying down on his side and helping to dig out a small latrine with a knife. By sunset, our signal fires were ready, and we had a cubic foot of excavated dunny. We knew that it was pathetically small, but it was still plenty big enough to cater for the non-existent demand. The most motivated member of our group also fashioned an animal trap out of sticks tied together with string, but it would undoubtedly have been useless unless one of the local animals saw it and died laughing! By the end of Day Three, we were completely spent! Done! Finished! Even our symposia about food had petered out.

Most of our time was now spent just silently gazing into the campfire—a phenomenon known in COMSURV Land as "Survival Stare." Even though our deliverance was now only thirty-six hours or so away, it seemed just as remote as it'd been when we'd first left the RAAF base. Time had passed slowly on the liferafts...in the Static phase, it virtually ceased to exist.

Day Four, our final day, was a carefree one in that we just didn't care anymore. Mother Nature had decided to hose us down gently with a steady drizzle of rain, and the leaden grey skies matched our collective mood. But we didn't care that it was wet, and when the instructors arrived, we didn't care that they considered our latrine too small, or that our animal trap was a joke, or that we hadn't gathered any bush tucker. We didn't even care that the wood for our signal fires had gotten wet. It was raining. What did they expect us to do? Put it in the tent while we slept out in the rain? When they told us "Rescue aircraft overhead in sixty seconds!" we didn't sprint off to light our signal fires, instead, we just stumblingly shuffled over to do so. When the damp timber steadfastly refused to catch alight, we didn't care about that either. In a real survival situation, our potential rescuers would have seen nothing and simply flown on. But in the contrived scenario of COMSURV, we simply didn't care. We were completely exhausted and knew that we were homeward-bound the next day, regardless of our efforts. The instructors took copious notes, said "Be ready to go around midday tomorrow" and left. As Group One were probably celebrating in their billiards room, we gloomily settled ourselves around the campfire for one final cold, hungry and miserable night.

Next morning though, it began to sink in that our deliverance might finally be at hand. A "runner" appeared to tell us that each group was required to send somebody up to the Group One area to be handed some food to share before we set off on foot for the trucks. We weren't advised what form this "food" might take, but it didn't take long to find an eager volunteer who was prepared to head on up and find out. He returned twenty minutes later...grappling with an agitatedly flapping live chicken that had its feet bound, and probably some idea of what lay in store. I guess the theory was that we "city slickers" would blanch at the prospect of killing a live chicken and then butchering it. But they hadn't counted on Group Seven's brawny Malaysian, whose eyes lit up as he grabbed the bird, dispatched it with his knife, bled it, plucked it, gutted it, dismembered it and had it boiling away over the fire in about twenty minutes flat. As soon as the meat was cooked, we divvied it up amongst ourselves and, with mouths watering in anticipation, bit into it. And it was...AWFUL! In my entire life, I've never eaten such a tough, stringy, flavourless chunk of meat. I don't know where the instructors found those chickens, but I had my suspicions that we'd probably just consumed the Best in Show of 1965. If our Malaysian colleague hadn't dispatched it so swiftly, it was surely only minutes away from dying of tremendous old age!

But with something now sitting in our aching stomachs (and an end to our suffering in sight), as midday approached, we summoned the energy necessary to return our campsite to the wild. We dropped down the tent, cut up the sleeping platform, filled in the still-unused latrine and, in a last act of malice, threw the bed posts and tent poles into the fire, so that they could never be used again. We wanted the next Group Seven to enjoy everything that COMSURV had to offer just as much as we had. When word filtered down to "Move Out," we did just that without a backward glance. After an hour or so, we were on our way back to the RAAF base. Unbelievably...our ordeal was over!

16
RETURN OF THE LIVING DEAD

Anyone witnessing our return to CSTS that Sunday afternoon would have sworn that they'd just seen an episode of The Living Dead—we would have certainly smelled dead, at least. Fortunately, we'd long since become immune to our body odour, although the birds dropping from the tree branches should have given us some indication of its severity. Again, we were individually summoned into the building to be weighed and, when my turn came, I discovered, astonishingly, that I'd lost a total of two-and-a-half kilograms. Yes...two-point-five kilos! Little wonder that there are no "COMSURV Miracle Diet" books around, and I planned to regain that weight just as soon as humanly possible. After we'd been told to report to CSTS the next morning for a final debrief, we were free to go. With our sunken cheeks, wild eyes, greasy hair and seven-day growth (Sharon notwithstanding) as we shuffled towards the blocks in our filthy uniforms, we must have looked a real sight. Even in our severely malnourished state though, the race was now on to get into the showers before the hot water ran out. After confirming an RV time with the others for our big upcoming feast, I went back to my room and assembled my toiletries for the blissful ablutions ahead. Already, the showers were running flat out, and by the time I'd pulled off my battered flying boots, peeled off my rancid flying suit, socks and jocks and wrapped myself in a towel, it sounded like the hot water was no more.

Unperturbed, I tucked my toiletries under my arm and soon found another bathroom nearby where I was completely alone. Skirting around the mirrors (to avoid scaring myself too badly), I turned on the shower, threw off my towel and let that hot, steaming, glorious, rejuvenating water pour all over me for about fifteen minutes straight. Washing my hair (which I still had in 1984) required about two handfuls of shampoo just to work up a decent lather. Then I cleaned my teeth, and the intensity of the toothpaste's flavour, combined with the strong scents of my soap and shampoo, almost resulted in a full-blown sensory overload. Finally, I reluctantly shut off the water, dried myself off and headed back to my room. After changing into some wonderful fresh clothes, it was time to...finally...*go out and eat!!!* But when our taxis pulled up in front of the Mess, it was already around three o'clock, and all the pub kitchens in town would undoubtedly be closed. So...what to do? "Pizza Hut should be open," I suggested hopefully and so, yea, verily, it came to pass that it was my campfire fantasy feast that was ultimately fulfilled.

Walking into Pizza Hut was like passing through the Pearly Gates and entering Paradise. When the waiter came over to take our order, we were drooling so much that we could barely speak. Even so, we ordered fairly conservatively and decided to partake in a cold beverage while we waited for our food to arrive. After a week's hibernation, my taste buds exploded back into life, and the flavourful sensation of truly the most magnificent beer that I've ever raised to my lips was nothing short of indescribable ecstasy. Had it only been a few hours earlier that we'd sat starving in the bush and dreaming of this moment? When the pizzas arrived, we each took a slice, cradled it in our hands and gazed upon it in wonder. Then, almost reverently, we raised it to our mouths, bit into it and...oh, immeasurable bliss! But after just one slice each, we all came to the same stunning realisation...we felt *completely full!* We couldn't believe it! After fantasizing about this meal for every waking moment of the previous week, COMSURV had cruelly shrunken our stomachs such that now we couldn't even enjoy it! Not only that, but the alcohol had gone straight to our heads, and we were giggling away and carrying on like lunatics. After just twenty minutes or so, we were as full as ticks and as drunk as lords, and our waiter must have thought that he'd either gone through a wormhole in the space-time continuum or that his watch had broken. Valiantly, we forced down another few slices before we reluctantly admitted defeat and headed back to the RAAF base. Lying on my thin foam mattress that night felt akin to lounging on a cloud, and I've never slept better.

The next morning, the trauma of the last three weeks was already being consigned to the memory banks, and everything suddenly seemed just so disconcertingly...*normal* again. There was no assault on Castle Hill, no more circuit sessions and, instead, we merely strolled into CSTS at nine o'clock for our final debrief. Again, the instructors emphasized that if we remembered "Protection, Location, Water, Food," then they'd done their job and, needless to say, it's now forever etched in my memory. Then, we were called into the CO's office individually for a few parting words. When my turn came, he was looking at a page of notes on his desk and, without looking up, said:

"I could make you come back and do the course again, but I don't think you'd do any better. So...get out!"

"Thank you, sir," I replied, before saluting smartly, doing an about-turn and leaving.

With the sentimental formalities concluded, it was time to head home for a glorious month of leave!

17
PRACTICE BLEEDING– A COMSURV EPILOGUE

My wife had been staying with her parents in Brisbane during my little getaway, so as soon as I got back to our rented house in Castle Hill, I packed up some stuff, threw it in the car and set off on the long drive north. I wouldn't arrive at my destination until the early hours of the following morning but, given the last few weeks, it seemed barely a hardship. I'd always quite enjoyed the drive and was looking forward to chilling out to some music along the way. But your mind tends to wander in such situations and, before long, I found myself mentally reviewing the events of the previous month. The saying goes, "You only get out of something what you're prepared to put into it" and to be completely honest, I knew that I'd put nothing into COMSURV whatsoever. But, even so, the CO's curt summation of my efforts rankled. I'd survived the course, hadn't I? Was I supposed to enjoy it as well? What had it taught me that I hadn't already suspected? On reflection, I could succinctly summarize what I'd learnt in Townsville, as follows:

1. Sitting in a liferaft is boring.
2. Beach beans give you dysentery.

3. In a desert, you WILL get thirsty.
4. In enemy territory, don't get captured.
5. Being hungry is bad...being *really* hungry is *really* bad.
6. Wet wood won't burn.

Now from this exhaustive list, only Number 2 (appropriately) was news—I either knew or suspected the rest. So why couldn't COMSURV have just consisted of a few days of theory in a classroom? If they'd told me, "Beach beans give you dysentery" I would've believed them. We could've sat around in rafts in the base swimming pool and built solar stills in a paddock somewhere. I just didn't see the benefit of putting all the theory into practice, although at least I now had a ready rejoinder for every complaint that I might ever hear throughout the remainder of my entire life.

"You're bored? You should try sitting in a liferaft for six hours. Now THAT'S boring!"

"You're starving? Try living on nothing but barley sugars and beef stock cubes for a week!"

"The bed's uncomfortable? Try sleeping face-down on a pile of rocks!"

For the life of me, I just couldn't see any reason why the course material couldn't have been taught in a classroom. Logically, it was like, "Bashing your head against a brick wall is painful! Now let's bash our heads against this brick wall to prove it!" They could've just told me. I'd have believed them.

COMSURV concentrated on the physical aspects of survival, but the psychological side was never really addressed. In the Static phase, we'd survived to a timetable. But what if there was no timetable? What if it was, "See you when you get back" or "Stay there till you're found"? The uncertainty, the not knowing, would surely be my undoing. Undoubtedly, the thing that keeps an individual going is their mental strength... their Will to Survive. I'd read about the terrible suffering that Allied POWs endured on the Thai-Burma Railroad. Those who'd survived did so because they did whatever it took, including eating rats and insects and weevil-infested rice. But others succumbed quickly to the horror and died. No question that the Will to Survive is much stronger in some individuals than it is in others. But for me on COMSURV, it'd been more a matter of testing my Will to Endure. If I was ever confronted with a genuine "do or die" situation, could I do the practically unthinkable to stay alive? This was the question that came back to me repeatedly on that long drive north and, after a lot of soul-searching, I finally realised that if I was ever in an Andes plane crash, it'd be far more likely that I'd become the first course than the first cannibal. And so, this confronting self-assessment became the most enduring legacy of my time at CSTS—that and the determination to resign if the RAAF ever introduced a Combat Survival Refresher Course!

Cresting the Northern Tablelands near the halfway mark of my journey, I noticed the unusual sight of snow piled up on the roadside and, in the pale reflected moonlight, saw that the paddocks were white with the stuff. The winter of 1984 had been one of the coldest on record, and this fact neatly explained our close encounter with hypothermia during the Semi-arid Phase. Later, I'd learn that one of the 33 Squadron captains had alarmed his Amberley-bound passengers by telling them that there was currently a great view of the ski fields below and that they'd soon be commencing their descent into Melbourne. It was around three o'clock in the morning when I finally pulled up outside my in-laws' place in Brisbane and, from my car, I could see my father-in-law asleep on the lounge-room floor with Wimbledon playing on the television. Eventually, my persistent knocking roused him, and he sleepily opened the front door to welcome me inside.

"G'day mate," he said, shaking my hand. "You want a cuppa?"

"No thanks," I said. "I think I'll just turn in. It's been a very long day."

"Yeah, I bet," he chuckled. "How was the course?"

"That's a looooooooong story," I said, lugging my bag up the stairs. "If I ever write my memoirs, Combat Survival Course is going to have to be a whole separate chapter!"

18
WHAT YOU DON'T SEE CAN'T HURT YOU!

After a few more Butterworth trips, I was again on my way to Honolulu on an Army task that would include two of my most memorable and oft-recounted experiences. One of these anecdotes involves an advance in technology that was so profound that it lent its name to an entire 'age'...the jet engine. As I've already explained, the redoubtable JT3D-3B engines on our 707s were no longer at the forefront of technological advancement but, given the complexity of their axial-flow engines and the extraordinary rotational speeds at which their compressors operated, I was constantly amazed at how these aging jet engines continued to be as reliable as they were.

However, there are always some minor technical issues that accompany machines of such mechanical complexity, and many minor niggles can be carried without jeopardizing the safety of the aircraft or its occupants. During the certification process for every aircraft, its manufacturer produces a list of allowable deficiencies for nearly every aircraft system in a voluminous publication known as the Minimum Equipment List—the RAAF had incorporated just such a publication into its suite of 707 flight manuals. Items of equipment suffering a defect that are not essential to the safe operation of the aircraft (and for which the corrective maintenance procedure can be deferred) are listed in the front of a RAAF aircraft's Technical Log as 'Carried Forward Unserviceabilities,' or 'CFUs.' At the commencement of this task, one of the CFUs for our aircraft read simply:

"No. 3 N1 gauge fluctuates at takeoff thrust but operates normally at all other power settings. All other engine indications are normal."

Without getting too technical, the two-stage axial compressors on the 707 engines comprised the inner N2 'power compressor' and the larger outer N1 'fan compressor' (which is connected to the turbine and essentially free-wheels in the airstream to draw more air into the power compressor in flight). On the ground in strong winds, the N1 fan can spin quite rapidly—even when the engine isn't operating—and starting a jet engine in a strong tailwind can be particularly hazardous since the N1 fan will be spinning backwards, effectively "stalling" the flow of air through the engine just as it's about to be fed combustible fuel.

Of the two key engine components, the N2 compressor is the most critical, and the MEL stated that the N1 gauge could be completely inoperative for a sector if the other engine indicators functioned normally. Woofy briefed us on the problem as we prepared to depart Sydney, and on the takeoff roll, we observed the N1 needle fluctuating on Number 3 engine, just as stated in the CFU. When the thrust was subsequently reduced for the climb and cruise, the engine and its associated N1 gauge settled down into perfectly normal operations. The remainder of the flight to Nadi was uneventful, and after a refuelling stop, we were soon on our way to Honolulu.

The sun had already set as we tracked eastwards for Hawaii, and after about an hour in the cruise, the loadmaster came to the flight deck and informed us that, in the inky darkness, the Number 3 engine was looking decidedly strange. "It's got what looks like St Elmo's fire coming out of the front of it," he told us somewhat concernedly. It seemed highly unlikely that this could merely be a coincidence, but the engine instruments in the cockpit were all functioning perfectly normally. Each of us in turn, though, left the cockpit and walked back into the darkened passenger cabin to take a look at the troublesome engine, the inlet of which was now filled with a spectacular, swirling cauldron of blue static electrical discharges that would have looked entirely at home in a science-fiction movie. We all had vivid recollections of the British Airways 747 that had dramatically lost power on all four engines in thick volcanic ash over Indonesia less than two years earlier, and we knew that the first indication of trouble that night had been a strange glow in the engine intakes.

"There aren't any volcanoes around here are there?" asked Woofy.

It was a perplexing dilemma, but since there were no other accompanying abnormalities, there wasn't even a checklist that we could consult. Above us was a Qantas 747, also enroute to Honolulu, and Woofy decided to call them up on the radio to have a chat about our predicament.

"Qantas 3...Aussie 123," Woofy called.

"Yeah Aussie...go ahead," said the Qantas crew boredly.

"You got any guys with 707 experience on board this evening?" Woofy enquired.

After a short pause, a different, more polished (but also crustier) voice replied stiffly, "Yes, I flew them for a decade or so. Do you have a problem?"

Woofy explained the CFU, the otherwise exemplary engine performance and the now disturbing situation that, whenever we looked at it, the engine inlet was swathed in St Elmo's fire. The paternal Qantas captain asked us a few perfunctory questions, and after a long, deliberative pause, said:

"Well, there's only one thing you can do then!"

"And what's that?" we asked eagerly, anticipating a pearl of wisdom from our venerable colleague that would make our problem go away.

"STOP LOOKING AT IT!" he stated bluntly.

We decided to heed his sage advice, and Woofy placated the now-concerned passengers with a quick explanatory PA that outlined the situation, while also assuring them that the engine was otherwise operating perfectly. The rest of the flight was uneventful, and after arriving in Honolulu at about 9am, the flight engineer entered "NIL" in the Defects column of the Technical Log. We subsequently thought nothing more about our mysterious engine problem and instead enjoyed some more of the beautiful weather, stunning scenery and cold beers that the tropical paradise had to offer.

138 | BIG BOEINGS AND HOVERING HELOS

The return flight to Richmond a few days later was supposed to be empty, but when the US military found out, they quickly rounded up about fifty personnel to travel back with us on a "study visit." Our unexpected guests were all delighted to be heading "down under" and were in a happy and animated state as they boarded the aircraft at Honolulu International Airport. The takeoff from the Reef Runway was uneventful and before long we were again established in the cruise on our way home. Woofy, in the left seat, had reclined his seat-back and, in the warm morning sunshine, was soon dozing peacefully. In the right seat, I was being fed a stream of tacos by the flight stewards in the forward galley. These Honolulu specialties were fast becoming my favourite, but unfortunately, as soon as you bit into one, it exploded in a shower of corn chips, beef mince and salsa that inevitably fell onto the Navigation

Log and turned it into a squishy, unreadable mess. On one of her resupply trips to the cockpit, the flight steward asked me if some of the passengers could come to the flight deck for a visit. "Sure," I muffled through yet another mouthful of taco.

A few minutes later, an enormous Marine walked into the cockpit and sat down in the vacant first observer's seat. He immediately surveyed his surroundings and saw the flight engineer working away on his panel, with Woofy asleep in the left-hand seat and me, beside him, stuffing my face with tacos. From his body language, I could tell that something was wrong and, a minute or so later, with wide eyes and barely controlled panic in his voice, he leaned forward and almost shouted:

"WHO'S FLY'IN THE F***'IN PLANE, MAN??!!!"

Now, with hindsight, I should have probably thrown my taco away and lunged for the controls, but it would've been a bugger getting the brown stains out of the sheepskin on the first observer's seat. Instead, with my mouth full, I merely pointed out the autopilot controls to my technologically challenged friend. When we eventually got back to Richmond, the ground crew carried out a more thorough turn-around servicing on the aircraft before releasing it for its next flight. When they opened the engine cowling of the Number 3 engine, the N1 bearing simply fell apart and deposited itself onto the tarmac in a pile of ground-down cogs and wheels, metal shavings and other assorted debris. It was the friction from this bearing (as it ground itself to destruction) that had caused the spectacular light show that we'd seen during our night crossing of the Pacific. Had the same problem occurred in the load-bearing N2 compressor, the engine would undoubtedly have failed, and this experience taught me a very valuable lesson. The aircraft rarely ever gives you a false indication—sometimes it's just a little difficult to work out exactly what it's trying to tell you!

19
BLOODY LEGENDS!

In 1984, RAAF Base Richmond played host to a reunion of the past members of Nos. 463 and 467 Squadrons—two RAAF Lancaster-equipped squadrons that had been based in England throughout the bomber offensive of World War II. Over a hundred survivors of this campaign were due to meet in the Airmen's Mess to swap recollections and remember their fallen mates—the junior officers on the base would act as their escorts for the day. Our CO's instructions were simple:

"Make sure they have a beer in their hand, but stop them drinking too much..." he began.

"...because if they drink too much, they might fall over," he continued.

"So, when they *do* drink too much and fall over, make bloody well sure you're there to catch them," he concluded.

The afternoon presented me with the unique opportunity to meet some of the contemporaries of my old workmate Harry Wright and, during one memorable conversation with a spry, former Lancaster mid-upper gunner, I couldn't resist asking him something that I'd wondered about for a long time:

"How did you fly night formation during those thousand-bomber raids?" I asked him.

"How do you mean?" he replied, with a quizzical look on his face.

"Well…" I continued, "with a thousand aeroplanes in the air at once, surely you must have had to stay in some sort of formation."

"Oh no," he said immediately. "We never flew night formation. Every squadron was given a takeoff time and an altitude to fly at. The first aircraft took off at the pre-briefed time, and the rest of us took off at thirty-second intervals afterwards. Once we were airborne, we'd spiral up over the airfield until we reached our pre-briefed altitude, and then we'd set course for the target. But we never flew formation…we were all individual aircraft flying together."

"So, on a thousand-bomber raid," I asked, "how many aircraft would you see?"

"Ooooh…" he said in deep reflection, "two…maybe three."

"In fact," he continued, "once we got to the target, my job wasn't to look for German night fighters anymore. My job was to look for other bombers in the searchlights above us with their bomb doors open. If I saw one, I had to call 'Break Left' or 'Break Right' to the pilot, so that we didn't get a load of bombs landing right on top of us!"

The prospect of being aboard one of a thousand blacked-out aircraft, all flying individually to their target and then converging over a specified location at pretty much the same time would have been enough to give me nightmares…let alone throwing in the threat of night fighters, flak and the myriad other hazards that these men confronted every single time they flew. Little wonder, then, that Allied bomber crews suffered the second-highest casualty rate of all military forces during World War II, with only the German U-boat crews faring worse.

Years later, I would watch a fascinating TV interview with a venerable RAF bomber pilot who had been awarded the Victoria Cross for continuing to his target and dropping his bombs, despite his aircraft sustaining significant damage from flak while crossing the French coast. The interview must have occurred during the 1970s, because the gentleman in question was magnificently attired in a lavender safari suit, and sported some spectacular facial "mutton-chops". The interviewer initially set the scene for his viewers by explaining how the flight had transpired on that night, so long before:

"So, you encountered heavy flak crossing the coast that left you slightly wounded and the tail of your aircraft heavily damaged. To stay straight and level, you had to hold in a lot of back stick and a lot of aileron. Yet you continued to your target, dropped your bombs and managed to make it safely back to England. That was an incredibly brave decision to make. Just what thought processes were going through your mind at the time?"

"Well..." the VC recipient began. "I knew that it was a thousand-bomber raid and that we were close to being the lead element in the attack," he continued. "When we were hit crossing the coast, I essentially had two options...continue to the target, or turn around and try to find my way through nine hundred aircraft coming the other way! I decided to continue and when I got back, they awarded me a Victoria Cross! Now that was all very nice, but I just thought I was taking the safest course of action available to me at the time!"

Explained in those terms, his actions were understandable and yet, undeniably, they were also very brave. Little wonder that the veterans of World War II are referred to by many as The Greatest Generation. I would learn much more about their courage and selfless sacrifice on my very next trip.

20
EGYPTIAN AND EUROPEAN EXTRAVAGANZA

While the trip to Marseilles in April 1984 had whet my appetite to see more of Europe, in November of that year I hit the jackpot when I was tasked with a trip to the UK that encompassed a side trip to Marseilles, an overnight stopover in Rome (on the way back) and transits of Cairo (both ways). Since the task involved conveying the Chief of the Defence Force to Egypt for discussions regarding Australia's commitment to the Multinational Force & Observers (which monitored the neutral zone in the Sinai between the Israelis and the Egyptians), two very senior 707 pilots were crewed as captains for the trip—Group Captain Mike and Squadron Leader Mal, who, because of their first names, were promptly (and discreetly) dubbed "The Leyland Brothers" by the rest of the crew.

Our first overnight stopover was Kuala Lumpur, which was a surprisingly modern city with freeways far superior to anything that Sydney offered at the time. On the morning of our departure, we were grateful for their existence, because our transport didn't show up and we had to be shuttled to the airport in a couple of the hotel's Mercedes limousines.

Because we were running late, we asked the driver to hurry, but we didn't expect him to take our request so much to heart. Soon, we were hurtling down the freeway at nearly a hundred miles an hour, weaving in and out of the traffic in a display that would have made James Bond proud. Amazingly, we made it to the airport in one piece and, after yet another overnighter in Butterworth, we were off on our way to Cairo.

After a quick refuelling stop in Bahrain, we eventually arrived in Egypt, where we then flew one of the most unusual descents of my career. The capital had no radar equipment in 1984, and the complex instructions issued by ATC were as difficult to understand as they were to fly. Initially, we were instructed to overfly the airport and keep heading west. Then, we were told to turn left and track towards the northeast. Then we were told to turn right and track back out toward the northwest before we were eventually cleared for a visual approach in the hazy, evening light. On the ground, we were then delayed for over two hours while our passports were collected, taken away and presumably examined for evidence of entry or exit stamps for Israel—a strict no-no! Finally, we were cleared to leave for our accommodation but, out on the freeway, we quickly discovered that Egyptian road rules were unique in the sense that, as far as we could tell, there weren't any! Cairo was the only place I've ever visited where three-lane highways routinely carried five lanes of traffic. Drivers didn't indicate when they changed lanes, they just blew their horns and moved. It was a city of nine million people and (seemingly) eighteen million car horns, and even in our hotel rooms, all we could hear was the sound of car horns out on the freeway as the crazy drivers jockeyed for position.

The next day we had off, so four of us got together and hired a taxi for a day trip out to the pyramids, which are surprisingly close to the city's outer suburbs. After some spirited haggling, we secured a personal car and driver for five hours for just twenty US dollars. Very quickly, we picked up on the fact that in Cairo, things ran on "hard" currency (US dollars, British pounds, French francs etc.). You may as well have wiped your backside with Egyptian pounds...and, from the look of them, many people had done precisely that. Our taxi ride to the pyramids that day made the limo driver in Kuala Lumpur look like a wimp. Again, our driver seemed to rely on just two pieces of equipment—his horn, and his accelerator pedal. Approaching the crest of a hill, there was a miraculous break in the traffic, and our cabbie gunned his vehicle like it was a Formula 1 race. He then immediately had to brake violently in a long skid that only just prevented us from smashing into the stationary traffic on the other side. Finally, we arrived at the pyramids and, grateful again to be alive, we shakily got out of the taxi and (reluctantly) confirmed with the driver that he would be there waiting to take us back again.

Woofy had warned me before I left that if the "Gyppos" found someone who made them a decent offer on the pyramids (and had a big enough truck), they'd sell them in a heartbeat. As we wandered towards the surprisingly diminutive Sphinx (crouched protectively before the Great Pyramid of Cheops), I finally discovered what he meant. Hordes of hawkers descended on us like flies on fresh meat, offering everything from rides on their flea-bitten camels to postcards and bottles of water. They offered themselves up for photographs (for a fee, of course) and I simply struggled to equate these wretched people with the incredible ancients who'd constructed these colossal structures almost five thousand years earlier. I tried to imagine the scene as thousands of workers hauled each massive block into position, and how the pyramids must have gleamed and shone like a desert mirage when faced with smooth white limestone. But try as I might to project myself back in time, the onslaught from the hawkers was relentless. Just when we thought we'd managed to finally evade them, an old Arab in flowing robes and headdress ("tea-towel and fan belt" in RAAF slang) approached us and offered his services as a tour guide...for no charge whatsoever. In his heavy accent, he described himself as a "Custodian of the Holy Pyramids" and promised to show us around places that were out-of-bounds to everybody else. His free tour also included the chance to see some "Holy Griffins," and while we had no idea what Holy Griffins were, his persistence finally wore us down and we all set off together on his (totally free) guided tour of the Holy Pyramids.

Firstly, he took us to a ventilation shaft at the base of one of the pyramids that was about a metre square. He then took out a piece of

newspaper, lit it, dropped it into the shaft and encouraged us all to lean forward to see for ourselves just how deep it was. Fearing that there might already be a pile of skeletons at the bottom from his previous "tour groups," we were understandably reluctant to accede to his request (and only took a half-hearted peek). He then escorted us to one of the three smaller pyramids, which we all climbed and then, from its summit, took some very unique photographs. This practice, I'm guessing, is now probably forbidden, and so I guess we should at least be grateful to the Custodian for that experience. Finally, he showed us some of his beloved Holy Griffins which, disappointingly, were just mispronounced hieroglyphics and thus, with our tour concluded, it was time for us to give him some donations "for the upkeep of the Holy Pyramids."

"Mate...you said the tour was free," we protested, although we probably always suspected that we'd ultimately be hit up for some cash. After a brief discussion, we offered him twenty Egyptian pounds, but he wasn't happy and demanded (loudly) that we pay him in US dollars,

British pounds or any other type of foreign hard currency. "Sorry mate," we said, "that's all you're going to get" and as he grew ever more agitated, we walked ever more quickly towards the canteen to make good our escape. One of our young groundies didn't walk quite fast enough, and soon found himself isolated at the back of the pack, and haggling with the disgruntled and increasingly angry old Arab. He caught up with us a few minutes later and appeared a little shaken by the whole ordeal.

"So how much did you give him?" we asked.

"About forty Egyptian pounds in the end. But the old bastard said he'd put a curse on me!"

While relating his harrowing tale, the young fellow was nervously (and increasingly desperately) trying to light a cigarette using a cardboard match from a very well-worn matchbook. As he reached the point in his story where he'd been cursed, the match finally caught alight and burnt his thumb in the process. He yelled out in pain, swore loudly and shook off the burning match.

"See mate..." we said, cruelly, "the curse is working. You should have paid him more!"

Early the next morning, we returned to the airport to fly to RAF Brize Norton for a brief stopover before continuing to Marseilles. On our way through immigration at Cairo, we had to pass through a metal detector, which proceeded to shriek continually while we received the bows and well-wishes of the ancient Arab who was in charge of airport security. At Marseilles, we loaded up some more Squirrel helicopter components before heading back to Brize Norton the following evening. We now had five glorious days off and, while four of us decided to rent a car and travel to London, the Leyland Brothers opted to stay put and sample the fare of the local pubs of Swindon. Early on the morning of Sunday, the 11th of November, we set off on a scenic drive through the Cotswolds District where, despite the gloomy, overcast conditions, the natural beauty of the place was simply stunning. The little stone-walled villages, with their trickling streams, lushly-grassed village greens and charming, slate-roofed sandstone cottages, were like something straight from a postcard. It was truly one of the most picturesque regions I'd ever visited.

Strangely, though, nearly every little town and village seemed eerily deserted and, as we were discussing this very point in one of the larger towns, we turned out of a deserted narrow side street onto the main thoroughfare...and found ourselves slap-bang in the middle of the town's Remembrance Day parade. Of course, being military types, we all knew the significance of the date, but we were unprepared for the importance that Britain placed on the horrific events that had taken place in the blood-soaked trenches of World War I. Union Jacks waved proudly on both sides of the street and the crowds cheered as we drove slowly along between the marching formations and brass bands. But when the procession slowed down to a walking pace at one point, an observant "bobby" approached us and asked us what the hell we were doing in their parade. He didn't buy our initial explanation that we were a visiting Royal Australian Air Force contingent (even when we produced our ID cards), and after we finally admitted having simply taken a wrong turn, he told us to "booger off then" in no uncertain terms.

During the rest of the day, we visited some of England's many historical landmarks, including the ancient Roman baths (not surprisingly, in the scenic city of Bath), the "White Horse" at Westbury and the prehistoric ruins at Stonehenge out on the windswept Salisbury Plain. It was a fascinating day, but when we arrived back at the pub that night, the Leyland Brothers informed us that Robert Trimbole (a drug baron implicated in the murder of Griffith businessman, Donald Mackay) had been arrested in Ireland and that the Australian government was urgently seeking his extradition. If Ireland agreed to that request, we would be flying him back to Australia to face justice. As fascinating as it would have been to play private pilot for such an infamous Mafioso, we were somewhat relieved when Ireland rejected Australia's application, and we were able to leave for London, as planned.

To avoid the worst of London's inner-city traffic (and also partly to reduce costs) we decided to base ourselves in a quaint little pub called The Lancer in suburban Chiswick. Like many other English pubs, it was a themed establishment, and its walls were covered in memorabilia celebrating the feats of the brightly clad and courageous British cavalrymen of the Crimean War. The Lancer was also typical of so many other

English pubs in that it was almost impossible to determine its age—it could as easily have been forty years old, as four hundred years old. After a hearty English breakfast, we headed for the local station to catch "the tube" and visit some of the landmarks of London that I'd only ever dreamed of seeing as a boy. Our first stop was Nelson's Column where, after taking some obligatory photographs, we set off down Whitehall towards the Houses of Parliament and Westminster Abbey. The Abbey was probably the place that made the biggest impression on me and where "Is This Really It" syndrome kicked into full overdrive.

This imposing edifice had its origins before the invasion of William the Conqueror in the 11th century, and more than three thousand people are interred beneath its heavy stone slab flooring. In high school, I concentrated on technical subjects, and history didn't interest me at all. But in Westminster Abbey, history wasn't just something you read in a textbook—it was tangible. You could see it...you could touch it...and you could almost feel it. Many of the grave markers on the stone floor were in Latin, dating back to the 12th century, whilst many others had been rendered illegible by the passage of the multitude of visitors who've thronged to the Abbey over the centuries. Private chapels and niches throughout the cathedral provide the final resting places of departed English aristocrats and their families, with many tombs featuring a stone effigy of the deceased personage—lying at rest with closed eyes and hands forever clasped in prayer.

In elevated tombs around the central altar—the most hallowed site in the cathedral—lie many of England's revered and reviled former monarchs. Edward I, who invaded Scotland and captured William Wallace (famously portrayed by Mel Gibson in *Braveheart*), is entombed in Westminster Abbey, as is Richard II, who became king at ten years of age, and was then deposed and murdered at thirty-three. In a more remote chapel at the rear of the church is the tomb of possibly England's greatest monarch, Elizabeth I, where the deep indentations worn into the stone steps of her chapel by so many visitors attest to her ongoing popularity. Intriguingly, not far away is the final resting place of Mary, Queen of Scots, who was executed on Elizabeth's orders in 1587. But Westminster Abbey isn't just reserved for royalty and aristocrats. Many other notable figures rest within its walls including David Livingstone, Oliver Cromwell, Neville Chamberlain, Geoffrey Chaucer, Charles Dickens, Charles Darwin and Sir Isaac Newton. Of particular interest to me was the spot below the stained-glass Battle of Britain Memorial Window where the ashes of Air Chief Marshal, Lord Hugh Dowding (Commander of RAF Fighter Command during the Battle of Britain) were interred in 1970. The Abbey was a fascinating place, awakening within me an interest in history that continues to this day.

After a short boat ride down the Thames, we continued our history lesson at the Tower of London—a castle built by William the Conqueror and, later, home to Henry VIII. After paying our admission, we were formed into a group by one of the famous "Beefeaters," who were once entrusted with guarding the Crown Jewels but who, these days, are mostly retired British military warrant officers who play tour guide for the Tower's multitude of visitors. The Beefeaters deliver their oral history of the macabre (but also sometimes grisly amusing) events quite drolly, and two of their stories remain firmly lodged in my memory. When the Tower was first built, it was surrounded by a moat, into which all of the sewage from the castle flowed, making the Tower of London the most rancid, vile-smelling place in London. The other story concerned an English aristocrat who was beheaded at the Tower before his official portrait had been painted. When the mistake was realised, his head was rather hastily re-attached to his body to enable the completion of his rather grim and odd-looking portrait. It's the Tower's function as a prison though, that has captured the public imagination the most, with a young Elizabeth I and Sir Walter Raleigh being two of its most famous inmates. While Elizabeth survived her ordeal, many others didn't, and over a hundred people (including two wives of Henry VIII—Anne Boleyn and Catherine Howard) were executed at Tower Green.

When the tour ended, we headed for the Jewel House to take a look at the fabulous Crown Jewels, before returning to the White Tower (the original and oldest building in the complex) to examine the extensive collection of armour and artefacts from the Tudor era. On the floor of a small basement gallery that displayed swords, lances, pikes and other assorted weaponry was a small brass plaque that bore the inscription "On this spot at 2:30pm on July 17th, 1974, an IRA bomb exploded killing one person and injuring forty-one others". It was a sobering reminder of the grim past that links the British and Irish peoples, dating back to the Norman invasion of Ireland in the twelfth century that led to more than 700 years of despised English rule. In the early 1980s, there were some particularly bloody attacks in London by the IRA, with eleven members of the Household Cavalry being killed by bombs planted in Hyde Park and Regent's Park in July 1982. Another six people had been killed in December the following year by a bomb planted in Harrods department store and, with December rapidly approaching, media reports were warning of the likelihood of an IRA "Christmas bombing campaign." We visited Harrods to do some Christmas shopping and noted the heavy security in place—police officers in bullet-proof vests manned every entrance and trained sniffer dog teams patrolled regularly, checking any suspicious packages for traces of explosives.

Then, it was time to bid London farewell and head back to Swindon. But on the outskirts of the city, we stopped in at RAF Hendon—a Battle of Britain airbase that was now home to the RAF Museum, which displays an example of every aircraft type flown by the Royal Air Force. We wandered through the massive hangars looking at the mighty Avro Lancaster, the pioneering Gloster Meteor jet fighter of World War II and the sinister, Cold War-era, delta-wing Vulcan bomber. But it was the Battle of Britain Hall that I was most keen to visit. As we ambled up the long entry corridor toward the ticket window, we were absorbed in an animated conversation when, suddenly, the unmistakable roar of a Rolls-Royce Merlin engine flashed over our heads. As we struggled to regain our composure thinking "What the f*** was that?" we noticed the girl in the ticket booth looking in our direction and laughing uncontrollably. Then we noticed the speakers in the ceiling and deduced that, at will, she could broadcast the sound of a Merlin engine at full throttle whenever she wanted…particularly when the unsuspecting visitor was at his most unsuspecting!

Inside the Battle of Britain Hall were all the aircraft of my boyhood fantasies—the robust and reliable Hawker Hurricane, the majestic

Supermarine Spitfire, the evil Junkers Ju-87 'Stuka' dive-bomber, the coldly efficient Messerschmitt Bf 109 fighter and the lumbering, bulbous Heinkel 111 bomber—and all of them in pristine condition. I thought back to that wide-eyed ten-year-old who had sat in awe and wonderment at the cinema in Brisbane, watching these aircraft engage in a life-and-death struggle to control the skies above the very building in which we stood. I reflected on the personal journey that had taken me from that cinema to this very spot, and what a pivotal role these aircraft had played in that process. But as awe-inspiring as the Battle of Britain Hall had been, the highlight of the day for me was a temporary exhibit that honoured the RAF aviators who'd been awarded the Victoria Cross during World War II. In large glass display cases lay the citations that listed some extraordinary feats of courage, along with either a picture of the recipient, an item of his uniform or perhaps even his medal itself. We spent a long time there, and I still vividly recall a couple of those stories.

The first resonated with me because it featured a young British fighter pilot who'd been stationed at Butterworth when the Japanese attacked the base in the opening days of the Pacific War. The Allied aircraft based there were the heavy and sluggish American-built Brewster Buffalos, which were simply no match for the swift and nimble Japanese Zeros. Only a few British pilots even managed to get airborne to resist the attack, and ground observers watched as this brave airman dispatched two Zeros before he was overwhelmed, shot down and killed. Surely, I figured, the minute he started his engine he must have known that he had no chance, yet he still fought as hard as he could before paying the ultimate sacrifice. Could I have done what he did? Or would I have been in a foxhole somewhere with a helmet on, head down and praying to survive? Just what innate quality did these men possess that drove them to fight so hard when they had so little chance of survival?

The second story concerned a bomber pilot on a mission over Germany. What many people don't realise about World War II bomber crews is that the RAF were so short of pilots that the bombers were essentially single-pilot aircraft. The flight engineer usually sat beside the pilot in the cockpit and received just enough basic flying instruction to be able to fly the aircraft straight and level. On this particular mission, the aircraft had been heavily damaged by flak on its return journey, and the pilot had sustained some serious injuries. Bleeding heavily and in extreme pain, he then refused the offered morphine so that he could remain conscious in the cockpit and talk the flight engineer through an approach and landing back in England. Ultimately, the pilot achieved his goal, but when the ambulance arrived at the aircraft to take him to hospital, he had already died from shock and loss of blood. He had sacrificed himself so that his crew could get back on the ground safely and not have to bail out over enemy territory. There was story after story just like this, and before we knew it, it was five o'clock and the museum was about to close. The Last Post was then broadcast through the PA system and standing in the presence of such unbelievable heroism and sacrifice, my eyes welled up with tears (just as they are as I type this). They truly were The Greatest Generation.

On our last day in England, we made a quick day trip to Wales to visit Raglan Castle, a once-mighty fortress that had been destroyed during the English Civil War in the 17th century. After exploring the ruins, we popped into a little pub on the English border and noticed that a magnificent English country house nearby had a large "For Sale" sign out front. "Who on earth would want to sell such a beautiful house?" we wondered out loud. But no sooner had we said that than a pair of RAF fighter jets roared up the valley at just a few hundred feet and promptly changed course right over the top of the house. Mystery solved. Our final stop was at the magnificent 11th-century Gloucester Cathedral where, in the old church's dimly-lit interior we noticed a plaque on the wall that declared "On this spot in 1085, William the Conqueror decreed that the Domesday Book be written". In the cathedral's gift shop, I bought a small book about English monarchs and read it avidly for the rest of the trip. These experiences helped me to put my own country's history into context, and I could only marvel at the resilience of the early English settlers who'd willingly left this lush and fertile land to make a future for themselves in a harsh and relentlessly unforgiving country on the other side of the world.

On the morning of November 16th, we departed RAF Brize Norton for the short two-hour flight down to Rome, arriving at our hotel in the heart of the old city just after lunchtime. With less than a day available for exploration, we simply stowed our bags, got changed and hit the streets. Under gloomy skies, however, I must admit that my first impression of The Eternal City wasn't all that favourable. Compared to London, it seemed to be in a somewhat inglorious state of dilapidation and long past its prime. The narrow, crowded, cobble-stoned streets, were full of shadowy entryways that would have made the city the perfect setting for a murder mystery, or a tale of espionage and intrigue. But suddenly, we emerged from this tangled maze of streets and alleyways and there, right in front of us, stood the magnificent Trevi Fountain—the largest Baroque fountain in Rome, and surely one of the most famous landmarks in the world.

With a strict timetable though, there was little time to do anything other than take a few photographs. I didn't even have a coin to throw into the fountain which, according to folklore, would have ensured my return to Rome someday. Incidentally, throwing a second coin into the fountain means that you'll get married and a third coin means you'll get divorced. So much for romance. Whatever the reasoning behind the significance of the three coins, the tradition results in several thousand dollars' worth of coins being thrown into the fountain every single day, with the money then being collected and used to fund projects to help the needy throughout the city. After pausing for just a few minutes to take in the scene, we turned around and set off and were almost immediately consumed again by the city's maze of narrow streets and alleyways.

Our next stop was the Colosseum (dating back to 70AD), where gladiators had fought against animals and each other, where land and sea battles had often been re-enacted and where countless Christians had met a grisly end for the amusement of the Roman citizenry. The heavy grey clouds were, by now, producing a steady drizzle, and this only added to the sombre atmosphere inside what had once been the largest free-standing amphitheatre ever built. The Colosseum was a masterpiece of ancient architecture, but it had suffered over the centuries from the effects of earthquakes, and the stripping away of much of its marble façade for construction projects elsewhere in the city. With the original wooden flooring of the Colosseum having long since rotted away, the labyrinthine walls of the subterranean storage rooms, passageways and tiny holding cells were still clearly visible. As I surveyed the stadium's vast interior, I tried to imagine how terrifying it must have been for the combatants and prisoners to sit in those tiny rooms, contemplating their fate while listening to the roar of the bloodthirsty crowd of fifty thousand Romans above them.

After leaving the ancient arena, we took the chance to have a little juvenile fun. Sometimes, a theme emerged on lengthy overseas sojourns, and on this particular trip, the "schtick" involved classifying our pedestrian crossings on a scale from Category 1 (looking straight ahead and nonchalantly strolling across the road) to Category 5 (sprinting madly across in fear for your life with your head swivelling in every direction). The crew's objective was to achieve a Category 1 crossing somewhere, but our expeditions by foot in Kuala Lumpur, Cairo, Marseilles and London had, so far, resulted in nothing better than a Category 2. Now, here we were in a city famous for its wild and chaotic traffic and, approaching a major roundabout, there wasn't a car in sight. Certain that we were on the verge of achieving our goal, we casually stepped off the kerb and strolled sedately toward the centre of the roundabout. Since we were looking straight ahead, it was more the *sound* the tiny Fiat made as it roared around the roundabout on two wheels and headed straight for us that alerted us to its presence. We immediately broke into a flat sprint and, on narrowly avoiding death by reaching the sanctuary of the traffic island, we figured that we'd better average it out at a Category 3 (at best).

With daylight rapidly dwindling, we hailed a cab to take us to our final destination—St Peter's Basilica. Our guidebook told us that the construction of the cathedral had lasted from 1506 to 1626, and I could only imagine how such a long timeframe would possibly be acceptable in the present day. "Yes, I can build you this cathedral! It'll probably take a hundred and twenty years or so, but that's okay, isn't it?" The cabbie dropped us off at the long pedestrian approach to the Vatican and, up ahead, we could see the enormous statue of Jesus Christ (flanked by those of his twelve apostles and John the Baptist) gazing down at us from atop the massive façade of the Michelangelo-designed structure. Finally, we stood before the enormous bronze door that serves as the main entryway into the Basilica. A large sign in English warned that photography was not permitted inside, but it seemed to have little impact on the groups of Japanese tourists who were aiming their flashguns at everything in sight. On this trip, I'd already visited Westminster Abbey and Gloucester Cathedral, but *nothing* prepared me for the grandeur and majesty that awaited me within St Peter's.

The dimensions of the cathedral's cavernous interior are simply staggering. It's two hundred metres from the entry doors to the main altar at the rear of the church, and its vaulted ceilings soar up nearly fifty metres above the heads of the congregation. St Peter's Basilica is built in the shape of a cross, and where the two arms intersect is the holiest place in the cathedral—the burial site of St Peter, who was crucified (upside down) on the nearby Vatican Hill during the reign of Emperor Nero in 64AD. Marking the spot is St Peter's Baldachin, a sculpted bronze canopy that is supported by four twenty-metre tall twisted Solomonic columns. Above the canopy is the central dome of the Basilica—also designed by Michelangelo—which rises to a height of one hundred and twenty metres above the cathedral floor. It's an astonishing structure that must have made the early pilgrims feel that they'd already entered Heaven. I was simply agog at the grandeur of the architecture, the statuary and the atmosphere of the place as we slowly made our way to St Peter's Baldachin. On reaching its base, I looked at my watch and then turned round to take in everything surrounding me. When I next looked at my watch, thirty minutes had elapsed. Grudgingly, we then had to leave, because there was one more place nearby that I'd wanted to see ever since completing my high school art classes.

After re-entering St Peter's Square, we set off in the semi-darkness around the perimeter of the Vatican's walls until, twenty minutes later, we stood before the door to the Vatican Museum and Sistine Chapel on which a sign read simply: "CLOSED." I was so disappointed to have gotten so close to witnessing one of Michelangelo's greatest masterpieces, and our early departure for Cairo meant that a return the next day was simply impossible. Crestfallen, we decided to call it quits and have an early dinner. We found a little place not too far away where the waiter greeted us in about four different languages before trying out his English on us. He then continued to practice his multilingual skills as he circulated amongst his customers, taking orders and chatting with them in their native tongues. I figured I couldn't go wrong with spaghetti Bolognese but, unfortunately, what I was served was pretty bland and smacked of mass-production. The watery Italian red wine was served from a bottle that must have been a candle holder the previous night because I swore there was still wax around the bottle's lip. On the whole, the dinner was a disappointment, but on our way back to the hotel, I began to see Rome in a different light...literally. The soft hues of the city lights bathed away the dirt and grime and illuminated the landmarks in such a way that they looked to be straight out of the pages of a picture book. So, while Rome was a bit rundown and grotty during the day, at night it was full of alluring charm, and I sincerely hoped that I would return someday.

The following day was a Saturday, and when we reached Ciampino Airport (Rome's secondary airfield) at 6am, the terminal building was still completely deserted. We went wandering from door to door, rattling each one in the hope of finding one unlocked when we were suddenly confronted by a very large Italian with an even larger gun. Some animated conversation followed (mostly courtesy of some extravagant hand gestures) before we were finally allowed through to the aircraft. By early afternoon, after enjoying a magnificent view of the pyramids during the descent into Cairo, we were back amongst the honking horns of Egypt. This time around, though, we stayed at the very comfortable Sheraton Hotel...which would spectacularly burn to the ground just six years later, killing thirteen people. Sunday was a rest day before we headed off to Singapore and by this time, we were all pretty knackered. We'd planned to visit the world-renowned Egyptian Museum and look at the ancient artefacts, but we eventually decided to just have a sleep-in and then play some tennis. Trips to Cairo were fairly common occurrences during Australia's involvement in the MFO, and my diary entry for this day read "I'm sure I'll get back to Cairo to see the museum sometime." Of course, "sometime" never came...so Carpe Diem folks. Carpe Diem! What a trip!

21
OHHHH...THOSE RUSSIANS!

In late 1984, my mother-in-law received the devastating news that a small lump on the side of her neck was malignant and that an intensive course of powerful radiation was required. My wife, Tracy, understandably wanted to be with her mother, and so I contacted DPO—the Directorate of Posting (Officers)—to request a compassionate posting to RAAF Base Amberley. "You won't get an F-111 posting—they're too competitive," I was told over the phone. "But if you're prepared to fly rotary-wing, we can give you a posting to 9 Squadron flying Iroquois helicopters." I already knew that my time at 33 Squadron was drawing to a close, but my work colleagues were somewhat taken aback by the complete culture change that I was contemplating. Woofy, though, seemed genuinely thrilled for me and, as a former helicopter pilot who'd served in Vietnam, he usually returned serve to those who belittled his rotary-wing hours by saying, "Yeah, well how many combat hours do you have in your logbook, mate?" I knew that I was now about to experience a completely different style of flying, and this made me all the more determined to enjoy my last few trips at 33 Squadron.

* * *

On March 12th, 1985, I woke up late because I was programmed for some night circuit training at Avalon and didn't need to go to work until lunchtime. Tracy was still up in Brisbane, and so I had the run of our rented house to myself. The previous evening, the lead television news story had been the death of the Soviet leader—the rather grim-looking Konstantin Chernenko—who'd only been in power for thirteen months. He had succeeded Yuri Andropov, who'd himself dropped off the perch a mere fifteen months after the death of the Cold War Soviet leader, Leonid Brezhnev. But I didn't expect this event to be of much significance to me personally because, as far as I knew, Australia hadn't sent an official representative to Moscow for the preceding couple of funerals, so why should this one be any different? Even the leaders of the Free World were probably getting tired of periodically racing off to Moscow to farewell the latest deceased Soviet Supremo. So, anticipating just another day in the office, I arrived at the squadron around eleven o'clock feeling very well-rested and ready to kill a few hours before heading off to Avalon.

But immediately upon entering the headquarters building, I sensed an unfamiliar buzz of excitement and headed straight for the Operations Room. There was Murray, the new OPSFLTCDR, standing in front of the tasking board with about three phones in each hand and a throng of people surrounding him who were all engaged in quiet but earnest conversation. When he saw me in the doorway, he pointed at me and said, "You! Go home and get some sleep. You're leaving for Moscow at 6 o'clock tonight!" I was stunned and only had time to fire off a few perfunctory questions before Murray's attention was again directed toward the assembled hordes who were busily engaged in what was a hastily convened planning meeting. The trip was not yet approved, I learned, and I could expect a phone call around 2pm to confirm whether it was definitely on or not. No sooner had I arrived at work than I was on my way back home again to try for even more rest.

Lying on my bed at home, a million thoughts flew around in my head, not the least of which was, "What the hell am I going to wear in Moscow at the end of a Russian winter?" I didn't even know where most of my winter clothes were, so I decided to just wait and see and try to get back to sleep. Needless to say, that was simply impossible and at 2pm, with not a single thing packed, I received the expected phone call that astonishingly informed me that the trip was indeed on and that I should report to the squadron headquarters at 3:30. With just under an hour to shower and pack, I ripped out every bit of winter clothing that I could lay my hands on and threw it all into my suitcase. I didn't even own an overcoat and decided that my blue, RAAF-issue one (sans rank slides) would just have to suffice. Soon, I was on my way back to Richmond for the second time that day.

The headquarters was still a hive of activity when I got there, and I soon discovered that our long tour of duty would kick off with a quick hop over to Mascot in the back of a C-130 Hercules. The installation of some arrestor cables at Richmond for the newly-acquired F/A-18 Hornets had temporarily rendered the runway too short for 707 operations and, as a consequence, we'd been operating out of Kingsford-Smith Airport. Our government representative was being flown to Sydney aboard a 34 Squadron aircraft, and as soon as he arrived, we would depart for Tokyo. After a quick refuelling stop in Japan, we would then head off for Moscow, arriving at Sheremetyevo Airport a mere two hours before the state funeral was due to commence in Red Square. Thus, we were on an extremely tight schedule and any significant delays would result in our VIP missing the big event.

Murray and the headquarters staff must have worked their butts off addressing a multitude of problems. The trip had cleverly been planned via Tokyo, thus minimizing the required number of diplomatic clearances that we (as a military aircraft) required when flying through another country's sovereign airspace. The clearances from PNG, the US, Japan and the Soviet Union had all been granted verbally via a series of phone calls, and temporary crew entry visas had been provided for us in Russian by the Soviet Embassy in Canberra. The 707 Maintenance Section had hastily fitted a fold-down sofa-bed for our passenger, with some partitions forward and aft, for privacy. Lastly, since our tour of duty would exceed every official limitation in existence, a one-off approval had been specially granted by the Department of Defence. Every second set of passenger seats in the main cabin had been turned around and pushed together to make sleeping areas for off-duty crew members.

The only remaining unresolved issue was where we would be refuelling in Japan. At that time, Tokyo had one of the strictest aviation curfews in the world, and it was highly unlikely that we'd be granted a dispensation to land our noisy aircraft there at around 3am local time. To circumvent this problem, approval had been sought from Washington to let us refuel at Yokota USAF Base on the outskirts of Tokyo, but formal approval was still pending. When it was time for us to leave for Sydney, we were handed a piece of paper with the phone number of a RAAF staff officer in Canberra who'd be manning his desk throughout the night to await approval from the United States Air Force. A call to this number via a RAAF HF phone patch whilst enroute to Yokota would ultimately determine whether the mission would be a success or a failure.

The last thing I did on my way out the door was to grab the Jeppesen manual for Eastern Europe, which contained all the detailed requirements for entry into (and operations within) Russian airspace. I'd amended this manual many times over the previous few years, but I never imagined that I'd ever actually get to use it. All of us were mindful too, of the fate of the intriguingly-designated Korean Airlines Flight 007: a Boeing 747 that had been shot down by Soviet fighter jets over the Sea of Japan—quite close to where we'd probably be flying—less than eighteen months earlier. The Koreans had inadvertently strayed into prohibited Russian airspace whilst flying between Anchorage and Seoul on what, the Soviets asserted, was a US-coordinated spy mission. Not surprisingly, Cold War tensions had escalated alarmingly afterwards, and to avoid any similarly disastrous navigation errors in the future, President Ronald Reagan had promised that civilian aircraft would soon be given access to the data from American military satellites. GPS was still in the far-distant future, though, and our navigation equipment was very similar to that used aboard the ill-fated KAL007. While we had no desire to create a diplomatic incident, we certainly didn't want to end up like the Korean crew.

After arriving at Mascot, we quickly prepared the aircraft for departure, with the 34 Squadron HS748 duly arriving and deplaning our

VIP passenger—a government Senator—and his staff of three. As soon as they were on board, we closed our doors and as daylight faded into evening at 8pm, we took off and set course for Tokyo. The Senator didn't visit us on the flight deck during that first sector, but his staff advised us that he was aware of our lengthy tour of duty and was happy for us to quietly transit the VIP compartment to reach the rest areas at the back of the aircraft. Not long after being established in the cruise, we calculated a Point of Safe Diversion (PSD) to Port Moresby—a 24-hour, 707-capable airfield—to afford the senior officer in Canberra the longest possible time in which to receive the Yokota approval. We figured that we'd reach this point at about 2am, Canberra time.

At around 1am (and with considerable trepidation), we requested a phone patch to the Canberra number via the Air Force HF network which, on that particular evening, was incredibly free of the usual horrible static and interference. Having already prepared a preliminary plan for a return to Moresby, we were incredulous to learn that the necessary approvals had been granted. With this final hurdle cleared, I retrieved the Eastern Europe Jeppesen manual and we all began studying the procedural requirements for operations in Russian airspace. It was just all so *surreal*! At about 3:30am local time, we began our descent into the Japanese capital. The sky on that late-winter, pre-dawn descent was "gin clear" (completely cloud-free in RAAF-speak) and the glow of the city lights was visible from well over two hundred miles away. I knew that Tokyo was one of the most densely populated cities on earth (containing more than Australia's entire population) but I was still somewhat unprepared for the enormity of the brilliantly illuminated metropolis before us.

The landing was uneventful and, afterwards, we were directed by ATC to a refuelling hardstand that was bordered by mounds of snow. Again, miraculously, our flight plan and briefing package for the next sector arrived just as soon as we opened our doors. Our planned route of flight came as no great surprise because, at that time, there was only a single airway that traversed the gigantic expanse of Siberia: stretching for almost 3,500 miles from Moscow to Russia's Pacific coastline at Vladivostok. After takeoff from Yokota, we would initially track north:

passing only about 180 miles to the west of Sakhalin Island (where KAL007 had met its fiery end). We would then cross the Soviet coastline to the south of the city of Khabarovsk, before joining the sole airway that headed west to Moscow. The Jeppesen manual provided guidance that all inbound foreign aircraft required positive radio contact with Russian ATC by 27 miles to run to the airspace boundary, and that failure to do so would require the aircraft to either turn back or risk interception by Russian military fighter jets.

There was a smudge of light in the eastern sky as we climbed up out of Yokota AFB and headed north for the shores of the "Evil Empire." After about 30 minutes in the cruise, we began trying to contact Khabarovsk Control—the Russian agency that would provide us with our inbound ATC clearance. We'd written down every frequency we could find for them (HF, VHF and UHF) and, as we approached Russian airspace, we had somebody calling on every one of them. Our initial calls went unanswered, and at eight miles a minute, the boundary line was rapidly approaching. Finally, though, with 47 miles to go to Russian airspace—just three minutes before we would have had to turn back—a deep voice in heavily accented English replied to our call. "Ooozy aircraft calling Khabarovsk...GO AHEAD!" We presumed that "Ooozy" was about as close as our friend could get to "Aussie," so we gave him our ETA for the Russian boundary and received an inbound clearance in reply.

Having been well-rested when we left Sydney, I'd volunteered to stay on the flight deck for the entire nine-hour flight to Tokyo. Now though, crossing the coastline, I was no longer actively on duty and, with our clearance from Khabarovsk safely received, I decided to head down the back to get some sleep. As the morning skies slowly brightened outside the aircraft, I looked out the window at the snow-covered and heavily wooded countryside that rolled gently by below us. We were on our way to the very heart of the West's mortal enemy, and it was truly an extraordinary feeling. I tried to imagine how my old workmate, Harry Wright, must have felt whenever his Lancaster crossed the coast of Occupied Europe and entered hostile territory.

But after so many hours of excitement and drama, sleep still didn't come easily and, after just a few hours, I returned to the flight deck to see first-hand what it was like to fly in Soviet airspace. The first thing I noticed was that we were now flying by Russian metric cruising levels that, in the same direction of flight, were only three thousand feet apart—as opposed to the standard four thousand feet (at the time). Also, while the imperial levels were in whole thousands of feet, the Russian cruising levels (even in metres) didn't make a lot of sense— Flight Level 8,600 metres, for example, equated to 28,200 feet. The Jeppesen manual also told us that all altitude clearances would be issued in metres, and since our altimeters only indicated in feet, we had to extract the exact metres-to-feet conversion factor from the manuals to have it ready before our descent into Moscow.

Also of interest was that, even though we knew the Russians were tracking us on their ATC and Air Defence radars, they still insisted that we provide full position reports for every point enroute—some of which were only three or four minutes apart. Some of these positions had some very interesting place names for us to pronounce and, rest assured, the Russian controllers' grasp of English was infinitely superior to our feeble attempts at Russian. Nevertheless, given the scarcity of Western aircraft on that airway, whenever we were handed off to a new controller, there was a long pause after each of our transmissions as he grappled with how he should respond in his rarely-used English. I should mention here that international aviation protocols demand that all radio communications be conducted in English, with the only exception being for exchanges between an aircraft and ATC within their common sovereign airspace (which can be conducted in their native tongue). Often, it seemed that just as soon as we'd given our position report, there'd be a rapid burst of Russian between parties unknown (which, of course, we couldn't understand). Were we being shadowed by Russian fighters or were we just being paranoid? Fortunately, the closer we got to Moscow, the better became the controllers' English.

Navigating the aircraft was also quite tricky when the reporting points were so close together. Since our Inertial Navigation Systems could only store nine waypoints at once, it meant that the INSs had to be reloaded every twenty minutes or so. We really didn't want to wander off track, and when we discussed this point with one of the senator's staff who'd ventured forward to visit us, he was quite amused by our use of the term "flying telegraph poles" to describe surface-to-air missiles. Just a few minutes later, though, the controller got our attention when he asked us to confirm our position. Maps and charts flew everywhere for a few minutes until, once we'd confirmed our location, he said:

"Very good, Oooozy. My radar has broken down, so PLEASE BE VERY CAREFUL!"

As we finally neared our descent point, the Senator came forward to see how things were going and, at Woofy's invitation, returned a little later to observe the approach and landing. He was diminutive in stature and pretty relaxed, but he was also obviously highly intelligent and could fix you with a penetrating gaze that left you in little doubt that he wouldn't suffer fools gladly. The weather in Moscow was cold and cloudy, but apart from the precaution of having two people independently converting the cleared altitudes from metres to feet, the approach and landing was surprisingly straightforward. When the runway appeared out of the cloud ahead of us at about a thousand feet on approach, it looked just like every other runway in the world, but when we subsequently arrived at our advised parking spot, it became immediately clear that this was no ordinary, run-of-the-mill day. Not too far away sat an aircraft in the distinctive livery of the presidential Air Force One. Next to it was the RAF aircraft that had carried Margaret Thatcher (or her representative) to Moscow, and right next to us was Muammar Gaddafi's private business jet.

After shutting down our engines, a set of motorized stairs (complete with red carpet) appeared at the door, accompanied by a small contingent of Russian military in their distinctive leather boots, heavy woollen overcoats and oversized peaked hats. A fleet of black limousines arrived as the senator descended the steps, and just as soon as he and his staff had climbed aboard, they were all whisked off in the direction of the city. The red-carpeted steps then also immediately disappeared, and we were forced to await the arrival of some less salubrious stairs before we could leave the aircraft that we'd now been aboard for almost twenty-four hours. It would be the first instance of several that confirmed for us that, in the land where all were equal, some were clearly more equal than others.

With the aircraft finally powered down, we donned our overcoats and walked out into the lightly falling snow and the bracing chill of the Russian afternoon. Our next stop was the Pilots Hotel on the airport periphery which was uniquely partitioned with floor-to-ceiling wooden panels on every floor to segregate those guests who had a Russian Entry Visa from those (like us) who didn't. One of the Embassy staff who'd accompanied us to the hotel told us that, while we could leave the hotel and travel into town during the day, when we got back to the hotel at night, we'd have to surrender our passports to the uniformed officer who guarded the entry to "our" side of the hotel. The Embassy had arranged some outings for us, and we would get our passports back whenever we left the hotel. We quickly dubbed this procedure "crossing Checkpoint Charlie".

Our hotel rooms were shabby but functional, possessing all the warmth and charm of a hospital waiting room. Once we'd stowed our bags in our single rooms—a much-treasured aspect of VIP trips—an impromptu briefing was held in Woofy's room, where a senior Australian Embassy official provided a no-nonsense way of thinking about our new surroundings:

"The Soviet Union is considered a superpower by the West. It's not. Just think of it as the biggest, third-world developing country that you've ever visited."

This advice provided a very concise explanation for many aspects of life in the Soviet capital we would witness for ourselves in the coming days. Having neatly defined Soviet Russia in twenty words or fewer, he got down to the nitty-gritty.

"Breakfast is served at 8am", he said. "If you're not there then…you don't eat!"

When the briefing ended, we paid a visit to the "Berioska," a sort of duty-free shop on each floor of the hotel. Ours was gruffly administered by an ancient babushka, complete with a black shapeless dress, black stockings and black headscarf. She seemed more than happy though, to accept our capitalist US dollars as we each purchased a bottle of the local Russian "anti-freeze". Back in our rooms, we discovered that none of them had a minibar but this wasn't a problem—all that was required to keep your vodka chilled was to open the window, push the snow off the window ledge and stand the bottle on it, a process we quickly dubbed "putting a drink in the fridge." An unofficial welcoming party had been organized by the Embassy staff for 4pm, but at 3pm I decided to have a short nap. I woke up eight hours later.

After tossing and turning for the rest of the night, I was relieved when it was finally time to shower, change and head down to the dining room for breakfast. Gibbo was already there, and a very shabby and shaky-looking Hawkeye arrived soon afterwards. The welcome party had gone long into the night and the supply of vodka had been generous indeed. We soon noticed that there weren't any menus on the Laminex tables, and so we just assumed that you ate whatever they gave you. At precisely 8am, the unsmiling dining room attendants appeared from the kitchen to present the smattering of hotel guests with their first course for breakfast. It was some sort of curdled buttermilk that had the sour taste of natural yoghurt and the texture of clotted mucus.

"Look at this s**t!" said Gibbo disgustedly, as he raised a spoonful into the air and then let it slowly dribble back into his bowl. Hawkeye, whose constitution was still very fragile from the night before, had to put his hand over his mouth and momentarily look away to regain his composure.

The second course wasn't much better, consisting of some sort of smoked fish accompanied by tinned peas that were just like little green ball bearings (and which we subsequently discovered would accompany every meal served in the hotel). The dining room attendants then appeared again, collected the used cutlery and crockery, disappeared into the kitchen and hey, presto...breakfast was over!

At 9am, the crew assembled at "Checkpoint Charlie" to collect our passports and climb aboard the pre-arranged Intourist bus for the thirty-minute journey to the Australian Embassy in the city. Along the way, we noticed that every major intersection had traffic lights, but that they were manually controlled by an operator sitting in a small, elevated booth. When we got to the Embassy, we were greeted by an official and escorted into the administrative area where some local Muscovites worked as interpreters. One of them—Marina, a stout, cheerful middle-aged woman—was introduced to us as our guide for the next two days. We would have much preferred any one of her more gorgeous, young female Russian colleagues, but Marina had obviously pulled rank and together we reboarded the bus to travel to the Kremlin and Red Square.

Along the way, we passed the incongruously brightly-coloured head-quarters of the KGB (at Dzerzhinsky Square) and as I took in the cityscape it struck me how much it resembled how filmmakers of the 1930s had envisioned futuristic cities—imposing, mildly sinister and completely soulless. Most of the inelegant "skyscrapers" in the Russian capital (invariably topped with the obligatory hammer and sickle) looked very 1930s-like themselves, even though they'd only been built fairly recently. At street level, the Russian shop windows, unlike their garish Western counterparts, were sparse, drab and uninviting, with usually only a few solitary items on display between the threadbare curtains that served as decoration. Nevertheless, the locals queued up everywhere to buy whatever meagre stock was available, with food and everyday items drawing particularly large crowds. Marina told us that queues would form merely on rumours, and the largest queue we saw that day (six deep and stretching about thirty metres) was apparently in anticipation of a shipment of shoes arriving from Poland. Marina described all this in a completely non-judgemental way, merely describing what life was like for the average Russian citizen living in the capital.

We soon arrived at the broad, cobbled expanse of Red Square, bordered on one side by the fortress-like Kremlin and, on the other, by the formidable GUM department store. Guarding the southern entrance to the square was the majestic and iconic 16th-century Saint Basil's Cathedral, with its brilliantly-coloured onion domes. As we admired its magnificent architecture, the ceremonial Changing of the Guard commenced at Lenin's Mausoleum, just in front of the Kremlin wall (where the wreaths from the state funeral the previous day were still on display). As I watched the precision of the strutting Russian soldiers, I reflected on the newsreel images of past Soviet supremos like Stalin, Khrushchev and Brezhnev who had all stood atop that very building, proudly watching the might of the Soviet military as it paraded through Red Square every May Day. Such displays of Russian power seemed in stark contrast to the reality of Soviet citizens queuing up on the street to buy shoes.

Marina then took some photos of the assembled crew in Red Square (with Saint Basil's Cathedral in the background)—a photo that still hangs proudly on my wall today—before we briefly visited the museum-like GUM department store. We then reboarded our bus and headed to the most upmarket hotel in the city for an opulent lunch that included caviar and champagne. Marina said that the hotel had been built to cater for the expected influx of wealthy American tourists for the 1980 Moscow Olympic Games, but after the military intervention by Soviet forces in Afghanistan in December 1979, the US had boycotted the games, and the hotel had seen little use ever since. During the meal, we also began to suspect that Marina might be a KGB agent, because she kept unsubtly asking us questions about the capabilities of our aircraft, which, of course, we promptly referred to Woofy as our senior RAAF representative. Her clumsy efforts probably led the Russian military to later speculate on how the Air Force of a backwater like Australia could manage to develop a supersonic 707 that could seat three hundred passengers.

We then returned to our hotel to rest up and change for the official (albeit informal) reception with the Ambassador and the Senator at the Embassy that evening. Marina provided us with another fascinating insight into life in the city by drawing our attention to the black-uniformed policemen who stood on the side of the main road about every mile or so. If they observed a traffic violation in progress, they merely pointed at the offending driver with their truncheon, and he (or she) was obliged to pull over to the side of the road to explain. If the reasons given were deemed unsatisfactory, a hole would be punched in the offender's licence. Three holes meant you lost your licence for life, and we subsequently observed one poor soul who'd suffered that fate dejectedly trudging off up the road on foot as, behind him, a policeman removed his number plates and stowed them in his overcoat. Although the traffic on the streets was generally fairly light, a special lane was reserved in the middle of the major thoroughfares for the exclusive use of high-ranking Communist officials in their government-provided black ZiL limousines.

About halfway back to our hotel, I asked Marina about the significance of a large tank trap of welded metal girders that was on prominent display beside the road. She explained that it was a monument to mark the furthest point of the Nazi advance in World War II and that from there, the German officers had been able to watch the people walking about in Red Square through their binoculars. It was a sobering reminder of what could have befallen the Russian people if the Nazis had not been beaten back by the combined forces of the Russian winter and the Red Army. Back at the hotel, I visited the Berioska again and purchased an ushanka—one of those Russian furry hats with tied-up flaps that can be lowered on extremely cold days to keep your ears warm. Marina told us that Russians believed that most of your body heat is lost through the top of your head, so, by keeping your head warm, you can preserve your body heat more effectively. Given the brutal temperatures that Russians routinely experience every winter, it was certainly hard to argue with their logic.

That evening, we returned to the Embassy and assembled in the anteroom to await our invitation to join the Ambassador and the Senator for our reception. On the wall of the anteroom hung a garish abstract painting with the artist's name boldly inscribed in a flourish in the bottom right-hand corner. We were derisively critiquing this artwork when the Ambassador emerged and introduced himself. Surprisingly, he used the same surname as that of the painter whose dubious work was so prominently on display, and I could only surmise that the object of our derision had been painted by either the Ambassador, his wife or one of his children. I hoped that the rest of the crew had picked up on this point too, and that they would not describe the painting in anything less than glowing terms if asked for their opinion. Thankfully the matter never came up—the Ambassador and his wife were friendly and charming and everyone, including the Senator, was in a relaxed and talkative mood.

The Ambassador began by telling us all a little of the history of the elegant Embassy building, which had been commissioned by a former Tsar to accommodate his mistress (who'd been an accomplished opera singer). The high-ceilinged room in which the reception was held had been the lady's rehearsal studio, and its acoustics were as close to perfect as could be achieved in Moscow at the time. Being accommodated in such a historic building by the Soviet government was regarded as a great honour by the diplomatic staff, and our host assured us that if a Liberal/National Party government was elected soon, the Embassy would undoubtedly be relegated to far less prestigious offices elsewhere.

The Senator then told us a little of his experiences at the state funeral, where he'd joined an illustrious group of world leaders outside the Kremlin wall to watch the unfolding pomp and ceremony in Red Square. Beside him, in the lightly falling snow, had stood President Zia-ul-Haq of Pakistan who, at the height of all the spectacle, leaned towards the senator and muttered quietly, "What did you think of the cricket last week?" So, as yet another Soviet leader was being laid to rest, the two men had stood together discussing a World Series Cricket match that had seen Pakistan defeat Australia at the MCG. The Ambassador also told us that in the aftermath of the funeral, the Communist government was feeling somewhat embarrassed by the rapid succession of leaders, and was determined that the next one should be a relatively young man: the name Mikhail Gorbachev was being touted as one of the early favourites. The reception finished at about 9:30pm and capped off a truly fascinating and surreal first day in Moscow.

The following morning was bright and sunny and crisply cold as we boarded our Intourist bus after a bland breakfast of ball-bearing-peas-and-something and a successful transit of Checkpoint Charlie. I noticed Marina smiling at me as I proudly donned my new Russian furry hat and, when I asked her why, she explained that the fur of your ushanka denoted your status in Russian society. A hat made of black bear fur denotes a prominent person in the community or the Party, while one made from winter rabbit fur (like mine) denotes a poor member of the peasant class. As a young RAAF pilot officer, my peasant-class furry hat therefore seemed entirely appropriate.

Our first destination was the grandiosely-titled "Square of Soviet Economic Achievement" which featured enormous pavilions showcasing Soviet accomplishments in various endeavours such as agriculture, manufacturing and—the primary focus for us—space exploration. Somewhat fittingly, we noticed that most of the pavilions were closed, and the Square was practically deserted (although Marina assured us that this was only due to the cold). As we walked towards the Cosmos Pavilion celebrating Soviet achievements in space, we noticed that most of the visitors there that day were lined up in front of a small food stand. "Would you like some ice cream?" Marina asked us, before marching straight to the front of the queue and placing her order with the vendor. Intriguingly, not a single person complained about her rudeness, and I could only imagine that the locals assumed that anyone who could be so brazen must be well-connected enough to not be messed with. I can safely say that the ice cream we had there that day was the best I've ever eaten!

When we reached the gigantic, hangar-shaped Cosmos Pavilion, we were disappointed to discover that it too was closed and that its enormous steel doors were firmly locked. "Just wait here," said Marina, before heading off to a small side door and knocking persistently. The side door opened, and after an animated conversation in Russian, the side door closed, the massive hangar doors parted, and we made our way inside for an exclusive, personally escorted tour. Our guide proudly pointed out the replica Sputnik satellite (which had begun the space race in 1957), the capsule that Yuri Gagarin had ridden into space (on the first manned flight in 1961), and the mock-up of the docked Apollo and Soyuz spacecraft that marked the first joint US–Soviet space venture in 1975 (and which effectively brought the space-race to an end). Based on what I'd witnessed that morning, two things seemed to stand out—firstly, such impressive technological achievements were totally out of step with ordinary Russians queuing for food, and secondly, Marina really must have been KGB.

After having lunch in the city, we visited the magnificent, 16th-century Novodevichy Convent with its elegant, slender bell towers and gold-faced onion domes, lucky to survive an attempt to blow it up by a retreating Napoleon in 1812. We then returned to our hotel and showered and changed before heading back to the Australian Embassy for the staff's customary Friday night buffet dinner and booze-up in the basement "Down Under Club." At 1am, one of the diplomatic staff suggested that we crash the American Embassy, and after passing through some extremely tight security, we then enjoyed an hour of festivities in their private nightclub (complete with mirrored disco ball and *Billie Jean* blasting through the sound system).

Eventually, at around 2:30am, I was dispatched to check that our bus was still waiting to take us back to the hotel. Needless to say, our driver was none too impressed by our shenanigans, and I didn't need to speak Russian to understand what he was telling me (rather forcefully). To rebuild Australian-Russian relations, I traded him a packet of his Russian cigarettes (which smelled like burning horsehair) for a packet of my Marlboro Reds, after which we were immediately bosom buddies for life. I still have those Russian cigarettes somewhere in a drawer at home and they're still completely untouched. Given the way they smelled, I could just never bring myself to try one.

Understandably, we slept in late on our final morning in Moscow and consequently missed our last breakfast of ball-bearing-peas-and-something. Instead, we fronted up to the dining room for an early lunchtime helping of ball-bearing-peas-and-something-else, with our grim-faced hosts kindly offering us some local Russian beer (that we noticed was 18% alcohol by volume) to help wash it down. Naturally, we graciously declined the proffered beverages before packing up our belongings, vacating our sterile lodgings and heading downstairs to check out. When Hawkeye asked the receptionist for the crew's hotel bill, he was advised in halting English that the Soviet government was picking up the tab and that no payment was necessary. Somewhat surprised at this generosity, we perused the hotel gift shop while waiting for our transport. On the wall behind the counter was a large poster that showed the locations of all US military bases and there, near Sydney, we noticed a little black dot labelled "Richmond Air Force Base." In the very heart of the Soviet capital, our little RAAF base in its quiet, pastoral setting had been designated an outpost of Russia's mortal enemy!

We also had time to kill at the airport, because the Senator and his staff had spent the previous thirty-six hours in Leningrad admiring the cultural treasures of the Winter Palace and weren't due back in Moscow until just before we were due to depart. While we waited, Steve, our Chief Flight Steward, told us all about his "inspection" of the airport's catering facilities that morning. His Russian hosts had read the word "inspection" and so, when he arrived to see how the catering was going, all the staff were lined up outside waiting for Steve to give them the once-over. The manager then escorted him inside and began checking off each item of the catering order. "The tomatoes should arrive from Hungary by lunchtime," he said, "and some of the other items should arrive from Poland and Czechoslovakia in time for your departure." When he arrived at the area where the butter curls were produced, Steve noticed that the girl working there had instead fashioned the cold, yellow butter into intricately carved rosebuds. The manager looked at the rosebuds, checked Steve's order for butter curls on his clipboard, and immediately began to angrily rebuke the girl for not producing the requested product. Steve had to personally intervene to calm down the ruffled official by copiously thanking the girl for her craftsmanship, while she, in tears, appeared extremely thankful for being allowed to escape what she probably figured was going to be a one-way trip to the Gulag.

As our departure time drew nearer, the catering was loaded, the aircraft was refuelled and the flight plan was delivered. All these vital functions were overseen by a tall, burly Russian (presumably a senior Aeroflot manager or government representative) who, again, refused any offer of payment for services rendered. "Australia is a very long way away," he said simply. "Your country has honoured us by sending a representative to our leader's funeral." During our stay in Moscow, we had paid for precisely nothing—accommodation, meals, fuel or catering—and Woofy felt that we should at least present our amiable Russian comrade with a small memento of our visit. Unfortunately, we hadn't had time to arrange a formal thank-you gift and, between us, the best that we could come up with was a little Qantas koala that could be attached to the lapel of your shirt or jacket. When presented with this almost inconsequential symbol of gratitude, this great bear of a Russian man appeared visibly moved and, on the verge of tears said, "When you go home...tell Australian people...Russians not so bad." Watching all this unfold, I thought to myself, "If only the world's philosophical differences could be overcome by such simple, heartfelt exchanges between ordinary people."

The Senator arrived at the aircraft around 4pm and spent a few minutes standing outside with the crew to capture a photographic record of what had been a unique and unforgettable experience. As a final gesture of farewell, the Senator was presented with two cases of authentic Russian Stolichnaya vodka (complete with Cyrillic labels), one of which was immediately offered to the crew to divvy up between us as souvenirs. With the sun setting behind us, we took off from Sheremetyevo Airport and set an easterly course to fly across the vast continent and return to "The West" in Tokyo.

Again, the Senator joined us on the flight deck, but while he'd been quite animated and talkative during our arrival, on the departure he spoke barely a word and returned to the VIP compartment shortly after takeoff. From the galley area, we could hear the clinking of glassware as the stewards used the donated vodka to prepare pitcher after pitcher of Bloody Marys to supplement the copious amounts of booze that the passengers had already consumed on the flight down from Leningrad. We settled back into the business of flying, with our flight plan taking us over the Siberian oilfields where, at times, it seemed that the entire countryside was ablaze from horizon to horizon from the fires burning at the almost innumerable oil refineries. Little wonder then, that petrol in the USSR cost about ten cents per litre at the time. After about two hours in the cruise, Steve came to the flight deck to say that there was, "a bit of a problem": the Senator had gone to the toilet about thirty minutes previously, and hadn't yet emerged. Our always-prepared flight engineer retrieved his trusty screwdriver, headed back into the passenger compartment, unscrewed the hinges on the toilet door and removed it to reveal our VIP passenger still breathing, but blissfully a-slumber inside.

After an overnight flight of a little over nine hours, we were once more back in Japan, a place where (during our thirty-six-hour stopover) we could eat what we liked, where we liked and when we liked and where McDonald's had never tasted so good. Ensconced in our plush and comfortable lodgings in the Tokyo Ginza district, I wrote an entry in my travel diary that encapsulated my insights on Russia generally, and on Moscow in particular: "Nice place to visit...wouldn't want to live there. There are some gorgeous girls in Russia. I must start a business exporting tinned peas to the Soviet Union." The Ginza district, with its street after street of shops and neon garishness, was in such stark contrast to the drab austerity of Communist Moscow and, for the first time in my life, I could fully appreciate the freedoms and opportunities that we take for granted every day. The trip had been a seemingly never-ending list of "firsts" which, once our Senator and his still hungover staff had disembarked in Canberra, continued right up until the last sector back to Richmond.

Less than a week before we'd left for Moscow, I had successfully completed a route check and been awarded a Category C Boeing 707 command. I was duly proud of this achievement, which had gone some way to easing the painful memories from Pearce and made a complete nonsense of the CO's bleak prediction of what I could hope to accomplish. The route check itself had been a "bit of a detail" because it had involved a trip to (where else) Butterworth. Now in Canberra late on the night of March 17th 1985, Woofy climbed out of the captain's seat and said, "Okay Geoff, the aircraft's all yours. You can take us back to Richmond." And with that, he and Gibbo went down the back of the aircraft while Hawkeye and I prepared it for departure. To say I was nervous was an understatement, but with the assistance of my extremely experienced copilot and flight engineer, I managed to get us safely home in one piece. Afterwards, Woofy heartily congratulated me on logging my first 707 command hours. I owe him a great debt of gratitude for championing my cause in the unit—without his support, my achievements would not have been possible.

It had been an extraordinary trip during a period that would later be considered "the beginning of the end" for the Soviet Union. Within four years of our return, the enlightened leadership of Mikhail Gorbachev would see the Berlin Wall topple, and the Iron Curtain across Europe begin to unravel. In Pakistan, the cricket-mad President Zia-ul-Haq would die in a 1988 military plane crash that many suspected was a political assassination. And at home some years later, Andrei Krasoff, Tracy's Russian-born grandfather, would reverently open my souvenir bottle of Stolichnaya vodka and savour a glass of the most famous beverage of his former homeland. It had been a remarkable trip from a now long-gone era, and I will never, ever forget it.

22
HELLO BOB AND BYE BYE BOEINGS

Only three days after returning from Moscow, I was off on yet another VIP trip—this time taking Prime Minister Bob Hawke to Honolulu and back. VIP trips were always much sought-after duties, and I'd been especially disappointed to miss out on the "Royal VIP" that had transported Prince Charles and his attractive young wife, Princess Diana, to Australia in 1983. In the mid-1980s, a very popular Australian television segment was Rubbery Figures, where political journalist Mike Carlton used puppets with grossly exaggerated facial features to lampoon prominent public figures of the day. His puppet-likeness of Bob Hawke featured the trademark sweep of slicked-back silver hair, and the most common skit featured the Prime Minister greeting the press gallery who had assembled to grill him by drawling laconically: "Aaaaaaaahhhhhh...how's it goin' fellas? Eh? Eh? Eh?"

Late in the afternoon of March 21st 1985, with large contingents of the Canberra press gallery and the prime ministerial staff already seated onboard, we prepared for our departure to Sydney to refuel before heading off for Honolulu. Soon after the PM had stepped out of his Commonwealth limousine and boarded the aircraft, we heard from the senior RAAF officer who acted as the liaison between the PM and the crew that Hawke would like to come up to the flight deck to say a quick hello while we were taxying out. It seemed pretty unreal that I would soon meet the Prime Minister of my country: quite a feat for a graduate of Boonah High. Sure enough, after just a few minutes of taxying, the flight deck door opened, the unmistakable face of the PM appeared in the doorway, and he greeted us warmly with: "Aaaaaaaahhhhhh...how's it goin' fellas? Eh? Eh? Eh?"

* * *

I ruled off the final 707 hours in my logbook on the 4th of May 1985. In two years of flying the big Boeing, I'd logged just under a thousand hours of flight time but, whilst doing so, I'd also accumulated some incredible experiences, met some intriguing characters and collected a host of unforgettable memories. Even as I prepared to leave the squat 33 Squadron headquarters for the final time, I just couldn't wait to be back again. After saying my goodbyes to a few colleagues, I opened my logbook to count how many times I'd flown to Butterworth. The answer was twenty-eight!

PART 2

DOWN IN THE WEEDS

May 1985–December 1987

1
WHAT HAVE I GOT MYSELF INTO?

An oft-heard saying around 9 Squadron in the mid-1980s was "if you haven't had a near-death experience, then you haven't really flown helicopters." As a new arrival to the unit, it was a rather sobering adage to contemplate just before my 'rotary-wing' training began, and a large poster on the crew room wall amplified my anxiety even further. Portrayed in cartoon form, a wide-eyed helicopter pilot sits in the cockpit of his complex machine, sweat pouring from his brow as he surveys the conflicting indications on his flight instruments. A horseshoe emblazoned with the words "GOOD LUCK" hangs from his windshield and the caption at the bottom explains that, unlike extroverted 'fixed-wing' pilots, helicopter pilots are brooding, introspective "anticipators of trouble" because they know that if something bad hasn't happened yet, it soon will. I couldn't help but ponder the motivation behind displaying this poster so prominently. Was its sombre message meant as a warning, or merely as an example of black humour?

The RAAF rotary-wing world had certainly had its fair share of accidents and 1981 in particular had been a terrible year. In August, the B-model Iroquois used for Search and Rescue at RAAF Base Williamtown had been on a test flight when it suffered a catastrophic mechanical failure and plunged back to earth, killing all three crewmembers on board. Two months later, a 9 Squadron H-model Iroquois crashed whilst participating in Kangaroo 81 in North Queensland. Fortunately, only one crewmember had been killed on this occasion thanks to the heroism of three officers on board (including the copilot) who'd helped the injured to escape the burning wreckage. Both accidents occurred during my very first year in the Air Force, and I remember them vividly. Thus, I was already acutely aware that flying helicopters could be much more hazardous to my health than jetting around in a 707, where the biggest potential risk was contracting food poisoning from a dodgy meal.

In 1985, the Air Force's operational fleet of Bell UH-1H Iroquois helicopters was dispersed among three units—5 Squadron (RAAF Base Fairbairn in Canberra); 9 Squadron (RAAF Base Amberley in Queensland); and 35 Squadron (a composite Caribou and Iroquois unit at RAAF Base Townsville). Using Aerospatiale Ecureuil (Squirrel) helicopters, 5 Squadron provided ab initio training for all prospective rotary-wing pilots, as well as an Iroquois conversion course for those who would then fly that type in any of the three operational units. Pilots posted to fly the heavy, twin-rotor Chinook helicopters also completed their basic training at 5 Squadron, but they then returned to 12 Squadron at Amberley for their type conversions.

I had bid a fond farewell to 33 Squadron in mid-May, reluctantly departing with a treasure trove of memories, a modicum of sadness and no doubts whatsoever that my next posting would be very different to the one just completed. I was saying goodbye to my luxurious quasi-airline existence and heading for the tactical sphere of military operations—going from Sheratons to share-a-tents—and I wasn't particularly looking forward to it. As a teenager, I'd enjoyed grabbing a tent and some supplies and going bush for a few days, but the Army Reserve and then COMSURV, in particular, had completely put paid to that. But the 9 Squadron posting was the only opportunity for my wife to be with her mother during her mother's convalescence, and so my concerns over creature comforts just had to take a back seat for the time being. After vacating our rented house and farewelling our meagre possessions, we headed north and settled into the spare bedroom of my in-laws' place (where Tracy would be staying while I undertook my helicopter training). I'd allowed myself a week to settle in at 9 Squadron, before beginning the long drive south back down to Canberra.

* * *

According to the old saying, first impressions mean a lot, and on arriving at 33 Squadron, I'd been pretty underwhelmed by the blandness of its headquarters building. But the 707 crews were inhabiting a veritable Taj Mahal compared to the ramshackle collection of dilapidated, low-set wooden structures that accommodated the distinguished 9 Squadron. The headquarters complex consisted of three north-south wings connected by a central east-west walkway. The east wing comprised the unit's official entrance, CO's office and the Orderly Room; the central wing comprised the "nerve centre"—Briefing Room, Operations Room and executive offices; and the west wing housed the squadron crew room and an assortment of smaller offices.

The peeling paint adorning the headquarters was of a faded, lemony-cream hue, and the buildings' interiors were no more visually appealing than their rundown, shabby exteriors. The crew room, where the squadron pilots spent most of their time, featured sombre wood-grain wall panelling and some stained green carpeting that had probably once been beige when the complex was new in the 1960s. Completing the overall motif of inglorious decrepitude was an unkempt assortment of neglected shrubs and bushes that struggled to survive around the headquarters perimeter.

Unsurprisingly, 9 Squadron (like an unwanted step-child) was located far away from the glamorous F-111 units (1 Squadron and 6 Squadron) that commanded the prime real estate at the centre of the base's extensive flight line. Compounding this physical isolation was the RAAF's recent philosophical separation of flying units into Groups based on function rather than location. Therefore, while the sleek F-111 fighter-bombers comprised the prestigious Strike Reconnaissance Group (headquartered in Amberley), the ungainly "helos" of 9 and 12

Squadrons were part of the workhorse Tactical Transport Group (headquartered elsewhere). Essentially, 9 Squadron had become a 'lodger unit' on its own base; but at least its members were spared the tedium of Amberley's monthly parades.

The squadron's haphazard existence, however, seemed entirely consistent with its inconsistent past. My new unit had begun its operational life as a maritime surveillance unit in 1925, operating seaplanes off HMAS Albatross and providing aerial support to the navy until its disbandment in 1944. In 1962, the squadron had been reformed at RAAF Base Fairbairn with B-model Iroquois helicopters to operate as a Search and Rescue (SAR) unit. But after gaining considerable expertise in supporting army operations, the re-born 9 Squadron was then deployed to Vietnam in 1966, where it served with distinction until its return to Australia five years later. The unit crest reflected the squadron's heritage of maritime surveillance, featuring the head of an albatross above a naval crown with the motto "Videmus nec Videmur"—"we see without being seen."

Of course, I had little interest in any of this when I first arrived there in late May 1985. Sure, the place was a bit dingy, but the squadron pilots seemed a decent bunch and the CO had soon invited me into his office for a quick chat. In stark contrast to 33 Squadron, I was pleased to discover that 9 Squadron had a well-established process in place to progress its pilots through the various operational flying categories on offer. I was also informed that the unit would be re-equipping with the newly-ordered Blackhawk helicopters within a few years, and so I would ultimately have to decide whether I wanted to convert onto the new aircraft type or return to the fixed-wing world.

But the most welcome snippet of news that day concerned my anticipated involvement in the MFO (Multinational Force & Observers) that was based out of El Gorah in the Sinai Peninsula. Since the commencement of Australia's involvement in that peace-keeping operation in 1982, every graduating helicopter course had attached pilots to it in deployments that usually lasted about six months. But with Australia's commitment finally drawing to a close, our course would not be required to do so; this information came as a huge relief. I'd been dreading the prospect of spending four months in Canberra and then another six flying in the Middle East almost immediately afterwards. With the welcoming formalities concluded on a positive note, it was time to set off for Fairbairn.

2
5 SQUADRON

To say "Canberra is cold in winter" is to exhibit mastery of stating the bleeding obvious. As I headed south, so too did the temperature, and by the time I stopped for lunch in Goulburn under leaden-grey skies on Sunday the 2nd of June, it was hovering in the low single digits. A few hours later, I drove through the main gates of RAAF Base Fairbairn and spotted the little blue-and-white Squirrel helicopters—some of which I'd played a part in transporting to Australia from Marseilles—sitting out on the flight line, festooned in colourful safety flags and tie-down straps. Shortly afterwards, I settled into my room in the Mess, which was surprisingly modern and comfortable (by the usual RAAF standards) and featured a large, wall-mounted electric heater that was immediately switched on (and then remained so for the next three months).

When I ventured outside the next morning to drive over to 5 Squadron, the temperature was well below zero, and I found that my car had become enveloped in a layer of fine, white frost overnight. The windscreen washers and wipers couldn't shift it but, through trial and error, I eventually discovered that my newly-issued plastic card from the bank was just as handy for scraping frost off my windshield as it was for getting money out of those new-fangled automatic teller machines. With my visibility restored, I shivered uncontrollably during the (thankfully) very short trip. 5 Squadron was one of two flying units based at RAAF Base Fairbairn in 1985, with the other unit (34 Squadron) providing VIP transport for the capital's politicians. The 5 Squadron Training Section was located in some offices on the flight-line end of one of 34 Squadron's maintenance hangars where, amazingly, it always seemed to be much colder inside than it was outside.

By eight o'clock, all of my other course-mates had also reported for duty. Max, a slender "academician" whose Python-esque humour belied his quiet, shy personality, was a gifted pilot who'd fallen short of completing an F-111 course and found himself in the helo world instead. Dave, a diminutive retread, had completed a copilot posting at 34 Squadron and was now looking forward to logging some command time on helicopters. He quickly gained the title of "Course Consch" because he always seemed to have his nose in a flight manual or checklist, even though he seemed to have already memorised most of the course material. Nevertheless, he was a very likable guy who seemed to have a permanent smile on his face. Shane also enjoyed a good laugh but, since he was 12 Squadron bound, he only had to put up with us (and we with him) for the first half of the course.

My final two course-mates were undoubtedly the most unforgettable characters. Everything about "Gumby" was simply larger-than-life. According to "Rumour Control," at well over six feet tall, Gumby had had to convince the RAAF hierarchy to allow him to fly the little Macchi jet trainers at Pearce, owing to the "medicos'" concerns that he could be severely injured if he ever had to eject. If these rumours were indeed true, ultimately, and not surprisingly, Gumby had prevailed. His big frame was topped with a big head of curly, blond hair that framed a big ruddy face that turned bright red whenever he burst out laughing in his big, bold guffaw. He also had a big loping gait and a big loud voice. His chin was always thrust assertively outwards, and his mouth was perpetually turned downwards at the corners, accounting for his alternative nickname of "Beaker."

The last of my course-mates I'll refer to simply as "Jacko." Fresh out of Pearce on his first operational posting, Jacko was young, single and virile and, frankly, a bit of a shambles. He was always the last to arrive anywhere and invariably turned up with unkempt hair, rumpled clothes and a sleepy expression on his face. But, with a beer in his hand, Jacko became the life of the party and could "talk crap" to the sheilas that made even the seemingly-intelligent ones soon turn weak at the knees. His favourite "party trick" involved betting a likely-looking lass five dollars that he could make her boobs move without touching them. When, with a hint of intrigue, she said, "You're on," with cobra-like speed he would briefly "polish her headlights" before extending a five-dollar bill and saying, "Whoops! I was wrong. Here's your five dollars." Had I ever tried that, undoubtedly, I would have either been slapped across the face, slapped with a sexual assault charge or both. But in response to the innocent, baby-faced Jacko, the lady in question would usually just tousle his hair, smile at him saucily and invite him back to her place. How we hated (envied) him at times!

But such raunchy adventures were still in the future at this stage and, back in the classroom, once our official welcome had concluded, we were introduced to the QHI (Qualified Helicopter Instructor) who would be conducting our ground school lectures. "Miz" (short for "miserable ****") was one of several Navy helicopter pilots who were performing instructional duties on exchange at 5 Squadron. He unabashedly introduced himself as Miz, and his melancholy expression and rare, rueful smiles seemed entirely in keeping with both his nickname and his self-professed, gloomy outlook on life. He also stated (for the record) that both his nickname and his despondency had pre-dated the catastrophic helicopter accident that had nearly claimed his life only eighteen months earlier.

In December 1983, Miz had been ferrying personnel back to RAAF Base East Sale from the Bass Strait oil rigs when the transmission of his big, grasshopper-like Wessex helicopter had begun vibrating alarmingly. After descending to a hundred feet in preparation for an emergency landing on the approaching beach, his transmission had suddenly and explosively failed. His crippled machine had then plunged into the ocean and broken into two large pieces before quickly sinking. As Miz related it, one minute he was strapped securely in his seat, sinking into the depths...the next minute he was floating to the surface, and he was at a complete loss to explain his change in fortune. Two of his passengers, regrettably, weren't so lucky and were killed in the accident. Miz had barely survived his "near death" experience, and I began to think of his ground school lectures as merely a two-week reprieve from the dangerous business that still lay ahead.

3
GWOUND SCHOOL

The ground school subjects consisted of helicopter aerodynamics, aircraft systems and helicopter performance and, since they're all so closely interrelated, I'll attempt to explain them collectively rather than individually. Before arriving in Fairbairn, I'd decided to keep an open mind about the scientific principles (voodoo) that keep a helicopter aloft—or, to put it more accurately, I'd done no pre-course preparation whatsoever—and so, at the outset, I had the vague idea that it was somehow connected to the indecipherable science of gyroscopics. But I was wrong...it was all to do with the almost indecipherable science of helicopter aerodynamics.

Through necessity (and poor memory), I'll keep this discussion brief. Categorising an aircraft as either 'fixed-wing' or 'rotary-wing' actually comes very close to explaining how it defies gravity. On a fixed-wing type, thrust propels the aircraft forward until it reaches a speed at which the lift from the wing exceeds the weight of the aircraft when the pilot pulls back on the controls. On a rotary-wing type, the rotor blades have a very similar aerodynamic cross-section to that of the wing on a conventional aircraft. A helicopter's engine drives a shaft that (via the transmission) rotates the blades until they reach a speed and angle at which the total lift generated exceeds the weight of the aircraft.

Helicopters have a tail rotor due to Newton's Third Law of Motion which states, "For every action, there will be an equal and opposite reaction." The transmission develops torque (rotational force) when turning the main rotor and so, without a tail rotor, the fuselage of an airborne helicopter would spin in the opposite direction to its main rotor. Therefore, whenever the torque of the main rotor increases, it must be balanced by applying what is called 'anti-torque' control inputs to the tail rotor.

This naturally brings us to the flight controls that are used to manoeuvre a helicopter—which can be broadly thought of as "up/down;" "left/right/backwards/forwards;" and "round and round"—with this discussion relating primarily to a helicopter in a steady hover. The first control is called the 'collective'—a lever beside the pilot that resembles a large handbrake. The collective gets its name because it changes the angle of all the main rotor blades equally (collectively). Raising or lowering the collective increases or decreases the angle of the rotor blades, increasing or decreasing the total lift from the main rotor and, correspondingly, causing the aircraft to move vertically up or down.

The next control is the 'cyclic,' which resembles the control column of a conventional aircraft and performs a similar function (albeit in a different manner). In a fixed-wing aircraft, moving the control column sideways raises the ailerons on one side of the aircraft and lowers them on the other, producing more lift on one side (and less on the other), causing the aircraft to bank and turn. In a helicopter, moving the cyclic causes the angle of the rotor blades to increase on one side of the aircraft and decrease on the other. The 'rotor disc'—the term used to describe the main rotor acting as a single entity—effectively tilts to produce more lift in the desired direction of travel.

The final controls are the tail rotor pedals—don't *ever* call them rudder pedals, even though they're operated by the pilot's feet and perform a very similar function. Similar to the collective, applying pedal inputs causes the angle of the tail rotor blades to increase or decrease (equally) to either offset any changes in torque from the main rotor in flight or make the helicopter (with the collective and cyclic controls held steady) pivot left or right when established in a steady hover.

The trickiest part of helicopter flying is that all these controls are manipulated simultaneously. For example, if you're in a hover and you simply want to move the aircraft sideways to the right, as I've just explained, all you'd need to do is move the cyclic to the right. But it's not as simple as that. When the rotor disc tilts, its total vertical lift reduces slightly, and so more collective is required to maintain a constant height. More collective also requires more anti-torque tail rotor pedal input, and so, this seemingly simple manoeuvre becomes: right cyclic (whilst raising the collective a little and adding a little more anti-torque tail rotor pedal). Similarly, stopping the sideways movement requires centring the cyclic (whilst lowering the collective a little and reducing the tail rotor pedal input). Because these control inputs are so closely interrelated, manoeuvring a helicopter is usually likened to rubbing your stomach and patting your head at the same time.

The other significant concept in rotary-wing flying is 'ground effect,' whereby, a helicopter requires less power to hover when it's close to the ground—referred to as hovering 'In Ground Effect' (or IGE). Although not technically correct, you can think of it as the rotor downwash creating a cushion of air (like a hovercraft) that partially supports the weight of the aircraft. But if the aircraft slowly rises vertically whilst hovering, when it reaches a height of about half the diameter of the rotor disc, the downwash will dissipate, and the rotors will be required to support the aircraft's entire weight through the application of more torque—referred to as hovering 'Out of Ground Effect' (OGE).

Miz, of course, explained all this information via an abundance of complicated vector diagrams, force scalars and highly technical jargon. There was also a lot of discussion about 'relative air flow' although, in the freezing-cold early mornings, it usually sounded more like "welatiff aih fwow" (until our lips had thawed out). Thankfully, a helicopter in forward flight behaves much more like a conventional fixed-wing aircraft. But to leave the hover and enter forward flight, there was yet another new concept to grasp—'translational lift'—which occurs when a helicopter accelerates to about twenty-five knots of forward speed and its blades gain greater efficiency by biting into the "clean air" that hasn't been previously disturbed whilst the aircraft was in the hover.

So, there was a multitude of new concepts and terminology to get our heads around and, over the next two weeks, we learnt all about swash plates, blade grips, stabiliser bars and pitch change links in aircraft systems, and transverse flow, induced velocity, phase lag and flapping angles in helicopter aerodynamics. We were also warned about the numerous unique perils that only helicopter pilots face—vortex ring, retreating blade stall, mast bump and dynamic rollover, to name just a few—and were assured by the melancholy Miz that any one of them could kill us if we weren't vigilant. I kept thinking about that poster on the 9 Squadron crew room wall. "If there is any disturbance to the delicate balance," it warned ominously, "the helicopter stops flying, immediately and disastrously."

Helicopter performance, the final ground school subject, expounded on the concepts of IGE and OGE and how the characteristics of a jet engine play their part. The Squirrel is powered by a tiny jet engine (small enough to cradle in your arms), but like all jet engines, the thrust it produces will vary as a function of altitude and temperature. If the aircraft is "loaded to the gunwales" at high altitudes and/or hot temperatures, it may not even be capable of hovering IGE, let alone hovering OGE. Therefore, if a helicopter is flying close to its performance limits, the priority for the pilot is to calculate the weight at which his aircraft will be capable of hovering OGE (since he will be able to manoeuvre his machine much more freely from this point onwards).

To calculate our aircraft's expected performance, we were each issued a small, plastic gadget colloquially known as a "Prayer Wheel"—essentially, a circular slide-rule that calculated the power required to hover as a function of the aircraft's weight and the outside air temperature and altitude. I'd heard that the Iroquois pilots in Vietnam didn't have access to such high-tech gadgetry, and had sometimes attempted to hover OGE when they didn't have enough power available to do so. The newspaper accounts of the inevitable crashes that followed simply read, "The pilot attempted to hover above the trees, but the aircraft failed to respond."

In Vietnam, helicopters regularly carried very heavy loads to Army units in the field and, sometimes, in the tropical heat, it wasn't even possible for them to hover IGE. In such circumstances, a run-on landing could be carried out, but in rugged areas (where such landings weren't advisable), the pilots had to improvise. Anecdotally, they reduced the power demand on the transmission by not applying anti-torque inputs when they entered the hover. Instead, the aircraft was allowed to spin around (just a few feet above the ground) while the loadmaster frantically threw out boxes of ammunition and supplies until the aircraft was light enough to hover IGE, and then depart.

But such death-defying stunts were still a long way off for prospective rotary-wing pilots who couldn't even hover yet. After the ground school had finished, we sat in pairs in aircraft out on the flight line and repeatedly ran through the checklists until we had them all memorised. The RAAF had wisely decided that we should conduct our initial training at a regional airfield to prevent an out-of-control Squirrel from careering into the path of the Prime Minister's jet. And so, while my initial 707 training had been conducted in Hong Kong, my helicopter training would kick off with ten fun-filled days in the exotic holiday destination of RAAF Base Wagga. What a contrast!

4
WOKKING MY WAY TO WAGGA

When we all assembled at 5 Squadron on the morning of Monday the 17th of June to set off for Wagga, the QHIs succinctly laid out their training objectives for the next ten days by letting us in on the unofficial helicopter pilot's motto, "Well, you know what they say… you're a poofter if you can't hover." Now, as far as credos go, this very politically incorrect one certainly lacked the romantic imagery of the high-altitude USAF Reconnaissance pilots ("Up where the sky is black and the Earth is round") and wasn't as bluntly accurate as the blackly amusing motto of the bomber crews of the USAF Strategic Air Command ("Peace through superior firepower"). But hey…if we were soon to lose our "poofter" status as non-hoverers, well then that was just fine with us.

The air was crisp and bitingly cold, with a temperature of around minus five degrees Celsius, as I hefted my bulging RAAF duffel bag down to the 5 Squadron headquarters. Overhead, the high-altitude passenger jets plying the east-coast, inter-capital trunk routes had already woven a delicate web of gossamer white contrails across the otherwise spotless, winter-blue sky. To protect myself from the all-pervading cold, I was wearing my flying suit, jacket and gloves, but for all the warmth they were providing me that morning, I may as well have been ambling about in my underpants. As I trudged past the flight line, I watched the 5 Squadron ground crew ("groundies") readying the Squirrel helicopters for their upcoming mission.

A critical element of this preparation involved removing any overnight frost accumulations from the rotors, since the consequences of unbalanced rotor blades turning at extremely high speeds can be disastrous. One of the groundies was engaged on this task with a cloth and a bucket of boiling-hot water and, after he'd wiped down the rotor blades, he threw the remainder of the steaming-hot liquid onto the windscreen of the aircraft. I swear that by the time the last of that water had trickled down to the bottom of the fuselage, it had re-frozen. At the squadron, we were divided up into crews for the hour-long transit flight and, while the rest of my course-mates travelled as passengers, I was given the honour of sitting in the copilot seat of my aircraft. Six Squirrels headed off in a loose formation for Wagga that morning and, since the formation leader did all of the radio work, I was free to sit back and draw comparisons between my new "office" and the old one.

From a physiological perspective, it felt a little claustrophobic to be wearing a flying helmet and Mae West again (and communicating via an intercom). Also, having grown accustomed to being served hot meals by smiling young flight stewardesses, the creature comforts of the Squirrel were sadly lacking. The total absence of any inflight amenities also meant you had to either "go" before you went, or sit there with your legs crossed and your "pucker valve" clamped firmly shut until you were back on terra firma. But even more intimidating was the raft of operational changes that I'd now have to contend with. Foremost amongst these would be the need to navigate by "looking out the window" again, after several years just spent entering strings of latitudes and longitudes into a computerised navigation system. Fortunately, the Squirrel's expansive windows—affording excellent visibility in every direction, including downwards—would surely make a difficult task just that little bit easier. Visually navigating a 707 would have been virtually impossible, since its narrow windshields sometimes made you feel that you were steering a tank rather than flying an aeroplane.

Even the necessary change in flight rules would present challenges. In 1985, Australia's airspace was simply either CTA—controlled airspace, wherein ATC prevented you from crashing into everybody else—or OCTA—outside controlled airspace, wherein ATC provided you with traffic information, but it was up to you to avoid crashing into everybody else. Also, flights were conducted under either the IFR (Instrument Flight Rules), whereby cruising altitudes (even in cloud), prevented you from hitting both the ground and opposite-direction aircraft, or the VFR (Visual Flight Rules), which required the pilot to visually avoid the ground, the clouds and every other aircraft in his immediate vicinity. On the 707, I'd been a mollycoddled, ATC-reliant IFR CTA pilot. On helicopters, I would have to be a hyper-vigilant, self-reliant VFR OCTA pilot who entrusted his life to his "Mark One Eyeballs."

So, in summary, *almost every aspect* of flying a Squirrel would be very different to piloting a Boeing 707. In terms of aircraft weight, range, height and speed, I was essentially transitioning from the macro to the micro and in the hour it took us to fly the 160 kilometres to Wagga, a 707 could have flown from Sydney to Brisbane. After we'd finally landed, I calculated that the fuel consumed by our Squirrel on the entire flight would have been barely enough to get a thirsty 707 from the terminal to the takeoff runway. I was entering a whole new world all right, and after settling into the Mess and devouring a quick lunch, I was back at the flight line again to have my first crack at hovering...the skill that would finally and irrevocably bring my "poofter-hood" to a close.

5
JUST LIKE RIDING A BIKE

Now, if I'm completely honest, this wouldn't be my first attempt at hovering, since that feat had taken place on the first day of the course when each of us had ventured into the Training Area with an instructor to see what lay in store. After about half an hour of flying around at treetop height (and thirty minutes of me hyperventilating), my instructor had put the aircraft in a hover and, after no instructional input whatsoever said, "Okay Geoff. You have a go." I put my hands and feet on the controls, the helicopter started moving forward and, almost instantly, we were airborne again.

"Nice takeoff," said my laughing instructor, "but I thought you were going to try hovering."

"I did," was my rather dejected reply.

So, to say I'd already attempted hovering would have been a pretty gross embellishment.

Our temporary Wagga flight line consisted of six Squirrels (parked nose-to-tail) beside a draughty old wooden hut that served as a combination briefing room, crew room and safety equipment room. After the customary pre-sortie briefing, my anxious-looking instructor (Miz) and I headed out to the flight line where, after completing the walk-around inspection, I settled into the right-hand seat to run through the preflight checklist and then start the engine. With the initial three hours of training being solely devoted to hovering practice, as the rotors accelerated, so too did my heart rate. Despite being a fully qualified military pilot, I felt just as uncoordinated and nervous as I'd been when five-year-old me had tried to learn how to ride his older brother's pushbike without killing himself.

What people don't realise about a helicopter is that, if its engine is at full throttle and its rotors are turning at operating RPM, then the aircraft is flying...even when sitting on the ground on its skids. In such a state, any large, sudden or clumsy control inputs can cause the aircraft to tip over, resulting in a catastrophic, swirling cloud of dust and disintegrating rotor blades. Therefore, once I'd wound the throttle up to full power, Miz took control of the aircraft, picked it up into a hover and nimbly manoeuvred it over to a large, grassy area. Then he pointed its nose towards a large building and said:

"Okay, Geoff, the first controls you're going to use are the tail rotor pedals. Just keep the aircraft pointed at that building and I'll do the rest."

In a Squirrel, the control forces are relayed via hydraulic servos, and just tiny (almost imperceptible) control inputs will see the aircraft respond almost instantly. The full range of required tail rotor inputs can be made while the pilot's heels remain anchored to the floor. Initially, I was badly over-controlling, and Miz was having quite a bit of trouble keeping the aircraft stable. "Just make small inputs," I heard him say repeatedly. After taking some deep breaths to control my nervous energy, I found that eventually, I could keep the aircraft pointed in the desired direction. Pivoting the aircraft left or right to point at a different feature was the next step in the process.

"Okay...take a break," said Miz, assuming control again after what, to me, felt like about an hour but, in reality, was probably about ten minutes. "That wasn't too bad. Just remember...SMALL inputs, okay?"

"The next control is the cyclic. Try to rest your wrist on the top of your leg and move the cyclic around using just your thumb and index finger. Pick a spot on the ground and try to keep the aircraft over that spot."

Novice pilots tend to apply a vice-like "death grip" on the controls that impedes their ability to make the small, fine adjustments necessary for a smooth flight. I was no exception and it's a miracle that the top portion of the cyclic didn't explode in my hand in those first few minutes. To prevent myself from ripping the cyclic out of the floor, I kept saying to myself, "Relax... Relax... RELAX DAMMIT!" In my unskilled hands, the little Squirrel was as skittish as a dragonfly, flitting from place to place seemingly of its own volition. "Small inputs," Miz intoned repeatedly as I feverishly worked away to keep the aircraft stationary. "All you need to use is your thumb and index finger."

Then, it was time to tackle the collective—probably the most challenging of the three controls initially. While the pilot can anchor his heels to limit his range of tail rotor inputs and compel himself to use only two fingers on the cyclic, the collective is adjusted using his elbow and lower arm (which is much more difficult to regulate). If a trainee over-corrects for either an upward or downward trend, he may find himself making oscillating control inputs of escalating magnitude that result in the aircraft either rocketing skywards or plunging earthwards. As I levered the collective up and down like a hand pump, I noticed that Miz was working pretty hard in the other seat. When that first hour finally drew to a close, I think we were both equally exhausted. "You just need more practice," said Miz as he efficiently whisked our Squirrel back to the flight line. But inside, I felt just like that five-year-old on his brother's bicycle, awkwardly wobbling his way across the backyard.

* * *

That evening, we all assembled in the Officers Mess bar to rehydrate from the afternoon's sweaty exertions. None of my coursemates were boasting about how easy it was to hover and, if truth be told, a few of us might have been thinking that we'd made a bad career move. Thankfully, the QHIs were a supportive and sociable lot, and I soon found myself enjoying the company of "Sinkers," another idiosyncratic, young Royal Australian Navy QHI. But that was where any similarities between him and Miz started and ended abruptly. While Miz was a quiet, single introvert, Sinkers was a garrulous, married extrovert who, I also learnt, could be a bit of a pyromaniac when he'd had a few.

Legend had it that Sinkers' firebug tendencies had gotten him into a wee bit of strife after a Dining-in Night at Fairbairn a few winters previously. In the early morning hours of a bitterly cold night, Sinkers had found himself alone, inebriated and incapable of driving home. For some added warmth to help get him through the long night ahead, he decided to stoke up the main bar's fireplace. But when he awoke several hours later, there seemed to be far less furniture sitting around than he remembered from the previous evening. Most of it, he subsequently discovered, lay protruding, half-burnt, from the fireplace, where sooty, black scorch marks extended far up the wall. The morning sun blazing in through the now curtain-less windows just served to accentuate the carnage.

Sinkers, I believe, paid several thousand dollars to cover the replacement costs of the furniture and the curtains, but it was the immolation of the framed, grandly embossed "Freedom of the City of Canberra" parchment (presented with great pomp and ceremony by the Lord Mayor of Canberra just a few years earlier) that had seen Sinkers invited to fill the role of Orderly Officer for several consecutive months. Chastened but not cured, his pyromania became a little more restrained afterwards, but in social settings, a blazing paper-plane sailing just past your nostrils was always a good indicator that Sinkers had had a few. As I would soon discover, such adolescent exuberance was pretty commonplace in the helicopter world.

* * *

After three hours of training, I found that I could hover a Squirrel with a reasonable degree of confidence. The second sortie had involved manipulating two of the three controls together (in various combinations) and, in the final hour, I'd begun using all three simultaneously. More advanced manoeuvres followed—moving forwards, backwards and sideways, and performing 360-degree pivot turns around the nose or tail.

With each acquired skill came more self-assuredness and more innate muscle memory for future application. Takeoffs and landings were the next logical development.

Simplistically, a takeoff should merely involve raising the collective but, again, the other two controls have parts to play. Initially, the pilot slowly raises the collective until his aircraft feels "light on the skids," and then adds just a shade more to coax it into the air. But again, tail rotor inputs must be made to keep the aircraft pointing straight ahead, and cyclic inputs are necessary to keep it stationary. Once airborne, though, the collective input must be promptly re-adjusted to maintain a steady three-foot hover. My first few attempts were tentative and took far too long for my liking.

But, just like a fixed-wing aircraft, takeoffs were still far less demanding than landings. When inducing a descent from the hover, the reduction in collective is so minute that the instructors referred to it as "breathing down" on the controls—almost as much a mental process as a physical one. Again, accompanying tail rotor and cyclic inputs were necessary to keep the aircraft straight and stationary. Initially, the skittish little Squirrel felt as if it was trying to flit from side to side (with increasing amplitude) the closer we got to the ground (in what I referred to as "Falling Leaf Syndrome"). This phenomenon seemed much more pronounced when descending onto concrete or asphalt than it was when landing on softer surfaces such as grass or dirt. Once again, I was tentative initially, but my instructor soon found something that got me on the ground *very* quickly…simulated engine failures.

Flying training usually involves being taught how to do something with everything working and then, soon afterwards, being taught what to do if something fails. Engines, for example, are notoriously unreliable in the training environment…failing frequently (and usually at the worst possible moment). In a single-engine aircraft, the pilot must be capable of dealing with an engine failure and, in a helicopter particularly, these skills are a matter of life and death. Only the rotor blades keep a helicopter aloft and, since it's the engine that powers the rotor, if you're in a helicopter that's experienced an engine failure, there's only one way you're heading—DOWN…and quickly!

Helicopter aerodynamics explains how the rotor blades can be kept turning after an engine failure, but I won't even attempt to explain that here. Suffice it to say, if you mishandle a helicopter engine failure, you may soon find yourself at the controls of the world's most inefficient fixed-wing. Since hands-on experience is usually the best teacher, helicopter engine failures are routinely practiced in notoriously challenging manoeuvres referred to as 'auto-rotations' (or 'autos' for short). Since, by now, we could hover fairly competently, the syllabus required that engine failures should first be practiced in this phase of flight. And so, we were introduced to the 'hovering auto,' where the instructor simulated the failure by rolling the throttle back to idle while announcing "PRACTICE" over the interphone.

Immediately afterwards, there was just enough time for the student to mutter an expletive before pulling up the remaining collective to cushion the aircraft onto the ground. As with most rotary-wing training sequences, the hovering auto was practiced so frequently that reacting to it soon became virtually instinctive. Henceforth, whenever we were hover-taxying away from the lines, it seemed that our forward progress became a matter of "PRACTICE"..."*$%#"...land, (engine winds up), lift up, move off..."PRACTICE"..."@#$%!?"...land (engine winds up again), lift up again, move off again..."PRACTICE"..."$%^&#$%!!!!"...land (engine winds up yet again), lift up yet again, move off yet again and repeat (ad infinitum). At least a hovering auto prevented the onset of "Falling Leaf Syndrome," and some of us soon formed the view that if landing somewhere was becoming too difficult, we could always just roll the throttle off on ourselves.

One afternoon, I was watching Shane coming back to the lines when his aircraft suddenly dropped to the ground in the manoeuvre just described. Even to my untrained eye, the landing seemed pretty hard and, shortly afterwards, I noticed that the HF antenna (a long strand of wire running along the tail boom) had come loose and was flailing about in the rotor wash. Fearing what might happen if it became entangled in the rotors, I had one of the groundies rush outside to give them a signal to shut down their engine immediately. When this direction had been complied with, Shane's instructor unstrapped and climbed out of the aircraft to investigate. When he reached the rear of the aircraft, he became visibly agitated, and it was then that I noticed that the tail boom was sagging considerably. The aircraft's back had been broken by the impact of the heavy landing.

RAAF incidents were classified on a sliding scale from 'Category 1' (an easily repairable minor scrape) to 'Category 5' (either complete destruction or impossible to repair). The damage to Shane's aircraft was subsequently assessed as Category 4, and the little Squirrel was ignominiously returned to Canberra on the back of a truck a few weeks later. Such were the slender margins for error when practicing auto-rotations. I already respected the QHIs enormously, but my esteem for them only grew when we started practicing autos from circuit height soon afterwards. Not that a helicopter circuit was especially challenging. Since the Squirrel didn't have retractable landing gear, a circuit merely provided the opportunity to depart the hover for a quick scenic lap around the airfield.

But, if it's not your day and your engine suddenly fails, then you must immediately lower the collective to the floor to keep the rotor blades windmilling. If there's a suitable landing area directly ahead, you must then wash off any airspeed above sixty knots, then descend at this speed. At a hundred feet, you raise the attitude at a rate that will wash off all the forward speed by the point at which the tail is about ten feet above the ground. You then pull up about half-collective to reduce the descent rate (the 'first stage pitch-pull'), roll the aircraft level, and then cushion it onto the ground with the remaining collective. This final element is referred to as the 'second stage pitch-pull' (although it's essentially just a hovering auto).

Such is the theory, anyway. But when you consider that a helicopter with a failed engine descends at about 2,000 feet per minute, from a typical altitude of about 500 feet, the pilot may have as little as fifteen seconds to assess his options and then conduct the auto-rotation. If he misjudges the situation or mishandles his aircraft, then he's dead...it's really that simple. The QHIs repeatedly emphasised the conventional wisdom that achieving zero forward speed on touchdown would probably result in a survivable accident—albeit with likely spinal injuries. Any significant forward speed on landing, however, would most likely result in the demise of both the aircraft and its occupants.

So, while actual auto-rotations are life-or-death manoeuvres, even practicing them on grass runways has the potential for disaster. If a trainee flares too late, he could dig the tail rotor into the ground, causing it to depart the aircraft. If he doesn't flare enough, he might run onto the ground at a high enough speed to cause the aircraft to pitch forward onto its nose. Over-flaring (or flaring too early) can lead to free-falling the last twenty feet to the ground, likely "spreading the skids" and injuring the crew. While a 'run-on' speed of zero is essential in the real case, in the training environment, we were limited to a landing speed of at least forty knots (to reduce the potential for heavy landings).

The Squirrels were also fitted with 'stingers'—short pieces of spring steel mounted under the tail boom to offer some protection to the vulnerable tail rotor. Any evidence of dirt or grass on the stinger after a training sortie was considered a likely 'tail strike,' which required a thorough post-flight inspection of the aircraft by the groundies. Ultimately, though, it was the QHIs who were the last line of defence, and when it came time for me to fly my first auto from circuit height, my only thought was, "Don't break anything! Just...don't break anything!"

Approaching the grass runways at a thousand feet, the instructor rolled off the throttle and announced "PRACTICE." My heart started thumping as I lowered the collective and commenced a 60-knot descent. Initially, it all seemed fairly sedate but, the closer we got to the ground, the more everything sped up. Completing the first and second stage pitch-pulls was a real adrenaline rush and, with a pounding heart, I managed to achieve a landing that didn't break either the aircraft or its occupants. An added bonus was that we didn't observe a detached tail rotor careering past us (as had happened to some other crews on previous deployments).

After further sessions of simulated emergencies, I was assessed as 'safe solo' and found myself completely alone in an aircraft flying circuits around RAAF Base Wagga. But having spent the last couple of years sitting in crowded 707 cockpits, being solo again was, truthfully, just a little disconcerting. It was rather comforting therefore that, henceforth, we trainees would fly together on 'mutual solos' (where we could scare each other rather than just scaring ourselves). By Thursday, the 27th of June, 1985, we were no longer poofters (having each accumulated about eighteen hours of rotary-wing flight time) and were classified unofficially as "safe dangerous."

On the flight back to Fairbairn, the instructor continually directed my attention towards an innocuous little item on the exterior of the aircraft that would soon become the very bane of my existence. Between the windshields, and projecting out into the airflow, was a short piece of rigid wire to which was attached a four-inch-long strand of red wool. This simple device acted as a rudimentary 'slip indicator,' and visually betrayed any sloppy pilot who hadn't applied enough tail rotor input to counteract any collective changes. I'd never really mastered 'aircraft balancing' on Pilots Course, even though the importance of doing so was hammered into us at both Point Cook and Pearce. In a fixed-wing aircraft, when power is added or reduced, the nose will tend to pull to the left or the right, and small rudder inputs are required to balance out any 'skidding' tendency. I'd managed to avoid any post-flight canings of my lazy feet—something experienced by some of my peers—but imagine my joy at the beginning of my 33 Squadron training when Woofy had said, "On the 707, unless you have an engine failure, the rudder pedals make good footrests." Now, it was back to having to keep the aircraft balanced again, and "Look at the string...KEEP IT IN THE CENTRE" was a command that I would hear loudly, and often, over the coming weeks.

6
THE TRIALS OF TRAINING

Once back in the bosom of Australia's cosmopolitan capital, we were granted a long weekend off to recover from the hectic pace of life in the Riverina. Our remaining training flights would consist of multiple practice autos onto Fairbairn's grid of grass runways, and acquiring our bread-and-butter handling skills out in a vast expanse of countryside to the east of Fairbairn. This area of a thousand square kilometres contained dams and pine forests, as well as every type of terrain from gently undulating farmland to densely forested mountain ranges and pinnacles.

Also within the Helicopter Training Area was a multitude of Landing Zones—or 'pads,' in helicopter-speak—that were rated according to a degree of difficulty that ranged from green (expansive, grassy paddocks) to red (tiny clearings surrounded by towering gum trees). Tyres painted green, amber or red were placed at the centre of each pad to confirm to the more navigationally challenged trainees that they had reached their desired destination. Also, since operations in the Training Area increased the chances of our fragile craft inadvertently contacting the local flora or fauna, each crew was henceforth augmented with a loadmaster to serve as an "extra set of eyes" in the back.

My first venture into the Helicopter Training Area took place under Miz's watchful gaze on the 3rd of July and, as we flitted from pad to pad, it was sometimes necessary to retreat into its farthest corner to be capable of achieving an IGE takeoff. Here was where the loadmaster played a vital role in proceedings, by steering us around with verbal directions, like this:

"Okay...you're clear back. Come back fifty...forty...thirty...twenty...ten...HOLD! Now swing the tail to the right. A bit more. HOLD! Okay. Now back ten. Back five. HOLD! That's as far back as you can get."

But not every commentary was quite so calm and measured, and if you were manoeuvring a little too aggressively, it might more closely resemble:

"Come back forty...twenty...ten...HOLD, HOLD!"

While the odd leaf or twig could be flayed away without sustaining any real damage, hitting a solid tree branch or an unforgiving tree trunk was another matter entirely. Therefore, despite their usually good-humoured demeanours, the loadmasters took their responsibilities very seriously, and would often hang precariously half-outside the cabin to get a better view. To prevent departing the aircraft, they always wore a sturdy nylon-webbing safety harness that was clipped onto a recessed D-ring in the aircraft floor. But very occasionally, after shutting down back at Fairbairn, you might hear the loadmaster exclaim rather shakily over the intercom, "F***...I forgot to attach my harness!"

One of the early skills we practiced was hovering OGE, during which the biggest challenge was to find suitable 'hover reference points' to help keep the aircraft stationary. If an area has plenty of features, the pilot merely selects a close-up reference point (the fork of a nearby tree branch, for example) and a far-away reference point (such as a distant, distinctive tree). He then lines up these features (like the sights on a rifle) to keep the aircraft both in a steady longitudinal alignment and at a constant height. A side-on reference point is also required to help prevent the pilot from drifting backwards or forwards. In an OGE hover, the pilot's attention is constantly shifting, with a ratio of looking forward to sideways of about 4:1. As I soon discovered, accurate OGE hovering is quite a demanding exercise that requires intense levels of concentration.

For one particular loadmaster, this activity provided the perfect opportunity for him to have a little fun at a trainee's expense. As the student sweated away on maintaining his OGE hover, the loadie (exhibiting either supreme confidence in his harness or sheer stupidity—you decide) would clamber outside the aircraft and edge his way forward along the skids until he was standing directly outside the trainee's side window. Then, he would either knock loudly on the window or smile broadly when the student shifted his focus to glance out sideways. In either circumstance, the student's shocked reaction was always a source of great amusement for the loadmaster...right up until he tried it out just once too often and on the wrong potential victim.

Being forewarned of the loadie's antics the day before their flight together, the trainee visited the safety equipment section and cut off the clip end of a worn-out harness. Later, when he was out in the area and established in his OGE hover, he waited to hear the expected knock on his window. When it came, instead of appearing shocked, the student turned to face the loadie and held up the severed clip of the safety harness. The tables had been turned, and the loadmaster (believing that the student had unclipped his harness) spread-eagled himself against the fuselage and inched his way along the skids until he was safely back inside the cabin. Needless to say, many expletives and much merriment followed when the loadie realised that he had finally received his comeuppance.

* * *

So, by now, you've probably figured out that flying helicopters is a risky business, and the most significant hazards can be broadly described as the "Three Ws"—wires, wind and weather. Wires and whirling rotor blades simply *do not* mix...if you need proof, search YouTube. Consequently, Canberra's Training Area (which included a designated Low Flying Area, where we routinely flew around at a mere fifty feet) was one of the most thoroughly surveyed areas in the country. But even in the Helicopter Training Area, some landowners adhered to the belief that, on their property, they were entitled to suspend wires wherever and whenever they pleased.

The environmental movement was only in its infancy in the mid-1980s, but some of its members were already lobbying for the removal of the large, brightly-coloured plastic spheres that were attached to high-tension powerlines to increase their visibility to transiting helicopter crews. Furthermore, the "greenies" were pushing for the steel stanchions supporting these cables to be painted in colours that allowed them to aesthetically blend into the environment. Needless to say, rotary-wing pilots had ample motivation to maintain vigilance, with the most likely consequences of hitting an unseen cable being either a severed rotor mast or a detached "brain bucket." The venerable Iroquois helicopters were all fitted with blade-like 'cable-cutters' (above and below the forward fuselage) as a last-ditch counter-measure, but the phenomenal odds of severing a hitherto unseen wire and escaping unscathed meant that avoidance was, by far, the most effective form of defence.

But while wires can be avoided, the wind is something that affects every flight and, if Moses had been a pilot, the eleventh commandment would have read, "Thou shalt takeoff and land into wind." In recent years, though, homeowners living close to major airports—even long-established ones—have achieved considerable success in establishing laws that require airline pilots to land in crosswinds (or even light tail-winds) under the egalitarian auspices of 'noise sharing.' Fortunately, unlike their runway-bound counterparts, helicopter pilots are usually free to fly their approaches into wind, provided they know where it's coming from. At an airfield, you can simply ask ATC or look at the windsock, but being "out in the boonies," requires a little more resourcefulness. While some intriguing theories were proffered at 5 Squadron—including the notion that stationary livestock will point their bums into the breeze—the most reliable methods of determining wind direction and strength are to examine the 'wind lanes' on exposed bodies of water or, better yet, to observe rising columns of smoke.

In a training environment, though, nothing is ever so easy or obvious, and a popular story concerned a student enroute to the Training Area with his instructor. During this short transit, it was common practice for trainees to evaluate the available wind indicators, but on this particular occasion, the crew was distracted by a huge bushfire that, with an accompanying pall of thick smoke, was blazing away just outside the area. When the instructor brought his student back to the task at hand and asked him where he thought the wind was coming from, the student supposedly replied, "Ummm. I'll look for some wind lanes on this dam up ahead."

Once you've assessed the wind, it then becomes a matter of overflying your chosen pad to determine the most optimal direction for the approach. At a "green" pad, this usually just meant approaching into the breeze, but at a "red" pad, the *only* possible approach direction might not be into wind, and the approach could become extremely challenging. The wind is also a crucial factor in 'pinnacle approaches,' which refers to landings made onto well-defined hilltops or mountain peaks. On such approaches, the landing spot is the only visual reference point, and judging your closure rate with the ground can be quite challenging. Strong winds will then complicate matters even further.

When the wind encounters an obstacle, it rises smoothly on the upwind side, but then falls again in a turbulent downdraught on the downwind (lee) side. The boundary line between the updraughts and downdraughts is called the 'demarcation line,' and, as the wind speed increases, this line becomes steeper and more clearly defined. Pinnacle approaches flown above the demarcation line (through the updraughts) require less engine power, and provide a much smoother ride. But doing so in strong winds can result in quite a steep approach angle that only accentuates the depth perception problems approaching the ground.

As challenging as flying pinnacle approaches could be, the manoeuvres that caused me the most unease initially were 'slope landings.' A hovering helicopter is never quite level—one skid always hangs slightly lower than the other. But when landing on uneven terrain, one skid might be firmly on the ground, while the other is still in the air. If you want to shut down the aircraft at such a landing place, both skids must be on the ground, and this is where 'slope landings' come in. Again, such manoeuvres would become instinctive soon enough but, initially, we practiced them onto terrain that sloped in every conceivable direction (left-to-right, right-to-left and, worst of all, either front-to-back or back-to-front).

To perform a sideways slope landing, you initially put one skid onto the ground and then slowly lower the collective until the other skid has also settled. To prevent the aircraft from tipping over, into-slope cyclic inputs are applied at the same rate as the collective is being lowered. If you're facing uphill, both skids will initially be in contact with the ground, and lowering the collective will cause the aircraft to tilt downwards at the back, sometimes creating the sensation that it's about to start sliding backwards down the hill. Most unnerving! There's a limit to the acceptable amount of slope, of course, but the ability to make such "eyeball" judgments would only come with more experience.

Notwithstanding all of these challenges, I soon began to enjoy flying the nippy and responsive little Squirrel. The novelty of hovering, flying backwards or sideways, and "flogging along down in the weeds" was never lost on me. Despite helicopter flying being very different from anything I'd ever experienced before, I was now starting to become confident in my general flying skills...something that I'd never really felt on Pilots Course. But after two weeks of focusing my attention solely outside the aircraft, the training syllabus now demanded that we tackle the last of the 'Three Ws'—the weather—by acquiring some instrument flying skills.

* * *

I should explain, though, that teaching instrument flying skills to a helicopter pilot is like teaching a submariner how to swim...it's a necessary skill to have but is something that will hopefully never be used on the job. The fragility of a helicopter's rotor blades demands that, if possible, it always be kept clear of any extreme weather, particularly when there's usually the option to land somewhere and just wait for conditions to improve. Accordingly, helicopter instrumentation was fairly rudimentary, and primarily intended for quick transits in benign weather. Nevertheless, in mid-July, we all set off for Nowra for some training that would culminate in each of us attempting an Instrument Rating Test.

The transit to Nowra was flown as a tactical navigation exercise, and my instructor was Ken Vote, a Navy lieutenant commander who'd seen active service in Vietnam whilst attached to 9 Squadron. Ken was a vastly experienced, gruff old "salt" and flying with him loomed as an intimidating prospect. But an even bigger challenge would be navigating my way through the heavily-timbered Macdonald State Forest, which lies on the direct track between Canberra and Nowra. I'd flown a navigation exercise to Richmond and back the previous week, where the IFR of visual navigation in well-populated areas ('I Follow Roads and railway lines') had proven hardly a challenge. But in the featureless, rolling terrain of the State Forest, I feared a repeat of my COMSURV embarrassment. And so, it came to pass that within about twenty minutes of entering the forested area, with its continual succession of identical ridgelines and gullies, I became completely and utterly "geographically embarrassed." Ken had to step in to work out where we were, and I flew the remainder of the way in humiliated silence. Completing my disgrace in the bar shortly afterwards was the realisation that I was the only one on the course who'd experienced any such difficulties.

At least in the bar I was able to enjoy Ken's dry wit, as he regaled us all with tales of his wartime experiences in Vietnam, the most amusing of which concerned 9 Squadron's practice of crewing new arrivals with seasoned veterans so that they could quickly learn the ropes. The squadron's duties included flying 'dust-off' missions—aeromedical evacuation flights that transported wounded or injured troops from their forward positions to medical facilities in the rear. One evening, a new arrival and an experienced captain who were crewed together for dust-off duty the next day met up in the bar for a cold "bevvie" and a quick chat. The old warrior soon drank himself to the point where the floor seemed like a nice place on which to have a little lie-down. Horrified, the novice and his fellow rookies manhandled the snoring old warhorse back to his tent and laid him on his stretcher.

Murphy's Law states that "bad things usually happen at the worst possible moment" (with many pilots justifiably believing that Murphy was an optimist). Sure enough, early the next morning, the copilot was notified of a dust-off mission that would need to get airborne just after dawn. With the help of his long-suffering mates, the copilot managed to lug the still-slumbering warrior out to the dust-off aircraft and strap him into his seat. About twenty minutes later, as the aircraft thundered along just above the jungle canopy, the captain finally stirred from his repose. Now, given that his last conscious memory would have been of drinking in the bar, you might imagine that it would be rather disconcerting to find himself strapped into a low-flying Iroquois. But not so, according to Ken. The "old hand" merely took a second or two to appraise himself of his situation before calmly stating "Taking over" and, without another word, assuming command of the aircraft.

Our training commenced the next morning but, since the Squirrel was only fitted with an Automatic Direction Finder (ADF), we were limited to flying either Non-Directional Beacon (NDB) letdowns (using the ADF) or GCAs (Ground Controlled Approaches). On a GCA, ATC radars scan the lateral and vertical approach paths to a runway, and the military controller on duty provides an inbound aircraft in IMC with a verbal account of its position relative to the runway. A typical ATC talk down on a well-flown GCA would sound something like this:

"Okay, you're four miles from touchdown...slightly left of the centreline...slightly above the glidepath. Increase your rate of descent."

"You're now three miles from touchdown...on centreline...on glidepath. Maintain your rate of descent."

"Two miles from touchdown...approaching the minima...on centreline...on glidepath."

"You're at the minima...look ahead...land visually. GCA out."

How we yearned to put the aircraft into a hover during a GCA or, better yet, fly backwards *up* the approach path. How would the controller respond then?

"You were four miles from touchdown, you're now five miles from touchdown...on centreline...on glidepath. Will you be landing soon, or what?"

But only our instructors could have attempted such outrageous manoeuvres because we trainees were "under the hood," whereby large rectangles of black vinyl had been attached (by Velcro) to the front of our helmets to (supposedly) prevent us looking outside for visual cues and to keep us focused on the instruments. Just like Pilots Course, we practiced climbs, descents and turns on the instruments, and were also required to demonstrate proficiency at UA (unusual attitude) recoveries. Before a UA recovery, the student looks away while his instructor puts the aircraft into an unusual attitude. When the instructor then says, "Handing over," the trainee looks up, assesses his attitude and airspeed and then, on instruments, returns the aircraft to straight and level flight. Because of a helicopter's limited manoeuvrability in pitch, however, these UAs were far less dramatic than those we'd previously experienced in either CT4s or Macchis. Nevertheless, one instructor on a previous deployment had found a way to flummox his student by gently landing the aircraft while the trainee was looking away. When the student heard "Handing over," he looked up at his instruments and discovered that his aircraft was already in straight and level flight...but with zero airspeed!

After several training flights, I was ready for my IRT and, in my room the night before, I thought I'd better study up on the Squirrel's various flight instruments...a favourite interrogation topic for the examiners on such flights. I soon discovered, though, that the English flight manual provided by the French Aerospatiale was very poor, and I fully understood why 5 Squadron had decided to undertake the lengthy process of completely rewriting it. I decided to begin with the description of the Attitude Indicator—the most essential flight instrument—in which the manufacturer attempted to convey the simple fact that the 'ground' portion of the attitude display (or "ball," as it was referred to in the manual) was black, while the 'sky' portion was grey. The French-to-English translation read, "If the pilot pushes his stick too far forward, his balls will turn black!" The next day, I managed to avoid getting black balls and passed my IRT—a rather novel way of marking my twenty-seventh birthday.

* * *

Back in Canberra, three more weeks of training sorties stood between me and my Final Handling Test (FHT), but still more novel experiences lay in store. My first night flight took place in late July, and I soon discovered that autos were even more challenging when you couldn't see where you were going. Instead, you just plunged through the blackness until you reached the height at which your searchlight could provide enough illumination for the flare and pitch-pull manoeuvres. Some eerie night navigation exercises followed with only the stars for illumination, and I simply couldn't help but ponder my chances of survival if the engine were to suddenly quit and I had to perform a 'dead stick' auto onto the darkened countryside below. Far more enjoyable was a mutual-solo day navigation flight down to the Snowy Mountains ski fields, where flying laps around Thredbo and Perisher Valley under cloudless, cobalt-blue skies was a truly unforgettable experience.

Equally memorable, but for totally different reasons, was my sole formation sortie on the Squirrel with Sinkers, just a few days before my FHT. Formation flying was something that I'd enjoyed on Pilots Course (despite the incredible concentration it required). Not only do you get to see another aircraft in flight up close, but you can easily gauge your progress as you gain more experience. "Mustard, mud, sweat and blood, grit your teeth and stay there," had been the catch-cry at Pearce, and the thrill of sitting just a few metres away from another aircraft in flight was such an exhilarating feeling that it simply defies description to anyone who hasn't experienced it for themselves.

The risks of flying helicopters in close formation, however, increase exponentially when you consider the dire consequences of clipping another aircraft's rotor blades. Whilst fixed-wing aircraft in formation can survive the occasional nudge or bump (due to their relatively low closing speeds with each other), inter-meshing the rotor blades of two helicopters results in the destruction of both aircraft and the instant demise of all onboard. Our goal that day was to achieve a formation station of 'two rotor disks'—twice the diameter of the rotor disk—from the leader, in what was truly a high-stakes (but also very exhilarating) exercise.

Two days later, and with ninety hours of rotary-wing time in my logbook, I passed my Squirrel FHT and received a very complimentary post-test report from my examiner. Once the others had followed suit, a brief presentation ceremony was held in the crew room, after which Shane bade us farewell and departed for his Chinook conversion course in Amberley. In the warm afterglow of my FHT, I began to think that I'd finally found my niche flying helicopters, but then we started our Iroquois training...and that feeling changed dramatically.

7
FROM A SPORTS CAR TO A BATTLE WAGON

I can't explain why, but I think the psychology of the situation was largely responsible for my change of heart. We'd just spent two months coming to grips with all things rotary-wing on the Squirrel, and now we were back in the classroom, starting all over again from scratch. Our "new" aircraft—the Iroquois (that iconic symbol of the "Helicopter War" in Vietnam)—also promised to be a very different style of conveyance to that which we'd become accustomed. Transitioning from the nippy little Ecureuil to the venerable, noisy old battle wagon that was the Iroquois was like climbing out of a BMW sports car and into a "preloved" 1960s Holden utility.

I can also state categorically that by mid-August, the novelty of my situation had well and truly worn off. As comfortable as my Mess room was, I longed to be back in my own space, where I could dress how I wished, do as I pleased and eat whatever (and whenever) I wanted. When you 'live in' a RAAF Mess, you pay what is called R&Q ('Rations and Quarters'), whereby the deduction from your salary pays for both your accommodation and all your meals in the Mess Dining

Room. Now, on the surface, this seems like a pretty cushy arrangement, but after several months of being subjected to the mysterious cuisine that comprises Mess food, I was well and truly *"over it."*

My use of the word "mysterious" here is intentional because, on the menus for every meal, the Air Force cooks seemed to pride themselves on describing their creations in the most obfuscatory terms imaginable. For example, you might be drooling at the prospect of feasting on *Saucisses et pommes puree* only to discover when your plate arrived, that you'd just ordered sausages and mashed potatoes. My biggest disappointment came when I ordered *Mock Filet Mignon* and was served up a shrivelled beef rissole around which a skimpy strip of bacon had been wrapped. Some of us considered breaking into the kitchen one night and stealing the cook's dictionary, so that we might at least have some idea of what would be assaulting our palates on future dining extravaganzas.

While the main courses were always a mystery, the accompanying vegetables were not: boiled Brussels sprouts or broccoli. After enduring endless servings of these bland greens, we began to suspect that there was a cartel of retired RAAF senior officers who cultivated them on their hobby farms and sold them to the Mess...pocketing our R&Q in return. By the commencement of the Iroquois phase, my Brussels Sprout/Broccoli Overload Warning Light was illuminated continuously, and so I increasingly relied on the Queanbeyan Pizza Hut to provide some culinary relief.

* * *

The Iroquois ground school lasted all of four days and primarily dealt with the mechanical differences between the Squirrel and its much older forebear. The advances in rotor assembly design were the biggest distinction between the two and, while the Squirrel's composite three-bladed rotor head was deceptively sophisticated, the Iroquois equivalent consisted of a whirling collection of metallic thing-a-me-bobs that would have looked at home on a Jules Verne time machine. Atop this antiquated assembly, and securing the rotor blades to the aircraft, was the

"Jesus Nut:" so named because if it came adrift in flight, the only hope you had left was to pray to Jesus.

But a stray Jesus Nut wasn't your only potential concern. Because of its 'teetering' rotor head assembly, the Iroquois was also susceptible to a very nasty phenomenon called 'mast bump.' Essentially, the blades pivoted around the attachment point and, if the pilot bunted (pushed forward on the cyclic too quickly) and induced negative G conditions, the blade hinges could strike and sever the mast, causing the entire rotor assembly to depart the aircraft. Encountering severe turbulence could have a similar outcome, making it even more important to avoid areas of extreme weather.

But despite its design fragilities, the sound of an Iroquois in flight suggested nothing but sheer power and brute strength to those who'd lived through the Vietnam War era. While the finely-machined blades of the Squirrel cleaved through the air and generated a sound akin to a swarm of angry bees, the thick, metal blades of the Iroquois "beat the air into submission," almost going supersonic at the tips (and creating that distinctive WOK-WOK-WOK sound that was simply like no other). But what almost drove me to despair about the Iroquois rotor blades when I first flew the aircraft was that irritatingly, frustratingly, maddeningly, they turned in the *opposite direction* to those on the Squirrel.

Now this quirk might seem fairly insignificant until you remember that *every* adjustment to the collective position required the pilot to make a concurrent tail rotor input. When the blades rotate clockwise (as on the Squirrel) raising the collective requires a *right* tail rotor anti-torque pedal input. But on an Iroquois (where the rotors turned anti-clockwise) a collective increase required a *left* tail rotor pedal anti-torque input. It had taken me two months to establish the instinctive relationship between my left hand (collective) and my right foot (tail rotor pedal) on the Squirrel. Now, I had no option but to completely retrain my brain to quickly form a left-hand/left-foot connection.

Another major difference was that the Iroquois didn't have a rotor brake. In the Squirrel, after shutting down the engine, the rotor brake engaged and quickly brought the rotor blades to a standstill. In the

Iroquois, however, the blades only slowed down through friction and inertia, requiring the development of a very unique shutdown procedure. The loadmaster would stand in front of the aircraft and when the pilot felt that the blades had slowed enough, he would fly down the advancing blade into the waiting arms of the loadie. The "captured" blade would then be walked around the aircraft and secured to the tail boom. This seemingly simple manoeuvre required a surprising degree of judgement. If the big, heavy blade was flown down too soon, its momentum could knock the loadmaster off his feet. But if the pilot waited too long, the blades would just grind to a halt and the disgraced pilot would have to climb up onto the roof and push the blade down to the loadmaster. While the loadies were all very macho in their approach to catching a fast-moving blade, if a pilot and his loadmaster weren't exactly the best of mates, the loadie could be in for a real hammering.

* * *

For the next month, we essentially repeated the Squirrel syllabus on the Iroquois and, in the Training Area, the emphasis shifted to practicing takeoffs and landings with limited power availability to prepare us for life in the squadrons. The instructors simulated a 'partial power' condition by winding off the throttle a little so that the rotor RPM would decay if we tried to apply too much collective. Thus, regular 'power checks' became necessary to determine the amount of torque we had available for our approaches and departures. In the circuit area, we practiced more advanced emergencies—simulated tail rotor, hydraulics or governor failures—as well as 90-degree, 180-degree and 360-degree autos (depending on the amount of turn that was required to land into wind).

The 360-degree auto was essentially a very tight corkscrew to head for a point almost directly below the aircraft at the point of failure. An alternative method of achieving that same spot was the 'constant attitude' auto whereby, after an engine failure, *all* of the forward speed was flared off at altitude, and the aircraft was then descended vertically to the ground. When I first read the description of this manoeuvre in the manual, the margins for error sounded even slimmer than usual: particularly when the point stipulated for the first-stage pitch-pull was "at the appropriate height." I queried this rather vague wording with my instructor, who replied simply, "Don't worry...you'll know when you get there." I remained sceptical.

After a few warm-up autos, it was time to attempt the dreaded constant attitude auto. The instructor rolled off the throttle and announced "PRACTICE"... I lowered the collective, flared off nearly all the forward speed (we were still limited to forty knots run-on speed) and then commenced a near-vertical descent. Things seemed rather sedate at first, almost tranquil, as we floated gently towards the earth at nearly 2,000 feet a minute. But then, the ground suddenly seemed to start rising around us and, just as I was sure we were going to be splattered like a bug, I yelled "WHOA" and hauled up on the collective to arrest the (now-horrifying) descent rate. After I'd cushioned the aircraft onto the ground and regained my composure, my instructor said casually, "Yeah...that was about right."

* * *

The night before my FHT, I was feeling anything but confident and relaxed. I was nowhere near as comfortable in an Iroquois as I'd been in a Squirrel, and the hectic flying program of the past month had been exhausting. After four months away, I also just desperately wanted to go home and kept trying to console myself by thinking, "One more day, and it'll be over." Almost inevitably, my FHT was an unmitigated disaster. My aircraft handling was sloppy, I attempted a landing without first conducting a power check and, worst of all, I couldn't locate a remote (and therefore largely unused) pad out on the very periphery of the Training Area. "You're going to have to do better than that," was the succinct, but also warranted, post-flight critique from my examiner. It was like being back at Pearce again except that, this time, I'd made a great start to the course, before faltering on the home stretch and then falling short of the finish line. I felt deflated and defeated. Embarrassed. Depressed. That night, when I heard my coursemates joyously packing up their stuff to head off the next day, I had to admit that I'd failed my FHT, and would be doing some remedial training before my next attempt. They surprised me by being remarkably supportive and consoling during what was quite a low point in my professional life.

The next morning, I was back in the air with a senior instructor, doing power checks and approaches, power checks and approaches, and more power checks and more approaches, with just a little visual navigation thrown in too. Just before lunch, I went out for FHT Mark II, which involved some partial power approaches (which I flew flawlessly) and a quick scoot across to a remote pad (that I located unerringly). "Take me home," the examiner said. Back in his office, he asked, "Why didn't you do that the first time?" as he shook my hand and wished me well. Moments later, I trudged back into our now eerily quiet and deserted classroom. On the blackboard, in large letters was written, "Well done, Geoff," above each of my coursemates' signatures. It was such a simple gesture, but it meant so much to me at that moment. But there was no time for sentimentality. Not wanting to delay my departure a second longer, I rushed back to the Mess, packed up my stuff, handed in my room key and sped out through the main gate. Finally...I was heading home!

8
SWORD OF HONOUR

After a few precious days of R&R in Brisbane, it was back to 9 Squadron to finally begin the job that I'd spent months training for. Since I was now officially a qualified Category D Iroquois captain, all that was required before I was let loose on the unsuspecting soldiery of south-east Queensland was a local familiarisation flight with a squadron QHI. The Amberley Helicopter Training Area didn't quite live up to the grand scale of its counterpart in Canberra, although its heavily wooded bushland came complete with creek lines and pinnacles, pads of varying difficulty and a surveyed Low Flying Area for operations at fifty feet AGL. Flinders Peak (elevation 679 metres) marked the southern boundary of the Area, but its imposing summit was only infrequently visited by the curious, the adventurous or the just plain bored. We flew an approach and landing at its confined, rocky apex on my first training sortie, where my instructor delighted in pointing out the sign erected by some past squadron "wags" that welcomed visitors to "Mount Flinders International Airport."

With my familiarisation ride complete, it was time to put my feet up in the crew room and "learn by osmosis" what I should expect over the next few years. I soon gathered that the squadron's tasks fell into three

main categories. Firstly, there were "famil flights" that involved flying to a nearby Army unit, giving a quick verbal presentation on the aircraft to the assembled throng, and then taking the troops up in 'chalks' of six or seven for a handling demonstration. Next was a "squadron bush push," where three or four 9 Squadron crews supported Brisbane-based Army units out in the field. Finally, there were the eagerly-anticipated major exercises, during which almost the entire squadron deployed north in support of Brigade-level exercises. But after just one famil flight, I found myself participating in a couple of highly irregular tasks that simply didn't fit into *any* of these categories.

* * *

After two weeks back in the Squadron, a three-day task labelled "Sword of Honour" appeared against my name on the OPSROOM tasking board. The OPSO said that the squadron was sending a 'slick' (your garden-variety Iroquois) and a "gunnie" (an Iroquois 'gunship': complete with mini-guns and rocket pods) to participate in (supposedly) an ADF recruiting film that was being shot around Port Macquarie. We were advised to look as "warry" as possible, and so both aircraft were also fitted with M-60 machine guns at the side doors. The other novelty was that we would be staying in a motel that had been booked by the production company. *What luxury!* I felt right at home.

Unsurprisingly, the CO and one of his flight commanders (Squadron Leader Ian 'Tayls' Taylor) would be the two aircraft commanders (with me acting as the CO's copilot for the transit flight down to Port Macquarie). It also became immediately apparent that my navigational skills weren't about to be too seriously tested—we simply took off, overflew Swanbank Power Station, followed its high-tension power lines to the Gold Coast and then flew "coastal" the rest of the way. And this was the way the squadron usually operated: head to the coast and then keep the land either on the right (going south), or on the left (going north). As well as its simplicity, this style of navigation had the added bonus of providing some spectacular views of the coastline as we "belted along" at 500 feet.

Now, 500 feet isn't some arbitrary figure plucked from thin air: it's a limitation set "in stone" as the lowest permissible aircraft operating altitude outside a promulgated Low Flying Area. But once you're accustomed to being at tree-top height, 500 feet feels like a "low earth orbit," and some "old hands" joked that they'd need oxygen if they ever found themselves up at 1,500 feet. So, occasionally, the 500-foot minimum height requirement might become, say, a little...*rubbery*. Our executives regularly warned us, though, that there were hordes of retired senior military officers living in ocean-front Gold Coast apartments, who loved nothing more than to "dob in" illegal low fliers. Not surprisingly, our altimeters usually remained solidly at 500 feet...at least until we'd passed Tweed Heads.

But, even along the lonelier stretches of shoreline, there were still some potential pitfalls for the intrepid aviators of 9 Squadron. One squadron executive had gotten into some serious hot water near Byron Bay when an adventurous young lass (clad only in a bikini top) was thrown from her horse after it was spooked by an Iroquois that she alleged was being flown too low. Her injuries had rendered her incapable of "throwing pots" at the local commune, and so she'd insisted that the Federal Government pay her some hefty compensation. The executive pilot gave evidence under oath that he was no lower than 500 feet, and that he hadn't even been aware of what subsequently became infamous in squadron folklore as "The Bottomless Horse Incident." Afterwards, loadmasters on coastal transits carried binoculars to be "on the lookout for white pointers." But if that was their objective, surely, they should have been looking at the ocean, and not at the people on the beach.

Fortunately, my first coastal expedition passed without incident, and we were checked into our motel by about four-thirty. We immediately changed and headed for the bar where we were soon engaged in conversation with a couple of blokes who said that they were involved in "the shoot." Not being a devotee of Australian soapies, I had no idea that these two guys were, in fact, Andrew Clarke (soon to become Australia's biggest star) and Alan Fletcher (best known for his recurring role on *Neighbours*). But when the diminutive and shapely Tracy Mann slinked through the door to join us, my eyes nearly popped out of my head! Tracy had starred in the Channel 10 soapie, *The Box*, playing a naïve young secretary who worked in undoubtedly the world's most over-sexed television station. Let's just say that I'd been a fan of her past work, and so, the penny dropped that this was no Defence Force recruiting film. Somehow, the producers of a television mini-series had procured the services of two RAAF helicopter crews, all for the sum of two nights' accommodation and a paltry meal allowance.

At dinner time, Tony Rickards (the actor cast in the role of a US military helicopter pilot) joined us to learn all our flying jargon and explore what it was that made "chopper pilots" tick. He soon realised that it was largely alcohol consumption and, when our animated and highly entertaining evening drew to a close all too soon, we were advised by the production team that "Vietnam" was just a few miles north of the airport, and that we should be promptly "on set" just after sunrise. At a little after six the next morning, we quickly located Vietnam, landed in the corner of a large clearing and then began one of the longest "hurry up and wait" experiences of my life.

The set was a veritable hive of activity...except that nothing productive seemed to be getting done. We met the Director, the Assistant Director, the Second Assistant Director and the Third Assistant Director, and noticed that each level of director appeared younger, more subdued and more emaciated than his immediate superior. Bustling about were cast members, costumed extras, cinematography crews, lighting crews, sound crews, make-up artists, pyrotechnic specialists, safety consultants, medical orderlies, costume fitters and set dressers. I counted over seventy people milling about in the early morning sunlight, but still nothing productive seemed to be happening. For the first couple of hours, we were virtually ignored.

Finally, an enormous man with a shaved skull came over and introduced himself as the on-set Safety Supervisor. One of our more observant crew members identified him as a former member of the 1960s and 70s World Championship Wrestling ensemble, which had featured such luminaries as Killer Karl Cox, Mario Milano, Skull Murphy, King Curtis and Gorgeous George. He absolutely beamed at being recognised and was instantly our friend for life, checking up on us regularly and regaling us with hilarious tales of the many characters he'd encountered during a very colourful career. But although he was, without a doubt, one of the funniest and most entertaining people I've ever met, none of us were laughing when he told us that our major contribution wouldn't be happening until around three o'clock in the afternoon. When he shared this news with us, it was about eight-thirty.

More hours of industrious inactivity followed before a female set dresser came over to start getting us ready for our big scene. Since (according to the storyline), we were members of a US Airborne Cavalry unit, both our aircraft had "Flying Tiger" markings applied to their noses, and each of us had a US military patch stitched onto our flying shirts. We were even "muddied up" a little so that we weren't too pristine for the upcoming gruelling battle scene. This final addition was all completely ludicrous, of course, but I couldn't help admiring the production team for their attention to detail.

As we busily practiced our American accents on each other, Tony Rickards appeared on the set, resplendent in a military flying suit and topped off by a black US cavalry officer's hat. RAAF approval had been granted for him to "fly" the aircraft on-camera, and he wanted to discuss what he could say over the interphone to add some authenticity. Noticing how bored I looked watching the endless preparations, Tony took the opportunity to answer the question that I'd put to him the night before—"How do you find the time to learn your lines?"

"Now you know!" he said with a grin and a wink.

Tony took off (with Tayls at the controls) just before lunch but, according to Tayls afterwards, all of the actor's meticulous preparation had come to naught. Confronted with the exhilaration of actually being in an airborne helicopter, all he was capable of doing was chewing gum and looking ahead with a steely gaze.

By mid-afternoon, it was finally time for our big moment in the spotlight. The trouble was, after hours of sitting around, it was surprisingly difficult to get ourselves motivated enough to "commit aviation." Just before we took off, Tayls and the CO discussed some final details with the director, handed him one of our "yellow bricks" (portable UHF radios) and gave him some basic instructions on how to use it. This shot was the pivotal moment of the whole day and, given the logistics and the expense involved, the director was anxious that it all go off without a hitch. After assuring him that we'd do our part, we took off and headed out over the ocean to wait.

After about ten minutes of "drilling holes in the sky," the UHF frequency sprang into life:

"Hello? Hello? Helicopterth?" an unknown, but very "theatrical" voice lisped through our headsets. "*You can come in now!*"

With a broad grin on his face from the decidedly *unmilitary* transmission, Tayls smoothly rolled us out onto a heading that would take us over the clearing in the required direction. Approaching the coast, we started a shallow descent to overfly the clearing at about a hundred feet and then, crossing the edge of the make-believe battlefield, all hell suddenly broke loose. Huge plumes of mud and dirt were hurled suddenly skywards on either side of us, as the explosive charges buried in the swamp detonated in sequence, chasing us from one end of the clearing to the other. From my vantage point, it looked pretty spectacular, and I had no doubts that it would have looked even more impressive on the ground. The problem was, after only about thirty minutes in the air, we were back on the ground and "cooling our heels" once more.

At around five o'clock, things seemed to be finally wrapping up, and as the sun sank towards the horizon, we were asked if we'd mind flying along the coast for a while with the sun setting behind us so that their camera helicopter could shoot some aerial footage for use during the credits. We obliged, of course, and were soon back in the air with the camera helicopter beside us and only about half a rotor disk away. Having him sitting there so close was a little disconcerting at first, but we soon adjusted and then flew up and down the coast…up and down the coast…up and down the coast. After about thirty minutes, we were once again bored rigid.

"What do you reckon? Should I, or shouldn't I?" Stewie, our loadmaster, standing over his machine guns and looking at the camera, enquired over the interphone.

Stewie was a master at what an American would describe as "mooning," but which we more vulgar Aussies would refer to as "chucking a brown-eye." Tayls said, "Sure…why not," and we all turned in our seats to get a better view of the reaction from our nearby friend. Initially, nothing seemed to be happening, but then the aircraft began to wobble about before pulling away sharply and heading off into the distance. "Thanks, guys…you can head back to the airport now if you like," the pilot said with a chuckle over the radio. I can only speculate on whatever became of that footage.

Our big scene had been the final shot at Port Macquarie, and so the film crew held a "wrap party" that night in the motel's function room (to which we scored an invitation). The libations flowed freely, the snacks were plentiful, and the smoke emanating from some of the civvies' cigarettes had a decidedly pungent and unusual aroma. Tracy Mann was the centre of attention, in an impossibly short dress that was so tight that it seemed to have been sprayed on. Around midnight, somebody decided that it would be fun to leap into the motel pool fully clothed, and everyone else immediately followed suit, some whilst seated in a Coles shopping trolley (which still lay submerged the next morning).

As I finally squelched off towards my room for some much-needed sleep, I wished one of the senior members of the production company a good night.

"How much film do you reckon was shot today?" I asked, thinking back over the hours and hours we'd spent sitting around on the set doing nothing.

"Oh! Today was a great day," he replied with enormous enthusiasm. "I reckon we must have got at least *five minutes* of film in the can!"

9
HOW DO YA FEEL?

Monday, November 4th, 1985 began like every other day. Just before 8am, everyone assembled in the Briefing Room and then rose to their feet in unison, as a mark of respect to the incoming squadron executives. A few minutes later, the serial malingerers (who always arrived late) attempted to scuttle into the back of the room unnoticed. As usual, they failed. The first order of business was the day's weather briefing and, seemingly, just like every other day, there was a weak ridge along the coastline that produced an onshore breeze and some afternoon coastal clouds, but little likelihood of rain. Although accurate, I just wondered whether the same forecast was recycled every day.

A succession of mundane announcements followed before Ian Taylor rose purposefully to his feet. Tayls possessed quite a quirky sense of humour but, on this particular morning, he seemed deadly serious. Our growing feelings of disquiet were only heightened when he ordered (more than asked) all non-operational personnel to leave the room. As everybody (except pilots and loadmasters) filed noisily outside, those of us who remained exchanged some furtively raised eyebrows. The pervading feeling of intrigue increased even further when Tayls ordered the door to be closed behind the last of the departing stragglers. "What the hell is going on here?" we muttered quietly to ourselves.

Tayls then opened a side door to admit some imposing-looking chaps who were all dressed in black combat fatigues and carrying side arms. As these new arrivals introduced themselves to the squadron executives, we couldn't help noticing that their black baseball caps were all embroidered with the crest of the Queensland Police Force, with some wags in the audience fearing that their past Mess indiscretions might be about to catch up with them. Tayls then spoke again.

"Gents," he began earnestly, "our visitors here are from the Queensland Police Force. I don't want to get into the specifics just yet, but I can tell you that the squadron will soon be participating in a major operation with the Tactical Response Group and that there'll be an element of risk to everyone involved. Therefore, if there's anybody here who doesn't want to take part, they can leave the room now, and there'll be no questions asked."

What a bombshell to deliver first thing on a Monday morning! The room instantly fell into stunned silence, save for those who were shifting in their seats to see if anyone was going to take Tayls up on his offer. Nobody did, of course, and when he saw that this was the case, Tayls introduced the senior officer from amongst the seated constabulary.

"Gentlemen," our guest intoned, "there's a major drug-growing operation happening in western Queensland, and the State Government has asked for Federal assistance in shutting it down. Canberra has agreed to provide the resources of 9 Squadron for this purpose, however, since this will be a State-sanctioned action, only members of the Queensland Police Force will be carrying firearms. Your squadron executives will give you more information soon but, for now, we have to return to Brisbane. I look forward to working with you all, and I'm confident that this mission will be a complete success."

And with that...they were gone again.

We were told that the crews would be allocated within a few hours and that, since everything we'd already heard was strictly confidential, any programmed participants in the mission should just tell their families that they were about to go on an overnight "bush push." This day was suddenly *anything but* like any other and, with feelings of both excitement and apprehension, most of us adjourned to the crew room to await developments. At around 10am, the pilot who'd been staking out the tasking board walked in and said, "Crews are up" and so, with all the composure we could muster, we walked very briskly down the corridor to the OPSROOM to discover our fate. Jostling for position at the counter separating us from the Ops Room staff, I noticed a black Chino graph pencil line next to my name for the following two days with the simple annotation: "CREW 5".

I was in the very last crew and, because I was still largely untested operationally, I was designated as copilot for Mal Cotterell—a calm and experienced flight lieutenant who conducted the squadron's post-maintenance test flights. I'd heard him on the phone to the engineers sometimes, describing vibrations that he'd felt were "out-of-limits" or "a bit unusual" and could only admire a pilot who was so attuned to his aircraft that he could detect something slightly amiss in a contraption that otherwise handled about as smoothly as an old utility hurtling along a corrugated dirt road.

Back in the crew room, those who were going on the mission seemed a little keyed-up and nervous, while those who weren't, seemed disappointed (although their disappointment might have been tinged with just a hint of relief). 9 Squadron had earned its reputation flying into "hot LZs" in Vietnam and now, I suspect, some of us were wondering whether we could live up to that legacy of coolness under fire. By afternoon, though, I was feeling a little more fatalistic. "Whatever will be, will be," was how Mum countered Dad's constant worrying, and that advice seemed particularly relevant here. Everybody in the military expects to be put in harm's way at some point: I just never expected my "moment of truth" to come on a police drug raid in western Queensland. When I got home that night, I told my father-in-law that my flight the next day would probably make the news, but I also swore him to secrecy.

The next morning, the squadron was a hive of activity and, just after lunch, the mission crews were assembled for a preliminary briefing. After loading our passengers, we would be heading off in a loose five-ship formation to refuel at Oakey, before proceeding to our overnight staging post—"Point Alpha," an isolated clearing about sixty miles south of Charleville. The detailed mission briefing would take place there that evening, and the raid would kick off at first light the following morning.

The first thing I noticed at the flight line afterwards was that the mission aircraft had all been fitted with bulky, armour-plated pilot seats. With their thick steel seat-pans and side panels, these uncomfortable seats would protect us from gunfire that originated from every direction except directly ahead of us. Therefore, on the raid, we would also be wearing "chicken plate"—half-inch-thick, steel bullet-proof vests—to protect our torsos. Only our heads encased within our fibreglass flying helmets, and our other most delicate of organs would remain exposed... so to speak.

As we prepared the aircraft for departure, our passengers arrived and began loading their equipment onboard. They were dressed similarly to their colleagues from the previous morning and exuded an air of quiet confidence and professionalism. They also seemed to be loading enough ammunition to re-stage the D-Day landings. Mal offered one of them the opportunity to sit in the jump seat and chat with us over the intercom as we headed west to Point Alpha. Shortly afterwards, we departed in a noisy formation for Oakey, via an initial over-flight of Toowoomba. The Great Dividing Range lies about sixty miles west of Amberley, but so steep is the escarpment approaching Toowoomba, it's like flying towards the vast overgrown battlements of an immense, stone fortress. When a moist onshore breeze hits this escarpment, it cools rapidly during its precipitous climb, and its water vapour can sometimes condense to form a thick blanket of mist and cloud that obscures the lip of the range.

Such was the case on this particular afternoon and, to continue west, there was little option but to split up the formation, climb into the cloud individually and proceed under the Instrument Flight Rules. To assist with terrain avoidance, we could tune our ADF to the Toowoomba NDB, climb to an altitude 1,000 feet above the terrain, and then fly towards the NDB. We could then continue on instruments towards Oakey if required, until we were once again in visual conditions.

Trouble was, as the lead aircraft climbed up into the misty overcast and disappeared from view, the needle on our ADF steadfastly refused to point towards the nearby Toowoomba NDB. We then relayed this information to the leader, who confirmed that there was no alternative but to "go IMC." The rest of the formation would press on for now, and listen out for us later on the squadron UHF frequency. We were relieved not to have been "scrubbed," and so set course back to Amberley at top speed.

We were expecting a lengthy repair but, instead, the groundies just pulled out the ADF control box, found that it had become unplugged somehow, re-connected the leads and, voila, we were "good to go." Nevertheless, we were now over an hour behind the others and would be hard-pressed to reach our destination by nightfall. Approaching the Great Dividing Range for the second time, our ADF needle pointed unerringly towards the Toowoomba NDB, and so we climbed up into the cloud, passed over the city and then encountered clearer skies to the west. After a quick refuel in Oakey, we began to relax a little and started chatting to our passenger about the upcoming mission. "I'm a sniper," he said, "So I don't think I'll be playing a very big part in things." Naturally, we asked him about his accuracy, and he told us that he could hit his target to within a half-inch..."over a range of two hundred metres" he added as an afterthought.

As the miles rolled by, the countryside grew progressively less inhabited, with the sun, finally tiring of its onerous duty, slowly sinking towards the undulating horizon ahead. GPS was still a long way off in 1985, and navigating purely via the "Mark One Eyeball" and a topographic map was becoming increasingly difficult in the glare of the setting sun. With the Terminator—the imaginary line delineating daylight and darkness—relentlessly creeping up from behind, I needed to look closer and closer to the aircraft's nose to find any landmarks at all in the almost-featureless plains below. Finally, the sun slipped below the horizon and I found myself "navigating sideways" by looking outside to see where we'd just been rather than where we were going. Inevitably, the Terminator overtook us and, with map-reading now impossible, our only option was to climb up to a safe altitude and proceed via the comfortingly-named process of Dead Reckoning. "DR" involves reaching your intended point by flying a known track at a given airspeed for a set amount of time. As twilight faded into darkness, I calculated that we were still about forty miles (twenty minutes) away from the elusive Point Alpha.

For SAR operations, our Iroquois had all been fitted with UHF Direction Finding (UHF/DF) whereby tuning into a UHF radio transmission and selecting UHF/DF resulted in the ADF needle pointing in the direction of the radio transmission's source. In the hope of getting a bearing to Point Alpha, I began calling up the other aircraft on the squadron UHF frequency...but my initial calls went unanswered. A few minutes later, though, we spotted a pool of lights on the ground and started to think that we may have found our colleagues without even needing the UHF/DF. Mal began a gradual descent towards them, and at about a hundred feet, turned on the aircraft's powerful searchlight... brilliantly illuminating a remote farmhouse in a blinding shaft of light. He immediately switched the light off again and climbed back up to resume the search, but I've always wondered how that farmer felt, and how many years he bored his friends with tales of his Close Encounter.

Just as we began to think that we might have to spend a lonely night by ourselves in a nearby paddock, we heard a familiar voice calling us on the squadron frequency and were able to finally get a bearing on their position. Ahead of us, we could see their red and green navigation lights on the ground and, when Mal turned on his searchlight this time, we were relieved to see four other Iroquois helicopters parked in a large grassy clearing. We had finally arrived at Point Alpha. After being greeted with a cheery, "Bout time you lazy bastards got here," we took a moment to look around and take in the impressive array of military assets that had been assembled for this mission. Apart from the five Iroquois, there were also two Chinook helicopters that had ferried out the fuel that was now being pumped into our aircraft. The darkened clearing was crisscrossed by a web of refuelling hoses and electrical cables, as the groundies tended to their charges and "put them to bed."

With all his crews finally present, the CO was now keen to get the final briefing underway. We all huddled together around a flashlight-illuminated whiteboard to examine an aerial photograph of the 'target area' that had been snapped by the side-looking cameras of a photo-reconnaissance F-111 aircraft. Concealed amidst the scrubby countryside in the black-and-white image was a large circular crop of densely-concentrated shrubs, with two nearby buildings—a storage shed and a makeshift irrigation pumping station. Three aircraft, we were told, would assault the shed—the 'primary LZ,' while one aircraft would attack the pumping station (the 'secondary LZ,' which was believed to be unoccupied). The fifth aircraft (with the CO in command) would serve as an aerial 'command and control' (C-and-C) platform to coordinate things, and liaise with the police units that would move in once the LZs had been secured. "It will also be used for medical evacuations to Roma Hospital," we were informed matter-of-factly, "if any casualties occur during the attack."

According to police intelligence, the onsite "farmers" were heavily armed and, since they were also believed to have 'scramblers' tuned in to the police frequencies, the mission would be flown in strict radio silence. The authorities had been given a copy of our confidential flight plan for the mission and, while the raid was underway, no radio transmissions would take place with anybody—either ATC or any other aircraft within the formation. The element of surprise would be our main weapon, and Point Alpha was situated far enough away from the target area to both avoid suspicion and prevent any aircraft noise from reaching the offenders until the last moment. While five Iroquois would indeed create a hell of a racket, it was hoped that by hitting the objectives simultaneously just after dawn, the offenders would be caught off-guard and thus be incapable of resisting arrest. That was the plan, anyway. Mal and I were designated as #3 ("Tail-end Charlie") for the primary LZ, while Gumby's crew would be hitting the secondary LZ.

By this point, I was feeling pretty drained and decided to "hit the hay" just as soon as the briefing ended. Although our clearing was now home to a mini canvas city, I didn't feel like pitching a tent and, instead, just claimed some vacant floor space in the back of one of the big Chinook helicopters. In my sleeping bag on the floor, I soon drifted into an uncomfortable, dream-filled sleep during which, hourly (it seemed), my internal wake-up service roused me to ensure that I wouldn't sleep in. At 4am, I gave up, rolled out of my sleeping bag and began my morning ablutions: a dry shave and a change into a fresh flying suit. I then checked out of the Hotel Chinook and mingled with the other light sleepers who were milling about in the pre-dawn gloom. It promised to be a momentous day, but I didn't feel fearful, worried or even nervous, really...I just felt hyper-alert and very impatient for things to get started. It was almost a relief when word came down that the mission was still "GO" and that it was now time to start pre-flighting the aircraft.

With the eastern skies brightening slightly, we used torches to inspect our aircraft before donning the bulky "chicken plate" and settling again into the uncomfortable, armour-plated seats. Our passengers, clad all in black (balaclavas, bullet-proof vests and combat fatigues), were an intimidating sight, and carried assorted weaponry that included sniper rifles, pump-action shotguns, sub-machineguns and M16 fully automatic assault rifles. For the first time in my short military career, the passengers in my aircraft would have live ammunition "up the spout"...and they were primed and ready to use it!

Just after 5am, there was enough pre-dawn twilight for us to clearly distinguish the features of the nearby vegetation and terrain. On a cue from the lead aircraft, a thumbs-up signal was passed up and down the line to signify that we were ready to go. The lead aircraft then gave the "wind-up" signal for engine start, and the pre-dawn silence was shattered as five Lycoming jet engines burst into life. With Mal at the controls, we lifted into a hover and then, after another succession of thumbs-up signals, rolled in unison with the others, up and out of Point Alpha to head at low level towards our targets.

The skies lightened steadily as the treetops flashed by below us during the twenty-minute transit to the target area. In sharp contrast to the typical Hollywood-style bravado, all aboard Iroquois A2-773 were quiet, as both passengers and crew alike silently contemplated what might lie in store for us at the LZ. Would we catch the "enemy" by surprise, or would they be ready and waiting? Cosseted in my heavy chicken plate, it all just felt so *surreal*.

With a minute to go, we flew up a gently rising escarpment and passed over a perpendicular red dirt road, signifying that our targets were now just a couple of miles ahead. "One minute," I announced over the interphone as I snatched a brief glimpse of the dozens of police vehicles that were awaiting their cue to move in after the attack. We then bunched up tightly for the assault and, after identifying the secondary LZ to the right, I saw the clearing coming up ahead that was to be our target. When the lead aircraft began to slow and descend towards the LZ, I knew that we would be at our most vulnerable when we passed back through translational lift (with our nose up and our belly exposed at low speed). Crossing the tree line and slowing to land, we saw that the LZ was quite confined and that we would have to move to the right to find enough space in which to land. We were now sitting ducks.

But all on the pad seemed quiet. There were no "bad guys" or muzzle flashes, and just as soon as our skids were on the ground, the loadmaster yelled "GO" to the coppers and they were gone...in a heartbeat. Mal then hauled up on the collective and we rocketed back into the air, up and away from the LZ at high speed and low level. We'd completed our mission and had come through unscathed! Now it was just a matter of listening out on the C-and-C frequency for news of what was happening on the ground. What we didn't yet know was that it was the primary LZ that was unoccupied and that all the bad guys had been sleeping in the pump house. When Gumby's aircraft had astonishingly materialised in their backyard, two of the "baddies" had looked outside to see some very scary dudes in black running towards them carrying machine guns, and had decided to make a run for it. On the way out, they released their attack dog but were dismayed to see it felled instantly by one of the advancing coppers with a couple of instinctive shots fired from the hip.

On their way out of the secondary LZ, Gumby's crew were watching the escape attempt unfold and weren't sure whether the TRG troopers had yet noticed their hasty departure. As they circled overhead the fleeing criminals, Gumby's captain, in a moment of divine inspiration, said to his crew, "Make it look like you've got guns!" So, re-living their misspent childhoods, Gumby and his loadmaster pointed their flying-glove-clad index and middle finger "pistols" at the bad guys...who promptly stopped, raised their arms in surrender and were immediately waved back towards the waiting constabulary. The other offenders were arrested where they lay. Word duly reached us that the LZs were secure, with a rising cloud of dust indicating that the police vehicles were now on the move to assume control of the site and begin the formal process of collecting evidence and taking statements. Passing over the secondary LZ briefly, we could see all the bad guys (with hands now cuffed) lying spread-eagled, face-down in the dirt as the attentive TRG troopers rested their gun muzzles on the backs of their heads. Shortly afterwards, we were all ordered back to the primary LZ.

After landing and shutting down, I watched as one of the offenders was led past us in handcuffs. In 1985, a very successful TV advertising campaign featured one bloke asking his mate, "How do ya' feel?" before tossing him an ice-cold can of Tooheys. While bloke #2 proceeded to pour the icy brew down his throat, the iconic jingle sang in reply, "I feel like a Tooheys! I feel like a Tooheys! I feel like a Tooheys...or two!" As the restrained baddie trudged dejectedly past our aircraft, I noticed that he was wearing a Tooheys promotional tee-shirt, and on the back was emblazoned that famous slogan—"How do ya' feel?" I could only imagine how he was feeling at that particular moment and guessed that it would be quite some time before he enjoyed another can of the sponsor's product.

With great relief, we removed our constrictive chicken plate and mingled with the other crews to exchange pleasantries and reflect on the events of the morning. Naturally, Gumby's crew was the centre of attention as they regaled all and sundry with their tale of single-handedly accounting for two of the bad guys. As we listened, we were all a bit distracted by the acres of leafy marijuana plants swaying gently in the breeze nearby. There must have been thousands of them, and each one was about the height of a full-grown adult. I'd never seen a marijuana plant before, but the sophistication of the plantation's irrigation system attested to the street value of the ugly plants on the drug market. Their seizure would be a huge coup for the Queensland Police Force.

Mal and I were given one final task before returning to Point Alpha: flying a police photographer over the site so that he could record every detail of it on film for use in any upcoming criminal trials. Moving from vantage point to vantage point, our powerful rotor wash whipped the plants around violently and stirred up an overpoweringly pungent aroma. After twenty minutes or so, I started to experience a mild headache...and a dawning realisation that flying was *reaaaaally groooooooovy, baaaaaaaby!* The other crewmembers admitted to feeling similarly, and we thought that if we didn't get out of there soon, we'd all be a lot higher than the Iroquois that we were flying around in.

At Point Alpha, we saw for ourselves just how happy the coppers were with the mission. They were simply over the moon! Thrilled! Rapt! But they just had one small problem: they'd brought along a ton of ammunition and, to this point, they'd expended precisely *two* rounds. "Well," said their senior officer, "we signed out all this ammo...

it'd be silly not to use it." And so, an impromptu "Yippee Shoot" was soon underway with four RAAFies (in rotation) firing every weapon in the TRG arsenal, while four policemen re-loaded the magazines just as quickly as they were being expended. Even so, it took nearly forty minutes for us to exhaust their ammunition supply. Any stray bushwalker passing by would have wondered what the hell was going on.

In hindsight, not wearing any hearing protection for the shoot was probably a bit of a miscalculation. We always wore earmuffs on the rifle range, but who wanted to look like a wimp in front of the TRG? In *Combat*, Sergeant Saunders hadn't worn bright-orange headphones when he accounted for about ten thousand German soldiers in World War II! So, as we prepared to depart for Amberley, our ears rang like banshees, and we realised that any combat soldier with frontline infantry service must have been as deaf as a post by the time he turned forty.

Fortunately, our ears were back in working order by the time we all watched the news bulletin together in the 9 Squadron crew room later. Liquid refreshments had been chilled for our arrival, and spirits were running high in the Mutual Admiration Society that now existed between the 9 Squadron helicopter crews and the troopers of the Queensland TRG. Cheers rang out as we watched the news report on the raid and saw the uniformed policemen uprooting the ugly plants. The newsreader reported that the plantation was nearly ten acres in area and that the *fifteen thousand* marijuana plants had an estimated street value of *twenty million* dollars...a truly staggering sum in 1985!

I didn't linger long at the celebrations, though, because I couldn't wait to tell Tracy and her parents all about the excitement of the last two days. If truth be told, I also didn't completely trust the coppers not to have tipped off their mates to set up a breathalyser just outside the base.

"Was that you on the big drug raid today?" my father-in-law (an avid news watcher) asked when I walked through the front door about an hour later.

And with that, I told my tale of the last forty-eight hours—the defective ADF needle, the farmer's close encounter, the Hotel Chinook, the drug raid, "how do ya' feel?", groovy baby, the Yippee Shoot...

everything. I tried to explain how it felt to be encased in body armour and deliberately flying into a situation where you might get shot. The experience had given me just the slightest inkling of what it must have been like for the helicopter crews in Vietnam and made me admire them even more for putting themselves in harm's way nearly every single time they flew. After listening to all these stories, and with me now almost hoarse, Tracy (a real animal lover) gave her response:

"THEY SHOT THE DOG?!"

10
PERILS IN PARADISE

So, within six weeks of returning from Fairbairn, I could already have been either blown up at Port Macquarie or shot down at Charleville, but even more excitement lay in store before year's end. The skies over Papua New Guinea are amongst the most challenging aviation environments in the world, due to the country's unpredictable weather, inhospitable terrain and rudimentary infrastructure. Its location on the southern boundary of the relentlessly active "Ring of Fire" also makes it extremely vulnerable to catastrophic natural events such as earthquakes, tsunamis and volcanic eruptions.

Papua New Guinea was a mandated territory of Australia until its independence in 1975, but it continues to rely heavily on Australia for financial and administrative support. In the 1980s, the Australian Defence Force was expected to respond quickly if a natural disaster struck in PNG and, owing to their ability to reach even the most inaccessible regions of the country, the 9 Squadron Iroquois were a particularly valuable resource. Commonwealth funding was provided, therefore, to enable the unit to conduct practice deployments on "Tropical Trainers" every year, and let our crews gain some invaluable flying experience in this forbidding environment. Each RAAF C-130 could transport a partially disassembled Iroquois airframe within its cargo hold, and despite a Herc's pedestrian cruising speed, deploying in this way was still far quicker than 9 Squadron deploying under its own steam. Therefore, when the 1985 Tropical Trainer crews departed Amberley in mid-November for Mount Hagen (high in the mountainous spine of the PNG Highlands), we found ourselves rather reluctantly onboard the four Hercules transports that ferried our charges northwards.

Since the engine noise within the cabin of a C-130 renders any conversation virtually impossible, there was ample opportunity during the flight north to read, sleep and ponder the experiences that might await us over the next fortnight. My brother had visited Rabaul in the mid-1970s, and his tales of American bomber wrecks dotted along the coastline and decaying Japanese fighter planes lying in the lush New Guinea jungles conjured up images akin to some black-and-white movie from the 1940s. In contrast, my New Guinea experiences to date had been limited to overnight stopovers in the Port Moresby Travelodge—a far cry from roughing it with the natives up in the Highlands.

Before leaving Amberley, we'd received some classroom instruction on the unique challenges that are present when flying in high density altitudes over unforgiving terrain in tropical weather. Since our aircraft would not be fitted with supplemental oxygen, we'd be limited to 10,000 feet above sea level—a problem when flying around terrain that soars to well over 13,000 feet in places. Other light aircraft were similarly restricted, and so the valleys that offered safe passage through the ranges were well-known and well-used. The concentration of aircraft at these choke points had led to the creation of discrete VHF "gap frequencies" that allowed pilots to announce themselves and enquire whether the gap in question was still open. Transiting these areas was appropriately known as "gap flying."

Although the Iroquois performed reasonably well at sea level in mild temperatures, the high altitude and oppressive heat of the PNG Highlands meant that OGE hover capability wouldn't be available for the majority of every flight. At such times, we would be as vulnerable to getting caught under lowering cloud in a narrow valley as our fixed-wing cousins. Therefore, whenever approaching a gap, we were advised to fly along one edge of the valley at a height that would enable us to see the ground on the other side of the gap. If we were able to do so, we could proceed...but if we couldn't, we were then in a good position to "chuck a one-eighty." As a sensible precaution, the roof of each of our deploying helicopters had been painted white to make them more visible to search aircraft if they ended up in the jungle somewhere. A sensible precaution, no doubt...but hardly reassuring!

During our pre-deployment preparation, we'd also each prepared a laminated topographic map of the Mount Hagen area which, due to the orange shading applied to the more mountainous terrain, was dubbed "The Yellow Peril." We would also carry larger-scale maps that would enable us to navigate by individual roads or creek lines if ever the visibility became particularly poor. Two weeks before our departure, we also commenced our 'prophylaxis' of anti-malarial medication—primaquine and chloroquine (derivatives of quinine) tablets—that wouldn't prevent us from contracting malaria, but would keep the parasites dormant within us until we'd completed an 'eradication course' upon our return. Being keen to avoid the joys of malaria, I faithfully adhered to my prophylaxis every day.

Joining us were two QHIs from 35 Squadron, one of whom had "permanently parked" two Iroquois in the PNG jungle. I guess the rationale for his presence was so that he could teach us how to avoid what had happened to him. "Duffy" was an imposing character—tall and wiry with narrowed eyes, a shock of ginger hair, and a bristling red moustache. You could easily visualise him as a marauding Scottish Highlander or a savage Viking raider in a previous life. In the helicopter world, he was also a bit of a legend for having achieved his gunship command in Vietnam whilst still a teenager. After the war ended, a rice paddy was established near Cooktown to employ the Vietnamese "boat people" who were arriving regularly in Australia. Duffy had seen them all at work one day (complete with "coolie hats") and, in what he claimed later was a "flashback," he simply couldn't resist rolling in on them in his Iroquois for a low-level "beat up." The sound of the helicopter must have also given the refugees flashbacks because they all reportedly dived into the water in every direction.

Duffy had mellowed a little since then, but he still maintained a rugged individuality, with a very distinctive catchcry—a gruffly bellowed, "AAAAARRRRFFFF." By way of an example:

Briefing Officer: "Are there any questions?"

Duffy: "AAAAARRRRFFFF!"

We could also quickly tell which aircraft Duffy was in on a formation flight.

Formation leader: "Albatross Wheeler...check."

Formation Aircraft: "Wheeler Two...Three...AAAAARRRRFFFF!"

We began our descent into Hagen in the mid-afternoon and, after landing, the Herc boys were keen to enlist some locals to help them unload their aircraft so that they could get going again before nightfall. The "Paps," apparently, were happy to help manhandle the disassembled helicopters *out* of the C-130s—mother bird gives birth to baby bird—but if it came to putting an Iroquois back *into* a C-130, the locals wanted nothing to do with it. Fortunately for the Herc crews, we would be flying our own aircraft home at the end of the deployment. Activity around Hagen airport must have been the "hot ticket in town" because, as we stiffly walked out onto the tarmac and removed our earplugs, we noticed that the perimeter fence was already jam-packed with local spectators standing about six deep in places. One of the C-130 loadmasters assured us that not even being showered with stones by the Herc's propwash on departure would be enough to disperse them later.

After clearing Customs and Immigration, we set off for our accommodation in the hired vans that would be used for transport every day. Our home for the next week was the Plumes and Arrows Motel—a large central building (housing the kitchens and the dining room) and a collection of outlying guest rooms (each of which resembled a native hut, complete with thatched grass roof). The entire complex was surrounded by a formidable wooden stockade, and the owner (an expatriate Australian) met us as soon as we arrived to explain a few unique aspects of his establishment.

"The front gate closes at 6pm sharp," he said bluntly, "and we let the Rottweilers loose at 10. Wherever you find yourself at 10pm, I'd recommend you stay there!"

With dinner time approaching, he told us to allow plenty of time for meals—"things move at a different pace up here." He also explained the need for the imposing wooden fence around the motel's perimeter. "The locals here are a lazy pack of bastards," he said in a blunt assessment of his staff. "Every year, I sack the lot of 'em and hire a new bunch. The old lot then go into town, get on the p*ss, and come back here later to try to burn down the place by firing flaming arrows over the fence." At this news, we all hoped that his firing/hiring cycle didn't fall due during our stay.

Gumby and I shared a room and, at that very first dinner, we discovered exactly what the manager meant about the meal times—it took an hour for our entrées to arrive after we'd ordered them. I was starving by this point, but couldn't help admiring the presentation of my prawn cocktail. The prawns were served in a huge conch shell resting in a thick bed of fresh salad. How fresh? Well, after resisting the urge to quickly scoff the lot, I noticed that there seemed to be some movement in the greenery and, upon closer examination, discovered a live caterpillar. Not surprisingly, the squadron executives warned us afterwards to always carry a roll of toilet paper with us whenever we went flying, just in case something we'd eaten the night before "came back to bite us."

After a day off (during which the groundies re-assembled the aircraft), we all returned to the airfield to practice and then demonstrate proficiency in high-altitude autos. Mount Hagen airport sits just over five thousand feet AMSL and, given the high ambient temperatures, we were effectively flying autos at eight thousand feet. If a helicopter fell to earth in a normal auto...at Hagen it didn't so much fall as *plummet*. When my turn came, it was just a matter of hanging on for the ride and, having survived, I joined the others who, with great relief, lounged around in canvas chairs, grading the latest hair-raising attempts with large cardboard scorecards. A quick local familiarisation flight followed in the afternoon, and we were then qualified to experience everything that PNG could throw at us.

Over the next week, I visited numerous places including Mendi, Baiyer, Goroka, Tabubil (site of the Ok Tedi mine) and Kopiago. I flew with several different pilots but, since Gumby and Duffy were both big personalities, they usually seemed to fly together. After returning from their first sortie, Duffy dubbed his copilot "Vasco da Gumby" and later just shortened that to "Vasco." The briefing facilities at Hagen were pretty basic, but we didn't truly need any forecasts because the tropical weather pattern rarely changed—humid cloudy mornings, with showers and storms in the afternoon that abated by evening. In a 707, you could fly above the weather, but in an Iroquois, you had to fly *under* it, with the arrival of gusty winds often being the first hint of an approaching thunderstorm and accompanying wall of leaden grey rain. Of more interest were the local Notices to Airmen (NOTAMs), which occasionally featured some airfield closures due to "warring natives." The Highlands were so rugged (and so densely vegetated), that the cleared airstrips were the most convenient venues for opposing clans to get together for a clear shot at each other with their spears and arrows.

"Situational Awareness" (SA)—the ability to perceive, understand, and respond to your situation—was an absolute necessity in the Highlands and of paramount importance was knowing your aircraft's hover capability (OGE or IGE only) and its location at all times. On every flight, we calculated the weight at which we'd be able to hover OGE, as well as the corresponding amount of fuel remaining at that point. Mal Cotterell recounted a previous deployment where he'd just achieved OGE performance before getting trapped in a narrow valley by a torrential downpour. With the visibility down to just a few metres, he'd had to hover just above the treetops for over twenty minutes and was completely exhausted afterwards.

Accurate navigation was also crucial since weather diversions in PNG were commonplace and the consequences of becoming "geographically embarrassed" over rugged terrain could be fatal. This point was amply demonstrated early one morning when, while flying along a valley under lowering skies, we realised that we could soon be at risk of encountering a dead end. We backtracked while we could, found a large hole in the cloud, and climbed above the weather to proceed 'VMC on top' (visual conditions above cloud). As the navigating pilot, I calculated an appropriate heading to steer and ran a stopwatch to keep track of how far we'd travelled. After about ten minutes of nothing but clouds below us, we saw another gap in the clouds approaching, and I advised the captain to descend visually down through it. After doing so, I was enormously relieved to see a dirt road right where I expected it to be—this is still the only time that I ever had to rely *purely* on 'heading and airspeed.'

But despite the workload, there was the occasional opportunity to just sit back and admire the stunning, unspoiled beauty of the countryside around us. My most prominent memory is of flying along the Strickland Gorge one afternoon on the way back to Mount Hagen. As we hugged one side of the valley (at about seven thousand feet), I could see the silver thread of the Strickland River, stoically winding its way through the rugged landscape thousands of feet below us. From the base of this rocky riverbed, the terrain rose steeply up into mountain ranges on either side, with unseen cloud-covered peaks towering thousands of feet above us. It truly was an unforgettable sight.

Suffering an engine failure in the gorge would have been disastrous, but there were also other perils lurking unseen in PNG that could be equally catastrophic. One afternoon, we were returning to Hagen when the captain decided to fly a pinnacle approach to the lip of an extinct, almost-conical volcano. The weather was fine, but the wind must have been stronger than we thought because, at about a hundred feet, we hit the demarcation line. With the aircraft being tossed about in the turbulent downdrafts, the captain hauled up on the collective to arrest our alarming descent rate, and we skimmed over the lip of the mountain by about twenty feet. There was quite a protracted silence afterwards before the loadie said, "Ummm...let's not do that again, shall we?"

Much more interesting (and far less scary) were our occasional encounters with the native population. Despite the seeming remoteness, if we were loitering anywhere in our helicopter, we'd be instantly surrounded by locals who'd materialised from nowhere. One afternoon, we'd landed and shut down in a jungle clearing to wait for some weather to pass and by the time the loadie had secured the rotor blade, we'd been encircled by an audience of about fifty natives, with the male members all resplendent in "arse grass and feathers." Thankfully, they just seemed curious, but since they spoke no English, we could only communicate our friendliness by smiling and waving. Frankly, the little Pidgin we knew rendered the language a little comical—for example, Prince Charles' official title at the time was "nambawan pikinini bilong Mises Kwin" and South Pacific beer was "bia bilong yu me."

When it came time to get airborne again, our communication difficulties presented a bit of a problem. Head-hunting had long been forbidden, of course, so we were far more concerned about them losing their heads if they stood too close to our rotor blades when we started up the engine. As tempting as it was to try saying, "Big pela fan chop off head bilong yu," ultimately, we just got our big, scary loadmaster to chase them all away. On subsequent flights, we took along spare chocolate bars, lollies and fruit juice poppers that our loadies would toss down to the kids who quickly gathered whenever we went into a hover over a clearing somewhere. After a few days, I felt less like a pilot and more like an aerial anthropologist who'd travelled back in time to study an ancient native culture.

On our final night in Hagen, the squadron executives decided to hold an impromptu dining-in night in the hotel's conference room, with the manager and his wife attending as our official guests. An amateur talent night was scheduled to both liven up the festivities and fill in the interminable intervals between courses. Therefore, a few of us rookies got together to form the Boggie's Tubercular Choir, and perform a musical tribute to our PNG experiences so far. Having survived a week of demanding flying, we were all in fine spirits and after the main course had been served, we performed our number, which plagiarised the "Come on Aussie" jingle, but with original lyrics:

> It's been a long hot summer,
> and PNG's a bummer,
> but that's the way it's got to be.
> When you're stuck up on Mount Hagen,
> with no power margin,
> and the QFI is blaming it on me...
> Come on boggies, come on, come on.
> Come on boggies, come on.
> The groundies are all hiding in their tent,

> because the f***ing Iroquois are bent.
> Now we're all really trying,
> to keep ourselves from dying...
> Mal Cotterell's nerves are very nearly spent.
> Come on boggies etc...

The remaining verses pilloried all and sundry at a lively tempo before we reverted to a slower pace for the final, introspective verse:

> Now there are only seven days to go,
> before we head to Aussie down below.
> The odds are nine-to-five,
> that we'll make it home alive,
> but then again you never really know...
> Come on boggies etc...

Sure, it wasn't *Stairway to Heaven* but, undoubtedly, we were the stars of the show, at least by our reckoning. The celebrations continued until long after the Rottweilers had been released, but I took an early mark because, the next day, I'd be navigating the lead aircraft of our four-ship formation that, heavily laden, was bound for Madang on the northern coastline—our base for the next four days.

I was far more comfortable with visual navigation by this stage but, since we'd be without OGE performance for the first half of the flight, turning up a wrong valley could (quite literally) be a dead-end. On the hour-long flight the next morning, I "track crawled" on the map for the first fifteen minutes—tracking the progress of the aircraft every second of the way—before I directed the pilot to turn down a valley that would ultimately take us out of the Highlands. The "yellow peril" of the mountains gave way to the browner shading of the foothills and then, finally, the green-shaded coastal plain that extended on towards our destination. When we arrived at Madang Airport, we saw that a 12 Squadron Chinook was there as well and learnt from its crew that night that they were recovering the wreckage of World War II-era Boston bombers so that one could be restored for static display. An infamous wartime raid had resulted in most of the participating Bostons being lost due to either enemy action or fuel starvation, and their decaying hulks littered the northern coastline.

My first sortie from Madang was a coastal return flight to Siassi during which, whilst belting along the shoreline at 500 feet, I just couldn't help but be blown away by the area's breathtaking natural beauty. The Bismarck Sea that gently lapped onto the sandy coast was crystal clear, with the ocean floor visible below the outrigger canoes of the local fishermen. Gently swaying coconut palms provided valuable food, as well as some badly-needed shade for the grass huts that (elevated on stilts) housed the local villagers. Whenever we flew by one of these idyllic spots, the locals would smile and wave, and their kids would chase us along the beach as far as they could. Tragically, a tsunami devastated this region in 1998, killing thousands, and, on hearing this news, I could only think back again to these happy, friendly people and their picturesque, tranquil little hamlets.

I associate funnier memories with a "stream navex" (navigation exercise) that I flew to Lae on the 2nd of December. Four aircraft were planned to follow the same route just a few minutes apart but, as one of the pilots in the lead aircraft, it soon became obvious that the other crews were regarding this exercise more as a race. The second aircraft in the stream was valiantly trying to overtake us when we saw it bank abruptly to the left and start descending towards a large, coastal clearing. We called them up on the radio to make sure that they were okay and they responded with, "Just an urgent call of nature for the loadie! We'll see you on the ground in Lae." When they did so a little later, their loadie recounted for us his unique experiences of the morning.

"About fifteen minutes after we took off, I started to get this cramping pain in my guts," he said, "and I was really glad that I had my emergency roll of dunny paper with me."

There was only one nearby clearing that looked big enough to accommodate an Iroquois and, despite the approach being flown expeditiously (through necessity), by the time they'd landed, the inevitable crowd of curious locals had already assembled. The loadie (toilet paper in hand), then leapt out of the aircraft and raced desperately for the trees, pursued by the throng of intrigued spectators. "It's the only time I've ever taken a 'dump' with an audience," said the loadie, laughing and shaking his head at the memory. One day, an anthropologist may well discover a tribe on the north coast of PNG whose folklore includes the tale of an enormous grasshopper that landed next to them one day and disgorged a strange, green man who ran off and crapped in their bamboo!

That night, a number of us were guests of the Middleton family on Kar Kar Island, where they'd established a copra plantation over fifty years earlier. The island is dominated by a towering volcano, and the family's patriarch, an amateur vulcanologist, had requested that one of our aircraft give him a lift into the very caldera of the mountain to make some observations—a flight I was quite content *not* to be on. Instead, some of my colleagues and I spent the afternoon drinking tea with Mrs Middleton in the grand plantation house. As we sat chatting, a plainly exhausted and very muddy dog stumbled

into the room and plopped down onto the polished wooden floor. The lady of the house explained that all the bitches on the island had been in heat that week and that she hadn't seen her dog in five days. If a dog can smile, that filthy pooch was positively beaming as he lay there, eyes closed, panting away and contentedly recuperating on the cool timber floorboards.

The next afternoon, we headed back up to Hagen to pack up our gear for the long commute home via stopovers in Weipa and Townsville. The three-day journey would commence with a rather disconcerting hour-long overwater flight from Daru to Thursday Island, during which our eyes were glued to the "chip" lights throughout. Both the engine and the transmission were fitted with these warning lights to indicate a buildup of metallic fragments in the oil supply that could precede a failure. The advice from the old hands was to climb as high as possible over Torres Strait for an engine chip light (to stretch the auto if the engine failed) and to descend to just above sea level for a transmission chip light (so that, if the transmission then failed, the crash might just be survivable).

Fortunately, we all arrived back at Amberley unscathed on the 6th of December and immediately commenced our high-dosage Malaria Eradication Courses. By New Year's Eve, I was feeling decidedly unwell and, by mid-afternoon, I'd developed a raging fever. The RAAF advised me to proceed immediately to the Yeronga Army Hospital but, when I tried to stand, the floor simply tilted beneath me and then rose to rest (not so gently) against my cheek. I had to be half-dragged/half-carried to my father-in-law's car, and I can say with absolute certainty that I have never felt worse in my life. I have no memory of being admitted to the hospital and, when my fever finally broke that night, it was like I'd been drenched with a fire hose. A quick shower, some fresh clothes and a change of bed linen had me feeling much better though, and I gratefully accepted a glass of champagne from one of the nurses when it was kindly offered at midnight. I was discharged the next day, and the family were somewhat peeved when they discovered that I was the only one of us who'd seen in the New Year properly. My condition had only been a reaction to the medication, and so I've never had any desire whatsoever to experience what "real malaria" might be like.

From the snows of Moscow in March to the heat of the PNG Highlands in December, 1985 had certainly been a helluva year.

11
TACTICAL OPERATIONS

Tragically, 1986 got off to a horrendous start when I awoke on the morning of the 29th of January to the news that the space shuttle Challenger had exploded on takeoff, with the loss of all seven crewmembers. Space exploration had almost become passé before this event, but the Challenger disaster reminded everybody that the dangers of space exploration were still very real and ever-present. The mood around 9 Squadron was understandably subdued, and my early flying consisted of mostly local training sorties and some "famils" (a bit monotonous for us, but a real thrill for our passengers). The most exciting ride was reserved for the two troops who sat back-to-back on the aircraft floor because, despite wearing seatbelts, they always felt that they would surely have to fall out through the open side doors whenever we banked sharply. Sometimes they screamed...and we loved "screamers"—the more they screamed, the more we felt the need to make them scream even louder. Duffy referred to his Army passengers as "mangoes"... "green on the outside, yellow on the inside and too many of 'em give you the sh*ts."

I finally gained some experience working with the Army in the field (9 Squadron's raison d'être) in March and, in May, I participated in my first major exercise—"Exercise Ramalot"—at Cooktown. Ten days of tactical flying followed on "Exercise Eager Eaglet" in Townsville and, as we transited from one place to another, I noticed that the captains gave fairly standard enroute briefings:

Over heavily wooded terrain: "If the engine fails, I'll auto into the *tops* of the trees."

Over sparsely wooded terrain: "If the engine fails, I'll auto *between* the trees."

Over water: "If the engine fails, when settling in the water, I'll move the cyclic forward and to the right, so that the advancing blade hits the water first and the transmission separates aft."

Such briefings were, of course, highly fanciful, if not downright delusional. While it was always a good idea to have a plan, if a catastrophic failure occurred, it would just be luck that ultimately determined whether you lived or died. A case in point was the Kangaroo 81 Iroquois crash, where the tail rotor gearbox had suddenly failed, the aircraft began to fly backwards, and the pilot attempted a *backwards* auto! After a while, I started to feel more fatalistic about emergencies because, if surviving one was all just a matter of chance, worrying about it certainly wasn't going to change anything.

"Exercise Eager Eaglet" would become the template for the major exercises that I'd participate in over the next eighteen months. Apart from the occasional operational flight, the first few days were usually spent sitting around in the crew room before the aircraft and crews deployed en masse into the field. One of the more frustrating things about tactical deployments was that we each had to sign out a 9mm pistol from the armoury to take along with us "out bush," but since there was no blank firing attachment for this weapon and no blank ammunition, our pistols were useful for just two things...cracking macadamia nuts and getting us court-martialled if we lost them.

All three helicopter squadrons participated in the major exercises, with the flying tasks ranging from transporting men and equipment to carrying external loads (slung under the aircraft) to conducting medical evacuation flights. But, undoubtedly, the most eagerly anticipated missions were the evocatively-named Airmobile Assaults. "Airmobiles" were a legacy of the Vietnam War, whereby large bodies of troops were tactically inserted into the field (sometimes under fire) by helicopter. The huge scale of military operations in Vietnam had often required dozens of Iroquois for an airmobile, but ours were normally limited to about eight aircraft. Tactically, all of the troops are ideally inserted simultaneously, and so the limiting factor in such operations was always the size of the landing zone (LZ), which therefore had to be large enough to accommodate every aircraft.

Now you might think that this requirement would be easy to judge, but the Army was spectacularly bad at estimating the number of Iroquois that could fit into a pad. RAAF officers were usually attached to Brigade Headquarters to act as Ground Liaison Officers (GLOs) but often the size of a pad was purely a judgement call made by an Army officer out in the field. Even more challenging was the common practice of assigning the rearmost formation station to the least experienced crew. Being "Tail-end Charlie" was always heart-in-mouth stuff whenever you crossed the tree line and had to make a split-second decision on whether you could fit into the pad before you decelerated back through translational lift. From personal experience, if the Army told you, "Oh, this pad can take eight aircraft...easy," anybody beyond Number Four could be in for an exciting approach.

Nevertheless, airmobile assaults were exhilarating experiences of the "wariest" kind! The mission always kicked off with a detailed briefing, during which the crew pairings and formation stations were announced. The aircraft were then pre-flighted, before taking off in formation to head for the pick-up point. The lead aircraft was always responsible for timings, navigation and communications, and a strict protocol had been developed with the Army to ensure that we were where we should be and that they were who they said they were. The following scripted exchanges always took place:

Formation Leader: "Throw smoke, over."

Army radio operator: "Smoke thrown, over." A smoke grenade would then be detonated within the pad to produce smoke in any one of a variety of different colours.

Formation Leader: "I see red smoke [for example], over."

Army radio operator: "Red smoke is confirmed, out."

We would then land and load our awaiting troops, who had already been sorted into pre-determined 'chalks' of seven (or less in very hot temperatures). In the mid-1980s, Queensland was in the throes of an extended drought and, whenever a large formation approached the ground, the rotor wash would instantly whip up an enormous cloud of powdery red dust that reduced the visibility to practically zero. Our troops would then appear out of this red haze, running crouched over to avoid our whirling rotor blades. With everybody safely secured on-board, the formation leader would then announce "Rolling" and we would all takeoff in unison. Once again, the formation would become enveloped in red dust just as soon as the power was increased and, on one notable occasion, my crew had to avoid a large bullock that, spooked by all the noise, had appeared out of the dust directly in front of us. A "bird strike" could be bad enough in a helicopter—but a "cow strike?"

So, the adrenalin was always pumping when you pulled up on the collective and rolled into the thick, red cloud, knowing that there might be six or seven aircraft somewhere ahead of you in the murk. Thankfully, you usually popped out of the dust cloud at about a hundred feet, whereupon a frantic, head-swivelling scan of the immediate area was necessary to account for the other aircraft in the formation. Once they'd all been sighted, you could then relax a little for the low-level transit to the insertion point. A loose "battle formation" was employed during this stage of the flight, where each aircraft spaced itself out from the others and manoeuvred within an 'arc of freedom' to avoid any obstacles. It remained essential, however, to keep an eye on the aircraft immediately ahead of you, because if he went to the left of a hill while you went to the right, you could be in for a very nasty surprise on the other side when you were suddenly approaching each other head-on.

Sometimes, the 'chalk commander' would sit in a jumpseat with a headset on to communicate with us on the way to the insertion point. On one particular airmobile, this guy kept calling out:

"Reg...Reg...REG!"

Trudge, my copilot, quickly grew tired of this, so he turned around and said:

"Mate. Who the f*** are you talking to?"

"You!" our passenger replied (as if Trudge was a bit thick). "That's your name on the back of your helmet, isn't it?" Trudge did indeed have "REG" (typed on a Dymo label) on the back of his helmet—short for his helmet size (Regular). I guess the guy kept calling out to him because he couldn't work out how to pronounce my name..."XLGE."

The formation tightened up again nearing the LZ (as, undoubtedly, did the "pucker valves" of the Tail-end Charlie crew). For the landing, it was incumbent on the front half of the formation to squeeze up as tightly as possible on the ground, and for the back half to approach at an angle that allowed them to fly a "go round" if the pad wasn't big enough. If a "bug out" did indeed become necessary, the flying pilot would have to haul up on the collective as his heavy aircraft shuddered violently in the throes of losing translational lift. Only when the aircraft was safely flying away for a second attempt would the pilot mutter under his breath, "F***ing Army wankers!"

But airmobiles were pretty rare, and most of our time was spent hanging around the Ops tent in the hope of getting some extra flying. Major exercises operated under NATO protocols, and sometimes on tasks, you could find yourself being allocated some very interesting callsigns from amongst the NATO-approved list of two-syllable, tactical callsigns—"CERVIX" is one example that quickly springs to mind. The Ops tent also stored the NATO code books that were kept under lock and key and were only issued to crews heading out on a mission. These codes were used to avoid transmitting sensitive information (such as grid references) in 'plain language' to the enemy (or "ena-meeee," as one senior flight lieutenant referred to them to the muffled amusement of others. Losing a code book was even more heinous than misplacing your nut-cracker...err, pistol...and the legend was often recounted of one poor chap who, whilst flying around in the High Range Training Area on a very hot day, opened his window for some ventilation and then watched in horror as his code book was sucked out into the airflow. With all the codes now potentially 'compromised,' NATO had to shut down for several days while their new code books were being produced.

While tactical flying could be exciting, life in the 'bivouac' after hours was anything but. Meals consisted of cold cans of something from our ration packs and entertainment was non-existent. If deployed for more than a few days, we were each expected to dig a 'shell scrape' (shallow trench) for protection against enemy attacks, but these excavations usually just became the venues for "hole parties," where we gathered after dark to swap jokes and stories. Usually, we would soon be dispersed by a senior officer threatening us with court-martials for breaking 'sound discipline' and so, afterwards, there was little option but to head for our tents and try to get some sleep. Because I snored (reportedly) I was usually in a tent by myself and so, to prevent myself from sleeping in, I would take along my wife's little red electronic alarm clock (the "Red Peril") that was so loud that it probably woke up everybody within a hundred metres—including the ena-meeee.

One night, my routine was altered when I was tasked to transport a flu-stricken squadron leader back to the base. The flight to Townsville would be in daylight, but the return flight would be in total darkness, so my copilot and I got to work calculating safety heights and reviewing the method for flying an approach to a light source for when we arrived back in the field. The outbound flight was uneventful but, having overflown the area's rugged terrain for the previous week, I just couldn't ignore the realisation that if our engine was to suddenly quit...we were all dead. Undeniably, everything at 9 Squadron involved an element of risk but, following the old adage, I still hadn't *really flown* helicopters yet. What I didn't know was that that day was now rapidly approaching.

12
KEEPING THE KIDS OCCUPIED

Not all our time at 9 Squadron was spent on death-defying, low-level tactical missions. We were also military officers, and this obligation was sometimes reinforced in the most unusual ways. At the time, the Manual of Air Force Law (MAFL) allowed minor indiscretions to be dealt with in-house by unit COs (colloquially known as "March in the Guilty Bastard") and junior officers were required to witness a charge being heard as part of our officer development. Trouble was, such events were rare, and one poor "bastard" was paraded before his CO with about a dozen junior officers lined up behind him as spectators. A case like this would be over within a half-hour or so, but the military was just about to adopt a new system, whereby Reservist barristers would be able to argue cases over days or weeks, wasting exorbitant amounts of taxpayer money. But in 1986, Prosecuting Officers and Defending Officers were still being appointed from within the ranks of the junior officer corps.

I'd found the RAAF legal process quite interesting at OTS, and so I was *almost* excited to be nominated as Defending Officer for a young airman who'd been charged with a minor indiscretion by the RAAF Police. The RAAFPOL were often disparagingly referred to as "Elephant Trackers," since it was a commonly held opinion that most of them couldn't "track a bleeding elephant through the snow." But when I was duly handed a copy of the airman's charge sheet, I found that the incident in question didn't come close to matching the offence with which he'd been charged and that there were no secondary charges listed. I rang the RAAFPOL Warrant Officer for clarification, whereupon he stunned me by simply saying, "I guess we'll drop the charge then." My thrilled "client" regarded me as akin to Perry Mason, and thus my legal career concluded with a perfect record.

Also, despite what I said earlier, we weren't *completely* exempt from the occasional parade. In 1986, the Commander Tactical Transport Group visited Amberley, and a parade was held to allow him to review and address his troops. The members of 12 Squadron and 9 Squadron thus dusted off their rarely used dress blues and began shining their shoes. The base lacked a professional military band, but the Amberley Volunteer Band was on hand to lend the event some gravitas. On the day of the parade, we discovered that what they lacked in talent, they amply made up for in volume and, during the fifteen-minute inspection, we were treated to their full rough and raucous repertoire. I'm not sure who started it, but as the band eviscerated a variety of military melodies, somebody started giggling, and the contagion spread rapidly with every butchered note. By the end of the inspection, we were all rocking in barely suppressed gales of laughter. Mercifully, when the Commander mounted the dais to pass judgment on us, we could all finally regain our composure. He announced that he was generally pleased with our presentation, but his closing comment almost brought us undone once more:

"The band could use a bit of work!"

The squadron executives also observed the basic premise of Parenting 101—keep your kids busy and they won't get into trouble—and nominated us for a bunch of RAAF ground training courses. While some of them were interesting and valuable, others were "not so much"—such as the Introduction to Joint Warfare Course (at RAAF Base Williamtown) where the challenge for the instructors seemed to be to throw as many acronyms at us as they could within the allocated time. The socialisation in the Mess during the evenings, however, was so outstanding that I promptly dubbed it the Introduction to Bladder Obliteration Course. In March, I was attached to RAAF Base Richmond for two weeks to participate in a Flying Safety Officers Course which qualified its graduates to act as primary responders in the event of a serious aircraft accident occurring on base. While much of the subject matter was understandably confronting and grisly, the course was, nevertheless, a very absorbing one, since it revealed how skilled investigators could determine (often very quickly) the possible sequence of events that had ultimately led to the disaster.

For example, a crash that leaves nothing but a charred crater is the result of a high-speed, almost-vertical impact, whereas an extended wreckage trail implies that the aircraft hit at a shallow angle (with the size of the debris pieces indicating the likely speed at impact). In a jet aircraft accident, the post-crash state of the engines can also be very revealing. Sheared-off fan blades and turbine blades indicate that an engine was operating at high power at the time, whereas, badly-bent blades are more indicative of a failed engine (or one operating at reduced power). The absence of a post-crash fire strongly suggests that fuel starvation could well have played a part. As we studied case after case of misjudgement, mismanagement and often just plain bad luck, I couldn't help wondering what these pilots were thinking during their last few seconds. Did they fight to the very end, or did they realise that they were hurtling towards oblivion? It was a very sobering thought indeed.

Since aircraft accidents invariably attract public interest, we were also given some fundamental media training. I'd once spoken to a guy who'd completed a military media awareness course, and it sounded like a very interesting and entertaining experience. Some very prominent media personalities (including the legendary Peter Harvey) took part to provide some useful tips on how to avoid the pitfalls of appearing on camera. Each trainee was then interviewed by a very attractive female, who was seated and seductively attired in a plunging neckline and very short skirt. When the edited interview was then screened for the entire course—mostly consisting of red-blooded males—the criticality of maintaining strict eye contact at all times became immediately and glaringly obvious.

Our media training was much more serious and focused on how to handle media interviews in the immediate aftermath of a major accident. The official line was to say that the incident was being investigated and that any speculation as to the likely cause would be counterproductive before the release of the official report. We were also warned, however, that it might be necessary to go off-script occasionally, with a television interview recorded after a Chinook crash in February 1985 illustrating this point admirably. The reporter asked the "RAAF spokesman" whether it was true that the aircraft had hit wires and, while the interviewee faithfully followed the party line, the cameraman zoomed in on the wreckage to reveal severed wires wrapped tightly around one of the main rotor assemblies. By the conclusion of two very sombre weeks, we were ready to let off some steam, so we headed into Richmond by bus for a delicious Chinese meal and some cold beverages. Beforehand, though, I rang home briefly and was told that, before year's end, I was going to be a father for the first time. On boarding the bus, I naturally shared this news with my colleagues, and was greeted with the anticipated cheers of "Well done!", "Congratulations!" and, inevitably, "Your shout!"

In May 1986, I returned to Williamtown for the Total Bladder Obliteration Course, after which a 9 Squadron Iroquois arrived to fly me back to Amberley. We'd only travelled about ten miles, though, before the aircraft was recalled by Williamtown Tower to assist in the search for a Mirage fighter jet that had gone missing off the coast. An oil slick had been sighted in the water some distance offshore, and ATC required our helicopter to go and investigate the scene. I was dropped back at the base before the crew left for the search area, and I caught up with them at the bar later that evening. A crewman had been lowered on the winch cable to collect any floating debris at the site, and he was also able to collect enough human remains to confirm that the pilot had been killed in the crash. To date, no official cause for this tragic accident has ever been established. As this incident amply demonstrated, helicopters are incredibly flexible machines.

Later that year, a number of us participated in an Artillery Spotter's Course at the Army School of Artillery (at North Head in Sydney). After a few days of classroom instruction on how to calculate grid references and then call in (and adjust) 'fire missions,' it was time to climb into our Iroquois for a test run of our newfound skills at the Army Weapons Range in Moorebank. When my turn came, the first shot based on my coordinates landed just short of the quarry that served as our target.

"How do you reckon that looks?" asked my Army instructor beside me.

"Pretty good actually," I said, feeling rather pleased with myself. "If they just add a bit, they'll be right on the money.'

"Okay, then. Call it in," said my instructor.

"Add fifty. Three rounds...fire for effect," I said, using the standard evocative terminology. Barely ten seconds later, three giant columns of dirt and rock erupted "dead centre" in the quarry. It truly was exhilarating stuff!

Equally exciting, but for different reasons, was the Helicopter Underwater Escape Trainer conducted by the (now-defunct) National Safety Council of Australia in Sale, Victoria. The course aimed to provide us with the skills necessary to escape a sinking helicopter, and a large four-man training rig (two crew sitting in the front and two in the back) was plunged into an enormous water tank (and then capsized) for this purpose. With my memories of almost drowning on COMSURV still fresh, I was no longer a fan of the water, but the presence of a diver in the tank to help us if we tried to swim down instead of up whilst blindfolded was reassuring. Yes...I said *blindfolded*.

The course required us to complete *six* distinct training runs and, on each one, we had to wait for the rig to roll inverted and then stop moving before we made good our escape. On each run, we had to release our harness and then exit via either the door on our side (Run One) or the opposite door (Runs Two and Three). The final three runs were essentially repeats of the first three, except that we were blindfolded to simulate poor visibility or darkness. My partner was Gumby and, just before the final run I said, "You'd better move quick, mate, or I'll go right over the top of you!" He still didn't move fast enough for my liking, and as I lay recovering afterwards, I thought, "Man...I hope I never end up in the water somewhere!"

13
SAY AGAIN???

As well as conducting a multitude of training courses, the RAAF also sought to continuously broaden its corporate knowledge base by encouraging its officers to serve with Allied forces overseas and, reciprocally, allowing allied foreign officers to serve in Australia (on what were known as exchange postings). With its fleet of American-manufactured aircraft and its close ties to the Army, it was only natural that 9 Squadron would offer an exchange posting to a pilot from the US Army. In mid-1986 (after a very long flight from the States), Captain "Chuck", his wife Ginger and their family arrived at the 9 Squadron headquarters where we had all been assembled to welcome them. As Chuck and Ginger wearily filed into the barbecue area for lunch, my initial impression of them was that they were straight out of central casting as the quintessentially American couple. Both were in their mid-20s, with Chuck featuring an athletic physique, a great set of teeth and a blonde buzz-cut (circa 1960s), while Ginger was pretty, slim and tanned with reddish-blonde hair and sparkling eyes. It would not have surprised me in the slightest if Chuck had been the captain of the high school football team and Ginger had been the head cheerleader.

Understandably, they didn't stay long and we didn't see much of

Chuck for the next fortnight or so as his family settled into their on-base married quarter. But when he then began his Iroquois conversion course, we got to know him a lot better and found him to be an affable, humorous and humble guy who "shot the breeze" in an "ole boy" drawl that hailed from somewhere deep in the American south—Alabama, if I recall correctly. Chuck had accrued lots of hours on the Blackhawk helicopters that would soon be introduced into the Australian military, and we were especially intrigued to learn that he'd seen active service in them during the US invasion of Grenada in 1983. We were initially pretty dismissive of the Grenada campaign—little more than a Caribbean holiday for the US military in the Australian media—but by Chuck's account, it had been a lot "hotter" than we were led to believe, with several aircraft being lost to hostile enemy fire.

At the end of his conversion course, the CO asked me to take Chuck out on a navex to familiarise him with the local area and give him some practice in Australian radio procedures.

"Let him fly the first half while you do the radio," he said, "then you take over and fly the second half while Chuck does the 'comms.'"

"Sure, sir," I said, and plotted out a triangular course from Amberley to Caloundra, with a coastal run south as far as Tweed Heads before heading back to Amberley.

Just after lunch, I ran Chuck through the flight plan, discussed the requirements when leaving and re-entering controlled airspace and then advised him how such procedures were conducted over the radio. As the CO requested, I let Chuck fly initially and, not surprisingly, he flew the aircraft confidently and very capably. After leaving Amberley's Control Zone, I gave a few position reports to the Flight Service unit, before we turned right at the coastline and sought clearance to re-enter controlled airspace to the north of Brisbane airport. After passing the city, we headed out over the water and dropped down to 500 feet above the rolling surf for a spectacular Gold Coast transit.

About halfway down "the strip," I said to Chuck, "Righto mate…time for you to do the radios while I have a fly. Have a quick look at the flight plan, orientate yourself on the map and work out what you're gonna say at our next position report."

"Okay," said Chuck a little tentatively after he'd handed over control of the aircraft.

Minutes later, and in his rich Southern drawl, Chuck gave his position report to Coolangatta Tower, "Aaaah...Coolang...errrrr...Coolong...ummm...Coolin...Coolin-gittar Tower, this is Albatross 123. We're abeam...aahhh...Coolun...ummm...Coolang...errr...Coolin-gittar at one-five, tracking coastal below one thousand and estimating errr... Marywill...ummm...Mooriwool...ahhh...Moori-wool-oombaaaahhhh at two-five."

The Tower controller was laughing so hard he could barely speak, and while we initially tried to stifle our amusement, we all soon joined in with gales of laughter at Chuck's expense. In response, Chuck just looked at me with only the barest hint of a smile and, with a trace of menace, snarled:

"Geoff...you're a ****!"

While we got on well...later...Chuck never really believed that I hadn't set him up to fail on that disastrous first radio call between Coolangatta and Murwillumbah. His verbal discomfort with our fine Aboriginal place names became the running gag between us afterwards and, just a few months later, we were crewed together again as a medivac standby crew for an Army parachute training exercise at Toogoolawah. I prepared the map for the flight and called Chuck over to discuss it with him and write out our flight plan.

"Chuck," I said straight-faced, "this is where we're heading today" (indicating Toogoolawah) "and I reckon we should give a position report here" (pointing out Mount Gooneringeringi).

"Geoff...you're still a ****," drawled Chuck, "and you're doin' the f***in' radios, man!"

14
COLOURFUL CHARACTERS

Chuck was just one of the colourful characters at 9 Squadron, with two others sharing the same first name: Pete C and Pete Mac. Pete C had a loud voice, a raucous laugh, a perpetual smile on his face and such a cheery disposition that he'd been cruelly nicknamed "Brain Damage" ("BD" for short). After a while, Pete grew tired of this disparaging label, so he decided to go see the CO about it. After knocking on the CO's door, he poked his head around the corner, just as the CO looked up from his desk and said, "Yes, BD. What can I do for you?" "Nothing sir," said Pete C wearily.

Pete Mac was a RAAF Academy graduate with an anarchic sense of humour and an encyclopaedic knowledge of all things Monty Python. At the time, he was married to a dentist, who created a truly hideous set of dentures for him to use as a joke at parties. For a laugh, Pete would select a random stranger, pop in the dentures unnoticed, tap them on the shoulder and then smile broadly when they turned to face him. Naturally, their reaction to his terrible teeth would always be one of barely restrained shock, but of course, politeness prevented them from staring or making comments. Pete would then chat away for a while and let them squirm, before finally taking out the teeth and sharing a laugh at their expense. One night, however, Pete came badly undone when he tapped his "mark" on the shoulder, and she turned to face him and smiled back broadly to reveal teeth that were even worse than his...and *quite real!* The tables had been well and truly turned and Pete, gallant as ever, had had to wear his dentures for the rest of the night to avoid embarrassing her.

Occasionally, Pete and Pete flew together, and both of them carried black Chino graph pencils to jot down important information on the windshield. The two Petes were engaged in a single-aircraft Army support task, where they had the rare luxury of leaving their helmets hanging in the aircraft overnight. One morning, Pete Mac climbed into his seat, donned his helmet and lowered his clear visor to reveal an enormous huntsman spider sitting just an inch or so from his face. He let out a scream and, with its chin strap still fastened, ejected his helmet (and its unwelcome occupant) out his side window. Pete C dissolved into fits of laughter at his crewmate's expense and teased Pete Mac relentlessly about it for the rest of the day.

The next morning, Pete C was still chuckling, but when he donned *his* helmet and lowered *his* clear visor, he saw another enormous huntsman spider sitting just an inch or so away from *his* face. Another piercing scream ensued before Pete C's helmet suffered the same ignominious fate as Pete Mac's helmet the previous day. But now, it was Pete Mac's turn to laugh, especially when he revealed to his colleague that he'd spent most of the previous evening laboriously *drawing* a huntsman spider onto Pete C's visor. In the squadron Lines Book the tale was recorded for all to read under the caption: "Beware the deadly Chino graph Spider!"

15
GOING FOR A SPIN

In 1986, the Brisbane City Council decided to stage a Festival of the River and set about identifying activities that would entertain the anticipated multitude. With a squadron of Army landing barges based at Bulimba (on the south bank of the river) and a squadron of RAAF helicopters stationed at Amberley, somebody, somewhere soon came up with the idea for a display that combined the two military capabilities. The plan was for an Iroquois to drop an external load into the hold of an army landing barge that was underway along the river, and I was nominated to fly the display.

On Thursday the 28th of August, my crew of Glenn "Mouldy" Auld (copilot) and Macca (loadmaster) set off for Bulimba for a practice session with the Army landing barge crew. The external load consisted of four forty-four-gallon drums of water sitting atop a wooden pallet, and secured within a cargo net. This load would then be suspended from our cargo hook by a sturdy, forty-foot-long nylon "strop." On Flying Safety Officers Course, we'd been warned that most serious incidents were preceded by a chain of contributing events, and the first link in our chain had already occurred in the morning brief a few days earlier. 35 Squadron crews had experienced several "over-torques" (exceeding

50psi of torque from the transmission) and, due to the cost of the subsequent maintenance inspections, it was intimated to us that the next bloke who over-torqued his aircraft would be parting company with his manhood. This warning was firmly lodged in the back of my mind when we met the Army crew to discuss what might be a fairly marginal operation.

My briefing to the Army guys was ultimately a simple one: "You head east along the river at about ten knots and we'll do the rest." The afternoon sea breeze had kicked in by this time, and so an easterly heading would point us into the wind for optimum aircraft control. With the external load hooked up, the power required for an OGE hover would be about 44psi and, despite the already warm late-August temperatures, an inflight power check confirmed that the transmission could provide 50psi of torque if we needed it.

After a quick lap around the Army base, we approached the landing barge that was now slowly steaming down the middle of the river. But once we were established in the OGE hover, the total lack of nearby visual reference points made it extremely difficult for me to gauge my height, position and speed relative to the unseen landing barge forty feet below me. I had to rely completely on the calls coming from my loadmaster who, safety harness connected, was lying spread-eagled on the floor and looking through the skids to give me directions.

"Okay, come left five...bit more...okay, you're in line, but a bit fast. Slow it down a bit...bit more. Okay, that's good. Come down ten now... come down five...NO, you're drifting right. Pick it up. PICK IT UP!"

After several more abortive attempts, the space that I was aiming for on the floor of the barge seemed to have shrunk to about the size of a bucket and I was working very hard. Then the aircraft's nose started turning to the right and, momentarily forgetting about the landing barge, my eyes locked onto the torquemeter as I fed in left tail rotor input to straighten the aircraft. At 49psi, the nose was *still* turning right, and so I decided to "cyclic out" of the situation by applying right cyclic (rather than any more left pedal, which would have resulted in an overtorque). But just as I started to do so, the aircraft flicked around rapidly, departed controlled flight and began spinning around like a top!

I have no idea now just how fast we were spinning, but the world through my windscreen was just a crazy blur of blue sky and brown water. My only concern was to avoid plunging into the river by keeping the aircraft upright and, in my efforts to regain tail rotor control, I probably over-torqued the transmission about four times. My heart was pounding madly in my chest as I fought the bucking, spinning aircraft, and I realised that if I had any chance of regaining control, I'd have to reduce the aircraft's weight. The loadmaster, hanging on for grim death, was now screaming continuously over the interphone, "GET RID OF THE LOAD! GET RID OF THE F***ING LOAD!" I kept repeatedly stabbing the electrical load release button on the cyclic, but nothing was happening. Later, I would learn that Mouldy had been doing the same thing, but with similar results. "GET RID OF THE F***ING LOAD!" the loadmaster yelled again, to which I yelled back, "I'M TRYING!" without even enough spare grey matter to consider pushing the interphone transmit button.

Time now seemed to become suspended, and I have no idea of how long we were spinning like that over the river. I knew that we were getting ever closer to the water, and I remember thinking with crystal clarity, "We're probably gonna crash here!" I was surprised by my sense of detachment from this horrifying realisation. Nevertheless, I was determined to keep fighting and, just as the loadmaster called, "LOAD IN THE WATER" I kicked the mechanical load release lever between the two tail rotor pedals. Our stubborn cargo was finally jettisoned and, with that, our aircraft instantly stopped spinning, and the world came back into sharp focus. We were about ten feet above the water and, without another word, I flew back to the Army unit, landed the aircraft and shut it down.

Nothing much was said in the immediate aftermath—I think we were all probably in a state of shock from having nearly crashed into the river. I soon rang the squadron to tell them what had happened and was told to stay put while a "rescue party" was assembled with the crew and equipment necessary to inspect and repair the aircraft (if necessary). Macca and I then chain-smoked about half a packet of cigarettes while the three of us reflected, somewhat shakily, on the experience that we'd somehow just survived. During the spin, Macca said, the load had been swinging around like a pendulum, and he could see it rotating outside the plane of the skids. When we went back outside to inspect the aircraft, we found that the metal panel surrounding the "hell hole" (the recess that housed the cargo hook) had been smashed in by the gyrating load to within just a few millimetres of the tail rotor torque tube. Had this control mechanism been compromised, we would have lost all tail rotor authority and would have had no option but to ditch the aircraft into the Brisbane River.

By now, the incident had begun to replay itself on a continuous loop in my mind. Had I done something wrong? Should I have done something differently? Was it all my fault? When the rescue party arrived, I was feeling quite badly shaken and, anticipating that this would be the case, the squadron had some beers waiting on ice for us when we got back to Amberley. It was a simple gesture that meant a lot. When I rang Mum to tell her the news later, she told me that she'd already seen some film of it on television, and had wondered if I'd been involved. It was footage that I never saw and, with hindsight, that was probably a very good thing. By Friday afternoon, the necessary repairs had been completed and, to get me "back on the horse," I was instructed to fly the aircraft back to Amberley solo the following morning, with a groundie occupying the left-hand seat. I'll candidly admit that this flight was a real challenge—I'd survived our ordeal unscathed physically, but my ego and self-confidence had taken a real battering. Afterwards, OGE operations at high power settings would always make me feel decidedly anxious and uncomfortable.

Our cargo hook was subsequently removed and 'bench tested' extensively, with both electrical and mechanical release mechanisms reportedly working perfectly. The investigation found that the loss of tail rotor authority probably occurred as the result of a slight wind shift that caused the main rotor wash to blow over the tail rotor and aerodynamically stall it. The pendulous swinging of the load had generated enough centripetal force within the hook to prevent the load from releasing… even with the hook's jaws open. This force was only dissipated when the load hit the water and stopped spinning, thus allowing a successful cargo jettison to take place. I'd confronted and survived my "near-death experience," but the incident had taught me another valuable lesson about flying: "If you need it...use it!" Exceeding a limit may result in some expensive maintenance inspections and repairs, but a "bent" aircraft is preferable to a crashed one, and a badly shaken crew is better than a dead one. I was lucky to get the opportunity to learn from my experience: many others weren't so fortunate. I had now *really flown* helicopters and been given the briefest glimpse of what it must be like to think, "Well, this might be it!" If nothing else, at least (under great duress), I'd fought hard to resolve the situation the entire time.

Not surprisingly, the planned display didn't make the "final cut" for the River Festival but, had it done so, it certainly would have highlighted the flexibility of helicopters generally, and of the Iroquois in particular.

16
HERE COMES SANTA CLAUS

Night Vision Goggles (NVGs) were introduced at 9 Squadron in 1986, and suddenly, all of our regular tasks could be carried out in conditions of almost total darkness. Although NVG training wasn't offered to everybody, all of us were afforded a familiarisation flight to see the new technology in action. It was truly bizarre to fly around the local training area on NVGs, where just the starlight was enough to generate that strange green world that is the norm "under goggles."

Our unit SOPs (Standard Operating Procedures) detailed other specialised roles and, while some of them were practiced regularly, others were not. In the former category was rappelling, where a device was secured to the aircraft floor, and each troop inserted his rope into the device on the way to the pad. Approaching the drop zone, the troops climbed out onto the skids and, when the aircraft was established in an OGE hover, the troops let the remaining lengths of their ropes fall to the ground. Then, on a signal from the loadmaster, they jumped out and away from the aircraft and lowered themselves to the ground using karabiners. The loadmaster then released the ropes from the device to complete the drop. Most of these missions were uneventful but, occasionally, one of the troops might be too gung-ho and descend too quickly, landing either flat on his back or on top of his pack.

The rappelling device could also be used for 'water insertions,' whereby the troops stood on the skids holding onto very short lengths of rope and then leapt into the water as the aircraft skimmed the surface at twenty knots. This speed was stipulated quite specifically in the SOPs, and so I asked Tayls one day how it came to be determined. The procedure had been tested with the SAS, he told me, and the twenty-knot speed had been arrived at by trial and error.

"On the first run," said Tayls, "we gave the signal to jump at about ten knots, but the troops punched straight down into the water and practically sank to the bottom."

"So, on the second pass, we gave the signal at thirty knots but, this time, they rolled up into a ball on top of the water...and then sank to the bottom. Between us, we figured out that a speed of twenty knots would probably do the trick."

The aircraft could also serve as platforms for "calling in" artillery barrages by specialist observers. I participated in one such mission in the Wide Bay Training Area, where all we did was load two artillery spotters onboard and then fly up and down an imaginary line while they did their thing with the artillery batteries. Once we were confident that the line would keep us safe from being blown up, we settled in for an hour of flying up and down the line...up and down the line...up and down the line ad nauseam. Nearby was a large pine forest full of mature trees that were well over a hundred feet tall. Fire trails had been carved through the forest, and these were wide enough to permit an Iroquois to follow them at below treetop height. There were some quite sharp twists and turns and, with a bit of imagination, it resembled flying the attack on the Death Star at the end of the original Star Wars movie. Therefore, to 9 Squadron pilots, this area was known as "Star Wars Alley."

At the end of one very boring artillery spotting sortie, the captain decided to spice things up a bit by paying a visit to Star Wars Alley. As he threw the aircraft around vigorously, we fully expected to hear some audible excitement from our passengers...but despite our best efforts, we didn't hear *a sound*. After they'd disembarked back at the landing zone, we remarked on how cool they'd been.

"Are you kidding?" said the loadie. "They were *scared rigid*—too terrified to scream. I practically needed a pair of pliers to prise their fingers off the seat rails after we landed."

An Iroquois could also deliver ordnance itself, and 'helicopter gunship' was one of the aircraft's most celebrated roles during the Vietnam War. In October 1986, a training course was held at the Evans Head Weapons Range on the central New South Wales coast to qualify a new batch of "Bushrangers"—the famous 9 Squadron gunship callsign—and, on October 4th, Pete Mac and I flew down to Evans Head to play the part of "flare ship." Our job would be to drop illumination flares that would light up the range while the "gunnies" conducted their "night shoot." Without NVGs, landing an Iroquois at night was always challenging, since the only typical approach aids were either a 'single light' source or a 'T-light' source. A single light source was exactly what its name suggests—just a single lantern sitting on the ground. During such an approach, the aim was to maintain a steady speed and a constant angle that kept the single light in a constant position in the windscreen. On moonless nights, this was an incredibly difficult manoeuvre, since it felt as if you were suspended in a black void, while the point of light moved around on its own—a phenomenon known in aviation as 'autokinesis.' A T-light source (usually eight lanterns laid out in a "T" shape) was much easier because, on approach, the aim was merely to keep the aspect of the "T" constant as you descended.

But in truth, the objective was to have the approach stable by about 200 feet, so that you could then turn on your searchlight for a visual landing. Pete Mac had taken part in an MFO deployment to the Middle East where night approaches to T-light sources were reportedly quite commonplace. "But on one night approach," he told me, "I just couldn't shake the feeling that I had to keep continually changing my heading further and further to the right." Feeling slightly disoriented, he'd been relieved when he was low enough to be able to turn on his searchlight...brilliantly illuminating a group of surprised Bedouins who were trying to steal away into the desert with the lanterns.

But our night mission still lay ahead of us and, during the afternoon, I took the opportunity to sit in the back of Gumby's aircraft while he was on a "shoot." The aircraft flew circuits towards a large target that had been mounted on the seaward end of the range and, after rolling out on final to point at the target, the aircraft unleashed a veritable hail of bullets and rockets from its dual mini-guns and rocket-pods. When it then banked away on its crosswind turn, the closest loadmaster would open up with his twin, door-mounted M60s. It was an impressive display, and the back of the aircraft was soon littered with red-hot brass ammunition casings and rocket arming wires, explaining why the flying suits of Bushranger crews were typically adorned with a multitude of small, burnt holes.

That night, Pete Mac and I took off to drop our illumination flares that, when ignited under their small parachutes, would burn at millions of candlepower and light up the range like daylight. Our aircraft had been fitted with a large metal storage rack into which about a dozen flares had been placed, with each flare expected to burn for about five minutes. The flares were meant to be dropped from 5,000 feet so that they'd extinguish before reaching the ground, but the forecast cloudbase that night was only around 4,000 feet. Therefore, the challenge for us would be to overlap the flare drops so that there was always one alight and to drop them far enough offshore so that, still ablaze, they'd fall harmlessly into the sea. After we'd taken off and climbed to 4,000 feet, our spinning rotor blades were practically obscured inside the base of the dense cloud layer. Far below us, the gunships were loitering at a safe altitude, waiting for the launch of our first flare, which the loadie slid out of the rack, then pulled out its arming wire and tossed into the darkness.

Seconds later, it ignited into a brilliant orb of white light that lit up the range and allowed the gunnies to go to work, firing brilliant red streams of tracer bullets. It was difficult not to just sit back and admire the view, but there was still work to be done. At our reduced altitude, working out when to launch the next flare became purely a matter of "suck it and see," and our loadie tried to time it so that the next one was launched just before the preceding one struck the water. The only way of knowing that a flare had hit the water was when it suddenly changed from a brilliant white to an aqua green. They were so powerful that they usually continued to burn underwater briefly, and a few even leapt back up into the air again before finally being extinguished.

Overall, our mission went pretty well, but occasionally we got it wrong, and we would hear the gunnies scrambling back up to safety height after the range had been temporarily plunged back into darkness. Some of our flares also blew onshore while still burning, and we later learned that we were responsible for burning out quite a large swath of local bushland. Nevertheless, the sight of those brilliantly burning flares, and the gunships "hosing down" their targets with streams of tracer rounds, is a sight I'll never forget.

I would fly one more highly unusual sortie as 1986 finally drew to a close. Every festive season, each RAAF base would stage a "Christmas Treat" for its servicemen's children, consisting of rides and games and a very special appearance by Santa Claus. In 1986, Santa and his elves planned to make a grand entrance by parachuting out of an Iroquois from 10,000 feet—and I was given the job of getting them there. For parachute sorties, our SOPs required that all of our aircraft doors be removed and that all of the helicopter crew wear parachutes so that, if something went wrong—our tail rotor becoming fouled by one of the jumper's parachutes, for example—we would be able to bail out of our uncontrollable aircraft. Although we'd regularly flown at 10,000 feet in PNG, we were only ever a few thousand feet above the terrain. This time, it felt like we were in a low earth orbit, and it took nearly thirty minutes of gradually ascending spirals to reach this dizzying altitude. After finally levelling off, the rotors seemed to be struggling for air and the crowd on the oval far below us looked like a colony of ants. I then gave our passengers the signal to climb out onto the skids and, after an exchange of thumbs-ups (and a big cheesy grin from Santa)...they were gone. The aircraft wobbled briefly from side to side after they departed, and as I watched them plunging earthwards, I hoped that their parachutes had been well packed. I imagine the parents below were feeling similarly—if those chutes failed, they would be up for a fortune in counselling bills!

17
THE ONLY CONSTANT IN LIFE IS CHANGE

As 1987 began, there was a palpable feeling in the air that this would be a year of tremendous change. It certainly was already so for me, as my firstborn son had made his grand arrival in mid-November the year before. I'd attended as many pre-natal classes as I could, wincing during the more graphic videos but, frankly, all the screaming had been a bit much (despite it mostly coming from the male audience). Ultimately, the eighteen-hour birthing process had been exhausting, distressing and, at times, extremely undignified...and my wife hadn't fared much better! Now, at work, 9 Squadron was about to lose its pre-eminent role in the helicopter world, with the first of the new Blackhawks due to arrive by year's end. We were advised to have our Posting Preference forms up-to-date since most of us could expect a posting sometime in December. I opted first and foremost to be sent to Flying Instructors Course, with a return to 33 Squadron as my second preference.

A change had already occurred in the top tier of the Australian Defence Force, with the title of the ADF commander being amended from Chief of Defence Force Staff to Chief of Defence Force (CDF) in 1984. Also different was how the CDF was appointed, with the process going from one of simply rotating the position between the three services to that of requiring a 'time in rank' qualification. Since the Army usually promoted its officers faster than the RAAF and the RAN, this system greatly favoured the Army, with senior Army appointees dominating the position until 2005. Having secured its pre-eminence, the Army then embarked on a power play to assume control of the 'battlefield helicopters' using the argument that, "Helicopters support the Army, so they should be controlled and operated by the Army." To many long-serving RAAF helicopter pilots—some of whom had seen active service in Vietnam—this development was a real, personal slap in the face.

The incumbent CDF visited Amberley in 1987 to explain this decision, but his total lack of empathy did little to win him any friends amongst his audience. His argument that "Trucks are driven by privates. Tanks are driven by corporals. Why do helicopters have to be flown by officers?" was one that was particularly derided in the 9 Squadron crew room afterwards. But, as is customary in the military, there was little that could now be done. While a few RAAF pilots eventually joined the Army to keep flying helicopters, most of us knew that the writing was on the wall and that it was time to enjoy whatever flying remained before the relocation of all our aircraft to Townsville in late August.

18
TRAGEDY AT TENTERFIELD

While 12 Squadron has garnered a few mentions in this account so far, I realise that I've said little about our glamorous co-tenants at Amberley—the F-111s of Nos 1 and 6 Squadrons. With such hugely different roles and such a vast gap in the relative performance of our aircraft, there was usually only very indirect contact between "us and them." During one such occurrence, I'd just returned to Amberley from a local training sortie and was in a three-foot hover over the base's grass runway when ATC instructed all aircraft in the circuit area to land due to the imminent arrival of an F-111 on a simulated low bombing pass from the south. We immediately pivoted our hovering helicopter to face south and get a better view of the action, when the Tower called us up:

ATC: (With obvious irritation) "Albatross 123, you were instructed to land!"

Us: (With obvious incredulity) "Just how low is his pass going to be?"

A more dramatic F-111 Amberley arrival occurred when an aircraft on a low-level return from Evans Head struck a pelican, causing damage that resulted in the loss of its altitude and airspeed displays. A "chase plane" was quickly dispatched to escort the damaged aircraft home and, since word of the incident had spread quickly, the approach and landing attracted quite an audience. When the crippled aircraft came into view, there was almost an audible gasp at the visible extent of the damage that it had sustained. The aircraft's shattered fibreglass nose was splayed out into the airflow, almost as if it'd been taxied into a brick wall at about sixty knots. Fortunately, the landing was ultimately uneventful but, sadly, not all past F-111 bird encounters had resulted in such successful outcomes.

In 1977, an F-111 suffered multiple birdstrikes at Evans Head, shattering the windshields and severely injuring both pilots. While an ejection was initiated, ultimately both crew members were killed in the accident. Afterwards, the RAAF embarked on a programme to find tougher windshields and, to test the prototype transparencies in the laboratory, defrosted frozen chickens were fired at them using a compressed-air cannon. RAAF legend has it that one day the cannon was all primed and loaded when lunchtime rolled around, so everyone just headed off for the canteen. Meanwhile, a moggie wandered into the deserted lab and decided that the barrel of the cannon looked like a nice, cosy spot in which to have a little siesta. When the technicians returned and fired the cannon, the first shot proved that the new thickened glass was not only bird-proof, but cat-proof as well.

Undoubtedly, flying these aircraft on low-level strike missions was a very dangerous business, and when the type was finally retired in 2010, nine of them had crashed, with the loss of twelve lives. Tragedy struck the F-111 squadrons twice during my Amberley posting, with an F-111 engaged in simulating a Harpoon missile profile crashing into the sea and killing both crew members just the day before the *Challenger* disaster. In April 1987, another fatal F-111 crash occurred that would rock the RAAF "fast jet world" to its very core. At the controls of the accident aircraft was Flight Lieutenant Mark Fallon, a "high flyer" who'd achieved his "triple one" command at just nineteen years of age. His marriage to his high-school sweetheart had then seen the glamour couple appear in a host of newspaper, television and magazine stories. But recently, the fairytale had turned sour, and divorce proceedings were underway at the time of the accident. On April 2nd, Pete Mac was the

Amberley Orderly Officer, and his phone ran hot from dusk to dawn as the tragic events unfolded.

A few days later (in one of life's more confronting experiences), I was tasked to fly an Air Force safety investigator to the crash site at Tenterfield. Major accidents were usually investigated by both a Board of Inquiry and by personnel from the Directorate of Air Force Safety (DAFS). Although the DAFS investigators were usually more skilled in accident investigation, their findings resulted in safety-based recommendations only, while the Board of Inquiry report became the legally binding account of the accident. Approaching the crash site by air, the impact point was immediately obvious from the enormous black scorch mark that resulted from the aircraft's exploding fuel. But it was down on the ground that the full scale of the destruction became apparent. Nothing bigger than a square foot of the aircraft remained in the debris field, and the wreckage trail stretched for over a kilometre. Bizarrely, the trail ended with both of the aircraft's jet engines, stripped of their blades, lying quietly side by side in a paddock. For a place that had so recently witnessed such violence and devastation, the site was eerily quiet, and I struggled to comprehend the magnitude of the impact forces that could reduce a fully operational fighter-bomber to metallic fragments in just seconds.

Once I told the investigator that I'd completed a Flying Safety Officers Course, he was much more forthcoming about the reason for his journey and explained that they were searching for the attitude display in the hope that, when the fuel ignited, it had thrown a shadow onto the instrument that, under infrared analysis, would reveal the aircraft's attitude at the point of impact. Since the wreckage was precisely aligned with the heading of the low-level egress that followed the simulated bomb release, the investigators were looking for anything that might confirm a Terrain Following Radar (TFR) malfunction. As we spoke, I recollected how Mark Fallon had visited Pearce as we neared our graduation, and explained how unnerving it was, initially, to put his faith in the TFR to level off the aircraft by itself and then, on autopilot, hug the ground closely at very high speed...particularly at night. Had those initial misgivings been justified?

After an hour or so, we took to the air again so that aerial photographs could be taken of the crash site. As we hovered close by the impact point, the grooves in the ground from the twin jet engine exhausts and the wing pylons were visible, as was an imprint from the back of the wings that showed the sweep angle. Radiating out from the impact point were a multitude of gouge marks that initially ran parallel to the escape heading, but then slowly diverged as the aircraft disintegrated. It was a heartbreakingly awful thing to witness, and I just hoped that the investigation would answer the inevitable question from the victims' families: "Why?" Unfortunately, the final Board of Inquiry report found that it was not possible to determine the exact cause of the CFIT (controlled flight into terrain), but it was believed that the crew may have lost situational awareness regarding their altitude during a critical flight manoeuvre. A memorial service was later held at RAAF Amberley that featured an overflight of F-111s in the "Missing Man Formation." Sadly, it would not be the last such aerial tribute that I would witness, and one formation would tragically include a flight of Iroquois.

19
MINIMUM EFFORT—MAXIMUM RESULT

Amongst the list of contributory factors included in the final report on the Tenterfield accident was the likelihood of fatigue amongst F-111 instructors due to the increased workload caused by the continuing exodus of experienced RAAF pilots to the airlines. The initial recruiting drives for Qantas and Cathay had kicked off in 1983, and the stream of resignations had turned into a flood once the unpopular Chief of Air Staff, Selwyn David Evans, infamously described the departing pilots as "malcontents and deadwood," a malevolent description that was soon adopted as almost a badge of honour amongst aspiring airline pilots—"Are you deadwood...or just a malcontent?"

But to join an airline, it was advisable to have an Airline Transport Pilots Licence, which required a Senior Commercial Pilots Licence, as well as a Command Multi-engine Instrument Rating. After arriving at 33 Squadron in 1982, I'd been told to "get my finger out" and get my Senior Commercial Pilots Licence sorted, requiring me to pass Flight Planning, Navigation, Air Legislation and Commercial Rules and Procedures. I'd decided to tackle Flight planning first because the mythical Seagull Mark V (on which the exam was based at the time) was essentially just a Boeing 707 under another name. So, in 1984, I'd completed a Flight Planning correspondence course, enrolled for the exam, paid my $2.10 marker's fee and reported to a technical college near Bankstown to attempt the paper in a large hall with about a hundred other candidates. I found the exam *extremely* difficult, and when the result slip arrived in the mail a few weeks later, I found that I'd failed...by *two percent*.

I was so annoyed that I decided not to "open the books" for another two years, by which time the Seagull Mark V had become extinct and been replaced by the Boeing 727. So, I revised my notes, familiarised myself with the 727 Performance Manual, paid my $20 marker's fee and enrolled to sit the exam in Brisbane with about fifty other candidates. Again, the paper was extremely difficult, and the question with the most marks asked how long an aircraft on a Hamilton Island to Sydney flight could remain at 10,000 feet after takeoff before it had to climb to reach its optimum cruising level and then arrive at Sydney with the required fuel reserves intact. To answer it, I made a lot of assumptions but managed to arrive at a fairly reasonable answer (despite being unsure as to whether I'd tackled the question correctly). After another nervous wait, the result slip arrived, and I was thrilled to discover that I'd passed (with a mark of eighty-two percent). You little ripper! One down!

As our Iroquois flying started to wind down, I thought it might be time to attempt the Navigation exam. Pete Mac had recently passed the subject, so I borrowed his course material, did a fairly cursory amount of study, paid my $30 marker's fee, and sat the exam in Brisbane (again) with about twenty other hopefuls. Given my less-than-stellar preparation, I wasn't particularly hopeful, but when the result slip finally arrived, I was rapt to learn that I'd passed...by *two percent*. I regarded this as my most efficient effort since I'd achieved the best possible outcome for the least possible effort. Amazingly, the course material had primarily focused on Grid Navigation (a technique used in the polar regions), which I immediately forgot on leaving the hall, and have never thought about since.

20
ARMY INVASION

In mid-1987, the first Army pilots arrived at 9 Squadron to emphasise the fact that the end was now in sight for Air Force helicopter operations. Given the acrimony that surrounded the decision the previous year, we were all geared up to give these "grunts" a hard time. But once we got to know the very personable Nick and the easy-going Griffo, we found that try as we might, we just couldn't hate these two blokes. Barbecues and social gatherings were soon a regular occurrence at Nick's place, and Griffo was quickly accepted into the social circle of the 9 Squadron "single-ies." Nevertheless, they still exhibited some peculiar Army quirks. On a bush push in July, Nick and Griffo came along to get some operational exposure to the RAAF way of doing things, and during a temporary lull, we all sat around eating some snacks out of our ration packs. Our two "tame grunts" were sitting together under a large tree and chatting away happily, before the following exchange took place:

Griffo: (Excitedly) "Hey Nick. Check this out!"

Nick: (Boredly) "What's that mate?"

Griffo: (In utter astonishment) "The shortbread biscuits in my ration pack aren't broken! They're *always* broken. I don't think I've ever seen shortbreads that weren't all busted up!"

Griffo held up his pristine shortbreads to show Nick and then set them down reverently beside him.

Nick: (Peering off into the distance) "Hey Griffo. What's that over there?"

As Griffo turned to look in the direction that Nick was pointing, Nick picked up a large rock and dropped it smack-bang on top of Griffo's shortbread biscuits, shattering them into a million pieces. Griffo immediately leapt on top of Nick and the two of them started wrestling in the dirt. The rest of us just bemusedly watched the unfolding spectacle thinking, "F***ing Army wankers!"

21
END OF AN ERA

Unsurprisingly, 9 Squadron was awarded the 1987 Duke of Gloucester Cup as the Air Force's most proficient flying squadron. I say "unsurprisingly" because, although the award was intended for the "most proficient" squadron, every year it seemed to go to the most "politically deserving" unit and, on this occasion, I suspect it was the RAAF's way of saying, "Up yours" to the Army. But rather than being thrilled to receive such an honour, most of us just groaned, because we knew that a ceremonial parade would invariably be in order. After many hours spent drilling on the parade ground, the Cup was duly presented with much pomp and ceremony one rainy afternoon in June and was then proudly put on display in a large Perspex case in the unit's formal entryway. With the squadron about to go into premature retirement, Channel 10—or was it still Channel 0?—set to work producing a one-hour television special ("Brothers in Arms") to acknowledge 9 Squadron's contribution to the nation. We couldn't wait to see the finished product and, when it finally went to air, we were amazed by two things: firstly, our former XO had been shot down within days of arriving in Vietnam and, secondly, during our filmed local flyovers, some of us still couldn't "keep the string in the centre."

All flying was scheduled to cease by the end of August, and the second half of the month was packed with both formal and informal functions to mark the end of Iroquois operations. Alcohol abuse was rampant in these pre-RBT days, but surely the prize for overdoing it went to one of the loadies who, in the grip of the grape, decided to take the back roads home, ran out of fuel and then walked the rest of the way. The problem was, in the morning, he had no idea where he'd left his car, and spent the next week with a pair of binoculars, trying to spot it on the way to and from the helicopter training area. Of course, we officers weren't immune from such alcohol-fuelled hijinks either. At Richmond once, we'd been ordered to attend the Air Force Week cocktail party in the Mess, only to discover that the 707 flight stewards were on duty there that night and that our mixed drinks were about eighty percent spirits and twenty percent mixers. We were all pretty charged by the time the Chief of Air Staff arrived and, when the band struck up the RAAF equivalent of "Hail to the Chief," one of the 707 pilots slurred that "a fart in a bottle" would have been far more appropriate.

The social life in the Amberley Officers Mess was even more boisterous but it still didn't compare to the squadron dining-in night that was held in the unit headquarters on the night of the 24th of August. By chance, the Army commanders in Brisbane had decided to honour the squadron on the same day, with a formal lunch for the squadron executives at the Enoggera Army Barracks. The CO, XO, ADMINO (and other "Os") piled into the back of A2-649 for the thirty-minute flight from Amberley, landing in the football oval there just before lunch. As the XO left the aircraft, I called him over and asked if we should return to pick them up at about two o'clock. "No," he said. "We'll call the Ops Desk and let them know when we're ready to go." With that, my copilot and I departed for Amberley and, after takeoff, received the usual advice from ATC while they coordinated our airways clearance, "Cleared to depart—remain in the local area not above *treetop height*." I was always tempted to reply with, "Would it be okay if we climbed just a little bit higher?"

Loitering in the Ops Room at two o'clock...nothing happened. Three o'clock and then three-thirty came...and still nothing happened. Finally, at four o'clock, the phone rang, and the XO slurred down the telephone line, "Okay...you c'n come get us now!" Thirty minutes later, we landed at Enoggera, where a very strong August westerly was now blowing. Soon after, a crew van appeared and disgorged some familiar figures who stumbled towards the aircraft. I counted them off:

"One, two, three, four, five, six. That can't be right. We had seven before, didn't we? One, two, three, four, five, six. I know we had seven. Who's missing?"

To answer my question, the XO jumped up onto the skid beside me and knocked on my window.

"Yes, sir?" I yelled, struggling to hear him above the noise of our rotor blades.

"We wun yoo to hoist the CO out of the Officers Mess barbecue area!" the XO slurred, exhaling extremely potent alcoholic fumes all over me.

"Sure, sir," I said, waving away the fumes. "Are you authorising me to do that?"

"Yep. Yep," he said authoritatively. "I'm authorising you!" And with that, he climbed into the back of the aircraft to join his inebriated colleagues.

I had no idea where the barbecue area was, but the loadie thought that it might be just a bit further up the road ahead of us. I did some fairly hasty performance calculations and worked out that, with seven passengers onboard, we could *just* hover OGE with the required margins intact. So, I picked the aircraft up into a forty-foot hover and we set off slowly down the road to see if we could locate our errant CO. Sure enough, just a little way ahead of us was a large swimming pool and barbecue area that held our CO and an escort of similarly-wobbly senior Army officers. Clearly, a good time had been had by all! I established the aircraft in a hover over the pool, and the loadie lowered the winch cable and stole down to the awaiting CO, who initially donned it the wrong way round...an almost unforgivable crime. After some frantic hand gestures from above, the error was corrected and, as the Army officers saluted as smartly as they were able (and as their outdoor furniture disappeared over the fence from our tremendous rotor wash) the

CO was hoisted skywards towards his awaiting chariot. I guess it must have seemed like a good idea at the time. Throughout the CO's ascent though, my eyes were locked on the torquemeter—46psi...47psi...49psi...48psi...49psi.

"Come on, mate," I said impatiently to the loadie. "Let's get out of here!" There was no way I wanted to experience another Bulimba fiasco with all our squadron executives onboard.

"I'm trying, sir," said the loadmaster, as the seemingly lifeless CO appeared, hanging limply outside his door. "He's just a dead weight at the moment—no help at all."

"Well, get him in and let's go," I said, as the torquemeter briefly touched 50psi. With that, the loadmaster hauled the CO into the aircraft, threw him on the floor like a sack of spuds and we were off on our way back to Amberley.

It was well after five o'clock by the time we'd put the aircraft to bed, and pre-dinner drinks were due to kick off in the loadies' "donga" (office) precisely at six. Dress for the night was either dress blues or winter mess kit so, after a quick shower and change, I was soon back on the base in all my finery. So too was the XO, who seemed in remarkably good shape given the afternoon's festivities. But by six-thirty, there was still no sign of the CO, and it was simply unthinkable to begin such an auspicious event without him. The XO picked up the phone and asked the operator to switch him through to the CO's married quarter. The CO's wife answered:

"Hello? It's the 9 Squadron XO here. Could I speak to the CO, please? Sorry...he's where?? Okay, we'll be there in a few minutes!" The XO turned towards the assembled multitude and said, "Apparently the CO is literally *under the table*...and isn't going anywhere in a hurry."

"Rescue party!" rang out in reply, and within minutes, a thirsty team of enablers was enroute to the CO's house in the squadron crew van. There, protruding from under the dining-room table, were indeed a pair of RAAF black shoes (with the CO attached), and so he was immediately manhandled into the shower, decked out in his mess kit and medals, and then delivered back to the unit to keep drinking (whilst also presiding over the formalities from the Head Table). The function organisers had done an admirable job of setting up the crew room for the formal dinner, with the cuisine for the evening consisting of some local Chinese takeaway served to us by two topless waitresses. What they thought of the proceedings I can only imagine. Complementing the lavish banquet was some red wine of unknown origin that had been discovered sitting in a squadron office in a large plastic drum. We agreed that, provided it didn't kill us or send us blind, it was a pretty reasonable drop.

When the sumptuous spread concluded, it was time for some of the witty, post-dinner banter and repartee that was customary on such occasions. When none of that materialised, however, the XO, exhibiting some astonishing resilience, stood to address the squadron.

"Gentlemen," he began sombrely, "tonight, we're assembled here to mark the end of 9 Squadron Iroquois operations."

The crowd booed loudly.

"Look at the Battle Honours on our Unit Colours. This squadron has had a long and illustrious history...and I think it's only fitting that the CO address us all."

After a bit of prodding, the CO rose shakily to his feet. "Genelmen..." he muttered uncertainly, struggling to collect his thoughts. "On an occasion such as this...the only thing I can say is...I don hav a f***en' clue what I'm talking about!" And with that, he slumped back into his seat to the thunderous applause of all assembled.

This was the cue for another scantily-clad young woman to enter the room and then remove said clothing to some recorded musical accompaniment. Understandably, the decorum of the evening accelerated rapidly downhill afterwards, with a spirited game of Mess Rugby following, and then a challenge that resembled Tossing the Caber...except that, in the absence of a caber, we used the crew room furniture instead. At one point, I remember, there was a fire hose in use. Much later, I had to place a hand over one eye so that there was only one set of numbers on my alarm clock. When that alarm then went off (all too soon), it was time to return to the headquarters to clean up the carnage. Some of the hardiest party animals were still there, as evidenced by their loud snores from under various desks and behind curtains. The barbecue area was littered with coffee tables and chairs, and the crew room was a jumble of broken glass and discarded food scraps. A fire hose snaked its way along the corridor and some of the carpet was soaked. Most shocking of all, though, was that in an act of either sublime marksmanship or scathing political commentary, somebody had thrown up dead centre in the middle of the clear Perspex panel directly above the Duke of Gloucester Cup.

On the 26th of August, in the most stinging blow of all, 9 Squadron was required to deliver its aircraft to 5 Aviation Regiment, which was being established by the Army in Townsville. Contrary to orders from above, the RAAF steadfastly refused to stencil "ARMY" on the sides of the aircraft before the delivery flight departed. For me, this trip was also personally significant, because I'd been afforded the honour of leading the last Iroquois formation out of Amberley, and would be interviewed by a Channel 7 television crew (who were recording the event) beforehand. Despite developing a slight head cold overnight, I was determined to complete the interview and, afterwards, we flew a few final laps around Amberley before loading up our gear and then departing for Townsville. I have no other recollections of that final flight, but I do remember, on shutting the aircraft down in Townsville, that my overriding sentiment was one of relief rather than nostalgia.

22

SO LONG, FAREWELL, AUF WIEDERSEHEN, ADIEU

The final few months of my 9 Squadron posting were overshadowed by the tragic passing of my adored grandmother, who succumbed to a brain tumour just six weeks after receiving her diagnosis. With all of our aircraft having now relocated to Townsville, hanging around the squadron was like re-living the last few weeks of the year back in high school—all of the hard work had been done, and we were all now just going through the motions. Familiar faces started disappearing as the "early leavers" departed on their postings and attachments. Mal Greentree—the copilot on my final Iroquois flight—headed off to fly Winjeels in the Forward Air Control (FAC) unit at Williamtown, while Pete Mac and Tayls left for C-130E conversions at Richmond. Others were bound for 35 Squadron to keep flying helicopters, while some diehard rotary-wing pilots resigned to join the Army.

But most of the departing 9 Squadron pilots were heading to RAAF Base East Sale, to undergo QFI training. Despite amplifying (three times) to be amongst their number, due to the continuing flood of resignations for the airlines, I'd been posted back to 33 Squadron instead.

I was a little disappointed to miss out on an Instructors Course, but as far as second prizes go, being posted back to fly my big, beloved Boeings again was pretty hard to beat. Plus, I'd still be going to Sale: just not as a trainee instructor. Because I'd be flying "fast jets" again, in January 1988, I'd have to undergo a Fixed Wing Refresher Course—not that I ever thought I'd try to put a 707 into a hover. As old faces disappeared, new ones arrived to take their place and introduce the soon-to-arrive Blackhawks into service. The CO retired and was replaced by a tall, former 9 Squadron XO, who had a kindly face and a rich, mellifluous voice. When speaking to him, you always felt that you had his undivided attention, and his manner never changed, regardless of whether he was speaking to a civilian, a pilot, a senior RAAF officer or an enlisted man. He had a gentle sense of humour and his bearing suggested nothing but dignity, integrity and competency. He seemed destined to rise through the ranks very rapidly, and his name was Wing Commander Angus Houston.

As the year drew to a close, it was time to prepare to head back south. Whatever I might have thought of my helicopter flying at different times, I could certainly never say that it had been boring! Reflecting on my experiences of the previous two (plus) years, I came to think of rotary-wing flying as a "young man's game"—you knew the risks every single time you got airborne, you just didn't want to think about them *too* much. It had certainly been a different *style* of flying, and whether it was from taking part in police drug raids or television mini-series, or from flying in the PNG Highlands to being "Tail-end Charlie" on an airmobile assault, 9 Squadron had certainly provided me with a catalogue of truly unforgettable experiences. Henceforth, I would always be able to say…with complete honesty…that I had *"really* flown" helicopters!

EPILOGUE

Monday, January 11th, 1988, was shaping up to be another scorcher as I drove onto RAAF Base East Sale to commence my Fixed Wing Refresher Course. More than four months had passed since I'd last set foot in an aircraft, so the course designed to cure me of any lingering rotary-wing habits would, in reality, be more of a general flying refresher. Checking in at Central Flying School (CFS) shortly afterwards, I was advised by one of the senior instructors that my first flight was scheduled for just two days hence and that, somewhat worryingly, if it went okay in the morning, I could expect to go solo in the afternoon. After visiting the flight line to get fitted out with a G-suit and helmet, I was then handed an armful of flight manuals and textbooks and advised that any pre-course preparation would be strictly a self-managed affair. And so, with the three-week course revising the entire seven-month syllabus from 2FTS, it was time to "hit the books" in earnest. Ensconced in my Mess room, I initially focused on the Mass Briefs—the Macchi "How to" manual—and found that, amazingly, a lot of the stuff that I'd crammed into my grey matter six years earlier was still there. The Macchi was flown using formalised "patters" and the After Takeoff procedure quickly came to mind.

"Safely airborne. Brakes On/Off. Landing gear Up. Flaps Up. Speedbrake In. Landing light In. Three 'UPS', flasher out, flaps up, speedbrake in, landing light in by 145 [knots]."

More memories came flooding back and, by the end of my first night of study, I felt that I might actually be ready to climb into a Macchi again in just a few days. But I'll freely admit that the thought of squeezing back into that tiny cockpit and strapping myself onto an explosive ejection seat (all the while with gloves and helmet on, visors down, and oxygen mask in place) triggered some uneasy feelings of impending claustrophobia. I also knew that I'd really miss those "extra sets of eyes and ears" on solo flights. It wasn't that I didn't trust myself to do the job capably on my own, it was more a matter of just having grown very accustomed to (and extremely comfortable with) multi-crew environments in the years since 2FTS.

Fortunately, Gary "Gaz" Criddle, my instructor for the first few flights, was very easy-going, with a permanent smile, a ready laugh and a willingness to do whatever he could to put me more at ease. After a few dual flights together, it was time for me to go solo and, while taxying out for takeoff, I selected 'hot mic' on my interphone panel, just to hear the sound of my breathing for some company. As I recall, it was a beautiful, cloudless afternoon and so, initially, I just headed out to the edge of the Training Area for a scenic flight along the Gippsland coast. But my conscience soon got the better of me, and I figured that I should, at least, attempt some basic aerobatics. With all the extra experience I'd gained since Pilots Course, I reasoned that 'stall turns' might now come a little easier... I was wrong. I tried, I failed and, in disgust, resumed my sightseeing tour.

Returning to Sale a little later, ATC advised me that there were a dozen other aircraft in the circuit. Since CFS trained instructors on both Macchi jets and propeller-driven CT-4s, the East Sale circuit area was always a veritable hornet's nest of aeroplanes flying around at different heights and vastly different speeds. As I pondered how to safely negotiate my way through them all, I remembered that an aircraft simulating an engine failure had right of way, and so I notified the Tower of my intention to conduct a 'glide fullstop.' Now, *they* would have to stay out of *my* way...so who said laziness can't be a virtue? Before long, I was back in the CFS crew room, recuperating from my taxing ordeal.

Also there were the between-flights CFS instructors, who not only "trained the trainers" but also, in many instances, performed flying displays all around the country as members of the Roulettes—the RAAF's precision formation team. These pilots were preparing for a very busy display season in our Bicentennial Year, and exhibited that cocky self-assuredness (bordering on arrogance) that is simply a must when engaged in a high-risk activity that leaves no room whatsoever for self-doubt. I watched in awe one evening as they practiced their display in the fading twilight, and simply marvelled at the skill of the individual display pilot who (inverted) rejoined his teammates at the top of a formation barrel roll. Just two months later though during another training session the Roulettes narrowly avoided disaster when, after a mid-air collision, one of them had to eject, and another (the team leader) had to make a belly landing on the East Sale runway. Then, as even further proof of the dangers of display flying, in August 1988, two Macchis of the Tricilori—the Italian equivalent of the Roulettes—collided at Ramstein Air Force Base in Germany, with one of the burning, crippled aircraft plunging into the huge crowd of spectators, killing seventy people.

Fortunately, my adventures in the "Maccherschmitt" were far more routine...with just one small exception. While flying solo in the circuit one day, I noticed that I had to keep putting in more and more right aileron to keep the wings level, and suspected that the fuel in the left-hand 'tip' (wingtip) tank wasn't transferring. Fearing that any further asymmetry might render the aircraft difficult to control, I transmitted a PAN call to ATC and carried out a fullstop landing. Safely back at CFS soon afterwards (and congratulating myself on my coolness under pressure) I reported the incident to a senior instructor, who simply said, "Well, why didn't you just jettison the fuel out of it?" D'oh...it was just *so* obvious! But since all my recent flying had been on helicopters (where you couldn't dump fuel) and my course preparation had been so rushed, I'd simply forgotten that Macchi tip tank fuel could be jettisoned. I felt like such an idiot—thank God I didn't eject! Notwithstanding this minor blemish though, I soon began to really enjoy flying the nimble little jet trainer again. I was also particularly pleased to discover that my ability to "eyeball" (visually judge) a glide approach was light-years ahead of my mediocre efforts of 1982.

Away from the flight line, the social life in the Officers Mess could best be described as "hectic." Many of my colleagues from the "helo" world (as well as Tim Ellis from 117 Pilots Course) were at East Sale on Instructors Course and, although I felt like a bit of a "third wheel" at times, I was usually invited to join them on significant occasions. One such event was a Sinai Wine Appreciation Society (SWAS) gathering, convened on the night of January 25th by the former helicopter pilots who'd flown with the MFO in the Middle East. At 9 Squadron, I'd heard many tall tales of the shenanigans in the Aussie Mess—many concerning SWAS nights—with one pilot candidly admitting that, upon his return to Australia, he'd experienced full-blown alcohol withdrawal symptoms. Therefore, I was curious to witness firsthand the rites and rituals I'd missed out on by not having flown in the desert.

With twenty-twenty hindsight, I'll just say that "appreciation" was a pretty gross understatement, and that "adoration," or maybe even "worship," would have served as far better descriptors. The next day—Australia Day 1988—was planned to be a huge celebration of our country's history, with HRH Queen Elizabeth II attending as guest of honour. A flotilla of tall ships (re-enacting the voyage of the First Fleet) would sail into Sydney Harbour in the morning, accompanied by a massed flypast of every serviceable aircraft in the Australian military inventory. Having "appreciated" the SWAS wines for far too long, I'd collapsed into bed in the wee hours of our nation's birthday without even attempting to set an alarm clock. When I finally awoke the next day and blearily opened a bloodshot eye to check the time, I discovered, to my horror, that it was 1pm and that I'd slept through everything—the ceremonies...the tall ships...the military flypast...the lot!

A little over a week later, I completed the final flight in the course syllabus, and had thus gone solo (by both day and night), completed an instrument rating test, conducted an overnight navigation exercise down to Tasmania and back and flown in formation (including some formation approaches in IMC). Even though my hairline had retreated rapidly during this time, I *still* regard the Fixed Wing Refresher as the "hairiest" flying course of my career. Fortunately, on this occasion, there was no Final Handling Test for me to fail and so, being declared free of any nasty, lingering rotary-wing habits, I was cleared to return to Richmond to reacquaint myself with the Queen of the Skies...the Boeing 707. Or, at least, that's what I thought was going to happen!

To be continued...

Geoffrey (Geoff) Cowell was born and raised in rural Queensland where, even from an early age, he was enamoured with the idea of one day landing a job that entailed both excitement and travel. Like many boys growing up in the 1960s, his ambition to fly was born out of assembling plastic model aeroplanes and watching black-and-white war movies like *The Dambusters* and *Reach for the Sky*, which appeared on television every school holidays. He was also addicted to *Commando* war comics and, when one of the greatest air-war movies of all time—*The Battle of Britain*—was screened in Brisbane in 1969, it convinced him to pursue a future written in the skies. Two years later, Qantas took delivery of its first 747, and life's possibilities as a globetrotting Jumbo pilot persuaded the author to set his sights on one day captaining a mighty Boeing 747 in Australia's famous Flying Kangaroo.

But in an era where the cost of attaining a Commercial Pilot Licence was about the same as that of an average family home, the author soon realised that the only way to achieve his goal was for the taxpayer to fund his flying training. Despite lazily coasting his way through high school, Geoff was still able to obtain high enough scores in the required subjects to be eligible for entry into the Royal Australian Air Force Academy. But during a visit to the RAAF Recruiting Office towards the end of high school, he was taken aback at the requirement to serve at least ten years in the Air Force—a veritable life sentence for a seventeen-year-old—and so he commenced his working life as a trainee Civil Engineering draftsman in the Queensland Water Resources Commission instead.

The flying bug remained though, and when he discovered that one of his older drafting colleagues in the Project Planning Branch (Harry Wright) had flown seventy-eight combat missions during World War II as a Lancaster navigator in the legendary Pathfinder force, he decided to pursue his dream and applied for Air Force pilot training. In June 1981, he was accepted into the RAAF as a member of No 117 Pilots Course and, after the most gruelling sixteen months of his life, graduated in October of the following year. During the fifteen-year military career that followed, the author flew Boeing 707s, Iroquois helicopters and C-130 transports before being accepted into Qantas in late 1995.

For the next twenty-five years, he flew Boeing 747s and 767s, until his career was cut short by the devastating impact of COVID on the aviation industry in 2020. Deciding on whether to accept redundancy at a time when the world's airlines were grounded, most of its population were in lockdown and no vaccine was yet available was one of the toughest decisions of his life. Ultimately, though, as a sixty-one-year-old, with potentially only another four years of international flying ahead, he very reluctantly accepted the package. The author wore his Qantas uniform for the final time in July 2020, when reciting his original poem, *Benediction for a Queen*, on the occasion of the retirement of the final Qantas Boeing 747-400 from service. He now works as a casual court monitor at the Federal Court of Australia in Sydney, assisting in the production of court transcripts.

www.ingramcontent.com/pod-product-compliance
Lightning Source LLC
Chambersburg PA
CBHW060550080526
44585CB00013B/511